WOMANKIND

The Story of WOMEN, Prehistoric Times to the Present

By the author of WOMEN'S ROOTS

June Stephenson, Ph.D.

Library of Congress Catalog Card No.
86-071940
ISBN 0-941138-05-4

OTHER BOOKS BY JUNE STEPHENSON

WOMEN'S ROOTS

HUMANITY'S SEARCH FOR THE MEANING
OF LIFE

IT'S ALL RIGHT TO GET OLD

A LIE IS A DEBT

THE ADMINISTRATOR

Diemer, Smith Publishing Company, Inc.
3377 Solano Avenue, Suite 322
Napa, California, 94558

WOMANKIND

Table of Contents

Acknowledgements

With all my heart I thank my husband, my daughters, and my friends who have offered advice and encouragement as this book developed. My husband is always my greatest supporter in every way. He feels that what I do is worthwhile and should be done. One of my daughters, Christine Reed, more than ten years ago helped me clarify the first chapters of this book. My other daughter, Evelyn Smith, did the original laborious typing, offering comments as she went along. When there were only three chapters completed, Deborah Boisot enthusiastically asked to share it with her friends, lifting my spirits about the book. Then, because of other work, I let the manuscript sit, unfinished, for about eight years, until Gail Kenna convinced me it should not be abandoned.

When I completed the book, Dorothy Hansen and Katherine Smith advised me to rewrite the last chapter because they saw that I had gone "off course." I know that good critics can confirm a writer's worst suspicions, so I wrote the last chapter again, and recognized that solid feeling when I got it right.

Clara Coffied praised this book as the best of several I have written, and Florence Buehler told me of her anger at one of my characters, and I knew then that they were real. After

Margaret Paul thoroughly proofed the galleys, the book was ready for publication.

Womankind was completed because people care about what the book says. I thank them here with unrestricted love and appreciation.

1

Prehistoric

Whenever they felled a markhor with stones they clubbed it to death. Then they tore its flesh out and ate its dripping blood. After the hide dried they used it to cover their bodies, protecting themselves from the cold. Looking like a pack of animals walking on their hind feet, this small group of people in the mountain area of ancient Turkey, nearly 20,000 years before the birth of Christ, scooped up loose dirt with their hands and threw it on the mound.

The group was small. There were only seven left now that Toan had entered the Spirit World. They had scratched the earth with sticks and animal bones and made a Last Sleep Place for Toan's body, to hurry it under cover before his arms and legs grew cold. They tried to put him in a sleep position, but his head was stuck in the wrong way. Blood flowed down his arm to where the wild grain seeds had been placed in his hand so he would have food to eat when he started his new life in the Spirit World.

As the smallest member of the group, a little girl they called Chee, helped pile the dirt on Toan's body, she had bad thoughts. If they had left the Cold Place when Stoe had wanted to, Toan would not now be in the Spirit World. They would all be over the mountain, getting away from the cold wind that had been warning them.

Three suns ago Chee had seen Stoe pointing out to Toan the shadows on the ground when the sun was low. Then Stoe pointed to the top of the mountain, but Toan would not watch where Stoe pointed. Chee knew they would move only when Toan moved first, for he was the one they watched and followed. It was Toan who made them safe from large animals, he who knew where the caves were, he who knew where to look for new fields of wild grain when their stomachs hurt, and it was he who warned them when they might meet people of danger.

Watching the dirt mound grow higher, Chee felt the bad thoughts again. If they had left to go over the mountain to leave the Cold Place before yesterday's sun, they would not have been there where the big animal broke Toan's head. The picture came into her again, how they had been turning over large rocks to find small things to eat, rolling over the rocks and

2

laughing each time a new mass of bugs ran to escape the sunlight. Breg was the one who called the warning to Toan when the big animal's shadow fell on the rock he had in his hand.

"Toan! Back! Look!" Breg called, but before Toan could turn around, the animal had knocked him to the ground and was on top of him. Toan kicked and hit the animal with the rock he had picked up. When the animal moved to fasten its teeth on Toan's throat, they saw Toan's head fall to the side.

It was then that Stoe picked up a stick, still hot and red from last night's fire, and pushed it into the animal's face. The animal growled and made a fierce yell that echoed back at them from the rock mountains. Chee shivered but remembered that Stoe seemed not afraid as he continued waving the firestick.

The animal tried to fight the firestick but this was a different enemy than it was used to. Chee saw the animal put its big paw up to its face before it ran growling into the mountains.

Then they all rushed to help Toan. They called his name again and again, but when they saw how his head was crooked, they knew their calls were not reaching him, not even in the Spirit World.

All of them, the two men—Stoe and Vrev—, the women—Uria and Dena—, the children—Breg and Chee—, and even old Oolar helped carry Toan's big body to the large rock place, protecting him from the wind. There they scrambled on their hands and knees and scraped a hole in the dirt, putting his body into the shallow hole. Each of them took handsful of dirt and put it over Toan's body until he disappeared. They patted the dirt mound to make it firm and backed away, watching the swirls of dust rise from the earth's swelling as the cold wind from the bare rock cliffs above caught wisps of earth to spread the dust elsewhere. They paused, watching, reluctant to leave the one who had always told them where they should go, when they should leave, and what they should avoid.

It was a time for change, a time for a new leader, and from the feel of the cold wind whipping in under their animal hides, a time to hurry to the Warm Place before they were caught in the snow without any way to find food. They would have preferred to postpone the changes, to ease Toan's transition into the Spirit World with loud wails to the Spirits, but their instincts told them to hurry away from the wind. Was not Toan's death an omen that they should have left sooner?

When Stoe said it was time to move, they nodded to their new leader, turned their backs on the burial mound, and followed Stoe to the bottom of the rock mountain that had been their shelter for six moons.

At the base of the first cliff they formed into a line with Stoe in the lead. Vrev climbed up the rocks after Stoe. Vrev had big arms and thick legs that helped him scale the rock shelter. After him was Uria, a large woman, taller than Stoe. Then came Dena, a woman with a big stomach who was given extra blood to drink at animal kills.

4

Breg, the other child in the group, followed in the line, climbing the mountain after Dena. When Chee, one time long ago, started to go in the line before Breg, Toan moved her to a place in back of Breg and pointed to the difference in their bodies and scolded her. Chee never tried to walk in front of Breg again.

In the line after Chee, old Oolar fumbled along on the rocks. Even though they had only gone a short way up the mountains, Chee heard his breathing noises already getting loud. Both Chee and Oolar knew the others would not wait for an Old One, for it would be dangerous if they slowed down to Oolar's pace. They must get out of the valley before more cold came.

Oolar would have to keep up with the rest or stay behind. As one of the early leaders of the group, Oolar knew this better than anyone else. There were Old Ones and Young Ones in his memory who had been left behind, who were never seen again. It was the way. There could be no other way. If they left him behind and if he could live through the Cold Time, they might find him where they left him when they returned at the next Warm Time.

Chee climbed rock after rock, watching where Dena, ahead of Breg, put her feet. Then Chee tried to put her feet on the same rocks that Dena used. The rocks would have been made safe for her. It was another thing that Toan had taught them.

Chee wondered if the Child Spirit in Dena could feel that it was climbing up a mountain. One time when Dena had put Chee's small hand on Dena's stomach, Chee felt something inside Dena's stomach knock at her hand.

Others had put their hands on Dena's stomach too, and after they waited, Chee had seen their faces smile. When Chee asked about Dena's stomach, Dena told her that when the Child Spirit enters a body, that means their group has been chosen for good reason.

"Why doesn't the Child Spirit put a small one in Toan's body? Or Vrev? Or Stoe?" Chee asked Dena. "Or Old Oolar?"

"It is the secret of the Spirit," Dena answered.

"And when you have a big stomach, Toan and Stoe and all of us look at you and it makes us smile. You are different from us," Chee said.

"Yes. A chosen one *is* different. We are one with the Great Spirit."

"I have a body the same as you," Chee told Dena. "Am I at one with the Great Spirit too?"

"Your body is yet like a stick. When you have not lived many moons you are as nothing. If your body is visited by swellings, then you are as a tree, and not a small plant. Then you are one with the Great Spirit because your body can be visited by the Child Spirit."

"And Toan, and Stoe, and the others like them?"

"Never. If they lived all the moons left and grew as high as the highest tree, they could not be one with the Great Spirit because their bodies do not swell to tell the Child Spirit that they could feed a small one."

Chee wondered about Toan and Stoe and

about Old Oolar who could never know the Child Spirit.

"We who have bodies that swell, like you and me, and Uria, we are chosen?" Chee asked.

"Yes. But the Child Spirit puts small ones in other bodies. Do you not remember in the last Warm Time when we crossed the Fast Water, the people on the bank who were resting? There were many, and I saw the Child Spirit had been with some of them and it made me sad."

"Why? When the Child Spirit came to us it made us happy."

"I was sad because I thought if the Child Spirit goes to them and puts a child in the bodies of those that have swellings, will the Spirit have a child left for me?" Dena and Chee both laughed and cupped their hands on Dena's stomach.

That was long ago and now Chee saw Dena moving up the rock mountain, careful not to hit her stomach. She must not hurt the small one or all of them would be angry with her, afraid that the Child Spirit might not come to their group again.

Chee felt her body shiver. The animal hides flapped against her short spindly legs, but she didn't worry about the cold. The others spoke of the dangers of the cold, but it was not a thing to worry her. Except, Chee remembered she worried one time when they all had to stay in a cave because the snow was too deep for walking.

Then she was hungry and worried about

how they would dig for roots in the snow. That was before Mren and Hewl had been left behind more than many moons ago, and all of them trying to keep warm had gone into the dream world of sleep lying on top of each other like a pile of branches. Chee's body shivered then as it shivered now, but now it was because she heard Old Oolar struggling behind her on the mountain and she knew she would have empty feelings if Oolar had to be left behind like Mren and Hewl had been.

She had many empty feelings in the last moons. She thought of Mren and Hewl, and after that, little Sel, whose short legs couldn't climb fast enough. When Sel's mother, Uria, went back to pick her up to carry her in her arms, Toan tore Sel from Uria's arms and forced the little one to walk. Uria knew she could not do what Toan did not want her to do. Everyone knew they had to let Toan lead them to food and safety or they might all go to the Last Sleep Place.

On that move, when Toan was far ahead, Uria had turned and called to Sel many times. Then Toan came back and they all stopped. That was a new thing for Chee to see. For as long as Chee could remember, Toan had never come back.

"Fast River comes higher, faster this time," Toan had said to Uria. They moved forward again. Chee turned and called to Sel who was far behind again. Breg, too, called, but Sel was tired. She moved her short legs slower and slower, and made noises that they could hear in the distance.

"Fast River is far," Stoe scolded Chee and Breg. "Move!" They could not help the small one because that could mean they would not be able to get across the river and they would all be trapped in the Cold Place.

The snow would cover the wild food, the animals would be gone to warmer places and they would have emptiness in their stomachs. Toan had told them the bones they had once found were people who did not move fast enough when the cold came. Though they had wanted to help Sel, they could not. She had to learn. When a child can no longer get its food from its mother's body, it is time that it must walk by itself. And when a child with a body that would swell in many moons, could not keep up with the rest, that child was left behind. When a child with a body like Breg, who would never be visited by the Child Spirit, was slow on the move, he was carried by a leader because one day he would be a killer of animals.

"One day *I* will kill an animal," Chee thought, thinking of Sel left far behind that day long ago.

Chee's small feet slipped on a loose rock, and she clutched a firmer rock to brace herself. She turned and watched the rock bounce down the mountain, gathering pebbles as it went, glad that Oolar was not in its path. He looked up at her and smiled his wrinkled smile. She knew he was letting her know he was all right. When she found a level place for her feet, she looked far ahead up the mountain and saw Stoe taking long climbing steps without stopping to rest. She hoped he would get to the opening in the mountain to go down the other side while the sun lasted.

Breg was far ahead of her, and ahead of him, Dena moved clumsily over the rocks. Chee would not be afraid of being left behind for she could keep up with Dena and they would not leave Dena behind. Stoe would not want to anger the Child Spirit. They would even carry Dena if she could walk no more.

Chee wished they could have carried Sel the last Cold Time when they climbed this mountain. They had all comforted Chee, saying they would find Sel when they came back for the Warm Time, but, when they came back Sel was nowhere to be found. Sel's mother, Uria, did not smile for many moons. When they were on their way back to the Cold Place, Toan scolded Uria where they were hunting for food because Uria used too much time looking for Sel. Then when Dena was visited by the Child Spirit, Uria would not look at Dena except from the corners of her eyes. It was only when Dena one time groaned with pains that Uria went and laid down with her and stroked Dena's back, that Uria stopped looking for Sel.

The higher up the mountain Chee climbed, the more she noticed the cold of the wind, and then pains in her stomach started. When they had gathered wild grain to put in Toan's hands she had cupped seeds into her mouth, but that was a long time ago. She wished they had been able to kill the animal that killed Toan, instead of scaring it off. It would have made them strong for the long move.

The last Cold Time, when they had made this move from the Cold Place, they had killed an animal the night before they left and they ate all of it, leaving the bones to the large flying birds. Chee had looked down from the top of this mountain and watched the big black wings circle and swoop and then land on the bones to tear away the bits of flesh that were left. Last time, climbing up the mountain, she felt good. Her stomach was full, Sel was right behind her, Oolar was not so old, and Toan was leading them. She had thought then that it would always be so when they moved.

Oolar made breathing noises louder with each climb up to higher rocks. Chee wanted to help him, but if she slowed down they might both be left behind. She tried to catch up to Breg. She pulled herself up over a rock as big as herself and called to Breg, hoping to slow him. He turned to look at her and shouted back and then went on. Stoe was near the top of the mountain where the separation of two huge rocks was large enough for people to push themselves through to get to the other side and start down again. From the top of the other side they would be able to see the far away Fast River.

The last of the sun's slanted rays could be seen through the passageway. With relief, Chee realized they would all get to the top while the sun was still shining and then they would go down to the other side before dark came. Chee would not want to go down the mountain in the dark. If she couldn't see how to step on

11

each rock, the rock could roll and she could fall to the bottom of the mountain.

Stoe shouted and waved from the top, and the others waved to him. Even Oolar pulled his old body up and over a large boulder, standing up to wave and shout.

Stoe shouted again, pointed into the passageway and disappeared. The others climbed faster for they must not lose sight of him.

Vrev was next up to the top. He shouted and disappeared into the sunlit passageway.

Dena moved carefully. Because she found ways to go around boulders rather than pulling her big stomach up over them, it was slower for her. Chee could see that Dena stopped at times and waited before going on. Breg was going ahead of Dena now because he climbed up over boulders and found the shorter ways. Though Chee was catching up to Dena, she did not want to make too much space between herself and Oolar.

Uria called to the four below her when she reached the top and Chee wanted her to wait, but Uria squeezed into the passageway and disappeared. Breg made a few quick scrambles, knocking rocks down on Dena, as he made the last stretched climb to the top. His shout echoed back over the darkening valley and Chee saw his small body move quickly into the passageway.

Chee was glad when Dena stopped to rest again, because that stop would give Oolar time to get closer to them. She looked down at Oolar.

She had not known when Oolar got old. He

still hunted and killed animals and told the others what plants to eat when they were sick. When Vrev had a big hole in his arm from an animal's horn, Oolar tied a special grass on it and made him lie in the shade of a tree with no food until three days were gone.

Dena and Chee reached the top of the mountain together, and Dena looked at the thin passageway, saw that it was narrower near her head and wider near her feet so she put herself on her knees and crawled into the opening. Chee looked at Oolar still climbing up and she knew she couldn't wait for him, but he was going to make it to the top and then going down would be easier for him. She followed Dena into the passageway knowing that Oolar would not have to be left behind here.

Chee felt the weak sun coming in the passageway. She followed Dena out into the opening on the other side and there she saw the others already half way down the mountain. Dena stood up, pointing to the Fast River in the distance.

"We will cross the water when the sun comes again," she told Chee.

"Can you cross with your swollen stomach?"

"Yes. Uria will help me."

Last time Toan had carried Chee across when they came back this way, and now Toan was not with them. Dena seemed to know Chee's thoughts.

"Stoe will carry you," Dena said.

"And who will carry Breg?"

"Vrev will carry him as he did last time."

"Why do they carry us across the rivers when they wouldn't carry Sel across the land?"

"The land is forever," Dena answered. "The Fast River is a short time. Little ones cannot be carried forever."

"Sel . . ." Chee began.

"Was not strong enough." Dena put her hand on Chee's thin shoulder. "Weak ones who cannot keep up must be left behind."

"Oolar?" Chee asked. Dena did not answer. Instead she began the long walk down the mountain, carefully choosing the rocks that would hold her weight.

At the bottom of the mountain Stoe and Vrev had found a sheltered place and were piling branches and twigs for a fire. Vrev, who carried the fire circle, a piece of hard wood ground away by rock into a circle, would start the fire to keep the animals away at night. He twirled another stick in the palms of both hands rubbing it into the circle and the fire would catch dry leaves. Oolar had shown him how to make the fire and one day Vrev would show Breg.

Uria, reaching the bottom of the mountain, began to look for things to eat, but Dena went to the shelter to lie down. When Breg put his body down on the ground next to Dena's, Stoe pulled him up and told him to go find food. He overturned rocks, hit the round curled bugs with small rocks, and ate them quickly. Then he found some tall grass, picked off the seeds, put them on a rock and pounded them with another rock. He chewed the pounded seeds while he found more grass and made these seeds ready to eat.

Uria had cornered a lizard under a fallen tree, still sleepy from the day's sun. She swung it by the tail and shouted for everyone to admire. Chee and Oolar who were the last ones down the mountain, called to her for some of the meat. Uria would hold it over the fire on a stick and they would all have part of it.

The wind blew the fire into tall flames. They would sleep by the shelter near the fire and know that no animals would come near them as long as there were flames. They would take turns in pairs, keeping the fire aflame.

As the morning greyness showed at the edges of the sky they searched for food and then they moved toward the river, walking in the same order as they climbed the mountain, with Stoe going first.

Moving in a single line, they each carried a short part of a tree limb to fight off animals. Fearful that the trees could be hiding animals or unknown people, they moved forward together in a kind of running trot. Again, Chee saw that Oolar was falling behind.

The way through the trees to the river was long. The sun moved higher in the sky and Chee's short legs were getting tired. She wanted to stop and rest, but Stoe kept them at the same running trot. She could not go as fast as she did when they first started at the morning's sun, and when she looked for Oolar, she could not see him for a long time. When she finally caught sight of his old body coming out of the trees behind her, Chee knew as she had known yesterday that she could not wait for him.

The sun moved over the trees and when it was near the top of the sky, Chee heard a strange noise. At first it was like a wind through the trees, but it grew louder. She looked to the trees but saw that they were not moving. Then she could hear that it was the sound of water, and she knew it must be the river. She could feel the dirt under her feet getting softer and she realized she must be getting to the Fast River. This would mean a rest because Stoe would carry her through the deep, swift-swirling water.

When the noise of the water was very loud, she looked back for Oolar, but could not see him. In front of her she saw Dena and Breg run into a space with no trees, and then she saw the wide Fast River.

Last time Toan said there were people of danger here so it would be a bad place to stay long. Toan had hurried them across the river. If they stayed too long on the bank, he had said, they might be killed by other people, and their bodies would be eaten as they themselves had eaten other people when they could kill them. So it was necessary to cross the river fast at once. On the other side they could slow down because Toan had taught them that people of danger did not live on the other side.

Already Vrev had picked up Breg who wrapped his short legs around Vrev's waist. Uria tied a vine rope around one of Dena's arms and on her own arm. Uria was a big woman and she would help Dena swim the fast moving water.

Stoe picked up Chee from the ground and she put her small arms around his neck. They waited, not looking at the river. They watched the trees to see where Oolar was. He came out walking and shaking his head when he saw they were ready to cross. Then he sat down on the earth and the group moved restlessly.

"It is time for you to go," he said to Stoe.

Nobody said anything. Chee had the same empty feeling she had when Sel was left behind, and when Toan went to the Spirit World.

Oolar said, "This time it is the time for me to stay on this side of Fast River."

Nobody moved. Then Vrev took the fire circle wood and handed it to Oolar. Oolar stood up to receive it and the group looked at Oolar and then turned their backs to him and walked into the noisy, rushing waters. Chee looked back to see Oolar watching them. She wanted to help him but all she could do was comfort herself, telling herself they would find him when they came back in the Warm Time.

The swift river was difficult to swim. When Dena became very tired, Uria shouted to her to turn on her back so Uria could pull her along. Stoe and Vrev, with the small ones on their backs used all their strength to not get caught in the fast waters that would take them down the river and over a waterfall. The waters pushed at them from one side as they tried to stay in a straight path from the bank they left to the bank on the other side. Chee knew what Oolar knew. This time he would not have been able to swim the river.

Vrev pointed out to Stoe the place on the other side where it would be best to get up on the bank. There in a clearing where there were trees on three sides they might not be seen by large animals or other people.

The swim path they made across the river was not a straight one. When Stoe and Vrev pulled themselves out of the water and set the small ones down on the earth, they went back to the river's edge and helped the women. Out of the water they saw that they had been forced far down the river. They looked across the water for Oolar, but the bank where they had left him was far up the river and he could not be seen. Saying nothing to each other, they lay down on the earth, letting the sun warm their bodies and resting before they moved on to the Warm Place, a moon's walk away.

The Warm Place was a relief from the cold wind that had been blowing at them many suns before they had left the Cold Place. They found their sleep places again cut into the hills, and then they went about the dirt looking for fresh animal tracks and wild grain sprouts. It was good again to be here and it would be good to stay here until the warm turns to heat and the heat drives them back to the Cold Place where it would be cool for many months before it was too cold again. Then they would move back once more to this Warm Place.

Stoe and Vrev set out to find their old hunting places. When Breg asked to go with them, they told him when they came back next time to this place he would be big enough to hunt with them. For now he would have to go with Dena, Uria, and Chee to find food on the ground and in the trees and bushes.

Chee and Breg found the Quiet Stream again, splashed in the water and hit the lazy fish with their sticks. Later they would hold the fish over the fire when Vrev and Stoe came back.

With Chee and Breg splashing in the water, Dena and Uria walked on farther, gathering food. Uria stopped and pointed to dust in the air she saw at a distance. From where they were on a hill she thought she would see a large animal kicking up the dust, but when they were closer they saw a new thing laid out before them many walks away.

In a place where trees were knocked down, they saw people. They had never seen people around here before. These people were scratching the earth and making dust go up into the air. Dena and Uria looked at each other in confusion. They stayed behind the trees from above and watched. These people looked like themselves. They had no animal

19

hides on their bodies. Had they discarded them as Dena and Uria had because they were not needed now in the Warm Place?

From their distance they could see there were small ones and the kind of big people who could have visits from the Child Spirit. Were there others? If so, were they out hunting as Stoe and Vrev were? Were these people of danger? Uria moved back quietly and beckoned to Dena to follow her back to their place, a long walk away.

At the cooking fire that night Uria told Stoe of the people a half sun away.

"They were not there last time," Dena said.

"Toan never spoke of another people by the Quiet Stream," Vrev added.

"Toan said there were no people of danger on this side of the Fast River," Stoe said. "Were there many?" he asked.

"Many," both Dena and Uria said.

They were silent. They ate slowly when their stomachs needed no more filling, yet they ate what was left on the bones because they did not want animals to come near their caves, drawn by the food smell. When they were finished, they threw the bones on the fire to make the blood smell go up into the smoke.

"Toan did not say there were people of danger here," Stoe repeated. "We will stay here. If they make danger on us, we will make danger on them." It was decided. They would not move until it was too warm here again and then they would move back across the Fast River. Dena was happy. Here in the Warm

Place she would have the child. Chee, too, was beginning to forget about Oolar—was beginning to lose that empty feeling.

When Dena did not want to go looking for food on one of the warmer days the small ones stayed with her. Uria went by herself so they would have something to eat if Stoe and Vrev came back with no animals to eat as they had for the last two suns.

Uria walked far from where they had been before, as they had picked all the berries near their place. They had climbed all the nearby trees for fruit and nuts, and scratched the dirt around their caves for all the roots.

Uria was alone, but as there had been no animals around, she was not afraid, until she heard the breaking of a twig. She stopped, expecting to see or hear an animal coming at her. Instead she saw a person. Though he had a body like Stoe, she saw that it was someone else. He was so close to her she could hear his breathing. Was he a person of danger?

Uria did not move. *He* did not move. Would he kill her? Toan had told them the people of danger did not kill those like Dena and Uria who could have visits from the Child Spirit. He had told them it was a Great Evil to kill Child Spirit holders. That was why they did not kill animals that could have small ones, or if they did kill them, they would not eat that meat, for it was Great Evil if that blood touched them. Uria wanted to tell this person standing in front of her that she had had a visit from the Child Spirit, so he would not kill her, but she saw the hard look in his face was changing. His lips opened from two thin straight lines to a wide smile.

Uria moved her eyes from his face to the long pole he carried. She saw that one end had been smashed to make it a point. Was it to hit an animal, or to throw? Toan had one time put a stone in a pole and thrown it at an animal that he could not kill by running at it.

The person in front of her saw her looking at the pole. He dropped it to the ground and smiled wider, looking at her. When the pole was on the ground, Uria lost some of her fear. She smiled and he laughed. Then *she* laughed. In the grove of trees where nobody could hear them, they laughed and they laughed, and then they stopped and sat on the ground, their bodies touching. Uria laughed again and he put his large hand on her body. She put her hands on his shoulders and chest.

He laughed again and she laughed and after much time of laughing and putting hands on each other, he pulled away from her, tossed some pebbles at her. She caught them and tossed them back at him. They laughed. They continued this tossing for sometime until it no longer interested them. Then he put his large hands on her face and slowly moved them down her body and then he put himself inside her body. When it was over he rolled off of her body and muttered, "Shael."

Uria bent her head to hear him. He pointed to himself and repeated, "Shael."

"Oh," Uria smiled. She pointed to herself. "Uria."

"Uria?"

"Uria," she repeated. "Shael?" she asked. He nodded and pulled her over on top of him when Vrev found them.

Their strange noises had drawn him to them. Vrev came to the tree spot without making a sound, his hunting stick in his hand ready to strike.

Uria saw him first and yelled, and the one next to her ran from her and disappeared. Then Uria laughed, looking at Vrev with his stick in the air. Uria pointed to the long pole on the ground. Vrev picked it up at the same time another hand grabbed for it. The stranger and Vrev both held the pole looking at each other.

Vrev's anger turned to a smile and he offered the pole to the stranger. With this movement they know that the stranger would be free to come to their group in the night to be with Uria, knowing he would not be attacked by them, nor would he attack their group.

As the many suns rose and set, Uria was visited in her cave at night by the stranger.

"Why are you called 'Shael,'?" Uria asked him on one of his early visits.

"In our language," he answered, "it means 'born in the springtime.' "

They laughed at that and at many things. "I am a fox," he told her, but they did not laugh at that. He was telling her that his clan was the clan of the fox. Uria's clan was the clan of the leopard.

"Now my brother is your brother," Uria told him.

When she asked him about the dust she had

seen in the air when she had long ago come upon his people, he told her they did that with their "digging sticks" to make grain grow. "Our women plant seeds," he said. But Uria did not know what that meant, and so he came one early sun time to her place and they walked until she was tired and then she saw he had taken her to where his people were. When she did not want to go near his place, Shael coaxed her to go into the cleared area with him. He smiled and she followed him.

Uria knew there must be many faces hiding behind the bushes and trees, looking at her, but in the clearing there was no one but herself and Shael. Where there were no trees she saw grain growing out of the earth in straight lines. She knelt down and pulled her fingers across the lines made by the thin stalks.

"How does it grow like this?" she asked, pointing to the rows.

Shael broke off a stalk and dropped the seeds into one hand, knelt and scooped out a hole in the dirt, put the seeds in it and covered them over.

"It will . . . ?" she moved her hand from earth toward the sky.

"With right words, water from the river, water from the sky . . . or if that doesn't make it grow, blood from our most valuable small ones. That is called 'fertility sacrifice.' "

Uria said nothing.

Shael explained more. "When our people, you know, like you, not like me," he smiled, "put the seed in the ground, they carry water to put on the dirt."

24

"Carry water," Uria laughed. "One cannot carry water."

"Our women have carrying pots made from the earth . . ." He showed her a clay bowl. She took it, smoothing her hands over its surface. Uria shook her head. It was too much at one time. Grain in straight rows, this clearing with nobody to be seen but many eyes to be felt on her, this knowing about water on the earth, seeds covered on the ground, and blood from small ones. Empty of any good feeling she turned and ran. Shael did not follow her.

It was when she was no more to be seen, the people from the sign of the fox came out from their hiding places and jabbered at Shael with their curiosity and their scolding at bringing a strange one to their growing place.

Uria ran until she was back with her own people. She fell down on the ground near her sleep place. Chee went to her.

"She is wet from running a long time," Chee told Dena.

"And she has brought no food," Dena noticed.

"Why were you running," Chee asked. "Are there big animals? People of danger?"

"No . . . ," she answered swallowing her breath in large gulps. "It was strangers . . . Shael's strangers . . . on the other part of the Quiet Stream. He told me many things."

"What?" Dena asked.

"They put grain seed in the earth . . ." she started.

"In the *earth?*" Dena exclaimed. "Why don't they eat it? Are they hiding it?"

25

"No . . ." Uria laughed. "The people of the fox scratch the earth with sticks and put the grain seed in the ground and . . ." she sighed, "it grows in straight lines. Remember when we saw the dust and the people with sticks. They were planting . . . putting seed in the earth and . . . it grows . . . and makes more seed to eat."

Chee asked, "Why does it grow?"

"They put water on it," Uria explained.

"*They!* You mean the *sky*," Dena corrected her.

"No. They make carrying things, bigger than my hands and bring water from the river to put on the seed."

Chee reminded them the water from the Quiet Stream is gone when the Warm Time gets hot.

"Yes. When there is no water, or when seeds don't grow, they use blood from what he said was, 'our most valuable small ones.' That was when I ran away. My head hurt. I like it *here*." Uria pulled herself into the hollow of the hill in her sleep place and quickly fell asleep, leaving Dena and Chee with strange new thoughts.

Stoe and Vrev were lucky hunters that day. They had taken a pole like the one Shael carried, shaped the end to a point, and with it they had brought down a small animal. One person could have carried it back but they made it seem larger being carried by two. They shouted as they came into their place. Breg shouted back and ran to help.

Vrev worked his fire stick to get high flames and they perched the animal up on large sticks. They had not had an animal for many suns. Dena and Uria wrapped roots and grain in large green leaves to put in the fire after the animal had cooked. They sat around in a circle with good feelings, waiting. Stoe and Vrev were proud of their animal hunt and proud too, to bring good news.

"We are brothers with the others," Vrev announced.

"We know that," Uria said. It was her man Shael who related them together.

"No," Vrev said, "*we* meet women now in the other place."

Both Stoe and Vrev grinned and laughed.

"You mean," Uria asked, "you go to be with women at sundown the same way Shael comes here?"

The two men grinned again.

"We didn't know you'd gone," Chee said. "We didn't hear you."

"It is not a place of danger here," Stoe explained. "We do not need to protect ourselves from animals here, but we do not go every sundown. One time I go, next time Vrev."

They shared their good news with the good food eating until all the meat was gone. Full and lazy from the food they went to their sleeping and dreaming places where Uria was later joined by Shael.

As Chee slipped into her dream world, she wondered whether it was Stoe's turn or Vrev's turn to visit the other people, but she didn't stay awake long enough to hear or see which one left.

Dena, full of warm food, and having good

27

feelings about Stoe and Vrev, slipped easily into the dream world, until she woke up restlessly. It must have been that she ate too much food, she thought for she had terrible pains in her stomach. She tried to go to sleep again, but the pains came back. She held her stomach and wanted to cry out but she didn't want to wake the others.

The pain went away and she put her hand on her head and felt that it was wet. She moved her body to another position and tried to fall asleep again when the pain came back, this time hurting more. She bit her lips to stop the cry she wanted to make. The pain went away and she felt that she might fall asleep again, but the pain came and went, came and went.

At first the pains gave her time to feel better before the next one came, but as the moon moved from the top of one tree to another tree, the pains came without going away, and each one hurt more than the last one. She bit her lip and whimpered.

Then she knew the pain would not go away until the child came. She rolled over on her side and lumbered to her feet, trying not to cry out. She walked slowly away from her sleeping place to where the moon shone down on the soft leaves. There Dena squatted and moaned, pushing the child out from her body. With the last pain she brought the child out into the air. It feel onto the soft leaves and she picked it up. When it cried, the strange new noise disturbed Uria who rose from her place, not waking Shael. Uria ran toward the new sound. She knew what it was.

Without saying anything Uria bit the cord that had united Dena and child for many moons. Then she helped Dena to stand up. Together they walked back to Dena's sleeping place. Uria helped Dena lie down, handing the child to hold close to her, ready to give it food from her body when the child was ready.

Uria quietly crept back to her own sleeping place, to move herself close to Shael. She saw the moon had moved to where its light was shining on their place. Maybe it was the moon's light or maybe Uria disturbed his dreams, for Shael woke up and looked at Uria who had Dena's blood on her body, her hands, and where she had held her hair back, she had streaked blood on her face.

When Uria saw that Shael was awake she told him the news. "We have another one of our people now. The child in Dena came tonight." She was not ready for what Shael did.

"Is *that* what is on you? Is that woman's blood?" He jumped up and backed away from her. "If you touch me with woman's blood a curse will fall on me." He ran off into the night.

Uria watched him disappear. Why should he be afraid, she wondered. She looked at her hands and at the blood on her body. She rose and walked down to the stream. If woman's blood would scare Shael, then she must wash it away. Now she knew why several nights in every moon time, Shael did not come to stay with her.

The next day when they heard of Dena's child, Stoe and Vrev were happy and when they saw its body and knew it would grow up to be like them they were happier.

It was a good time. Dena was happy nursing her child, Chee and Breg caught fish every sun in the Quiet Stream. Only Uria was not happy. Each sun down she waited for Shael who had not come back since the child came to them. Should she go to him and show him that she was clean of blood? She did not know what to do. So many things were new in their thinking.

One day Uria saw Stoe and Vrev putting tree poles in the ground and making vine rope between the poles to hold up branches of leaves. This they told Uria is to be the "Men's House."

"It is only for men," Vrev said.

"Why?" Uria asked.

"So women won't go inside," Vrev answered.

"Why not?" Uria persisted.

"Because there will be Spirits inside who speak only to men. That is the way it is with the others."

Uria remembered when she had gone with Shael to the others there had been something he called the Men's House. Uria was confused. Too much had been happening. She was missing Shael and now all this about a Men's House when they never had any house before.

"What Spirits talk only to men?" she asked.

Stoe and Vrev continued to pile large leaves and handsful of grain stalks over the vine rope. After a long silence Stoe answered, "When the Men's House is built, the Spirits will enter."

"If we build a Women's House will Spirits come to that?" Dena asked.

Stoe and Vrev laughed. "Maybe. But not the

same Spirits." Vrev told her. "A Child Spirit visits you. It doesn't visit us."

"This is all things your women told you?" Uria asked.

"No," they both said. Then Stoe added, "Our new brothers tell us. They tell us bad things we have been doing that we must not do any longer or an Evil will happen to us all."

"What?" Dena asked listening from her sleeping place.

"You should not touch us, or our hunting poles, or our food when you have the moon blood."

"Why?"

"Because if we see your moon blood we will not find animals and we will lose our strength," Vrev explained.

"Your brothers tell you this?" Dena asked, watching her child feed himself with loud sucking noises. "What do your women there tell you?"

"Our women say their blood is taboo because they do not want a man near them when it is time for their moon blood," Stoe told them.

Dena laughed. "I do not want a man near me when I have made a new child. My blood is taboo now . . ."

"What other things are taboo now?" Uria asked.

"We must not enter your bodies because we are of the same family . . ." Stoe said quietly.

"Why not?" Dena asked.

"Because they say it is the greatest taboo,"

31

Vrev said. "For women we must go to others."

"You have learned many things to *not* do . . ." Dena told them.

"And," Stoe interrupted," things *to* do."

They waited. Stoe looked at Breg and Chee. Chee could see he did not want to tell them what things he had learned *to* do. Then he said slowly, "To make the grain grow they form a body out of earth and call it the Fertility Goddess. They put the Fertility Goddess in a special place on a mound near the grain and they dance around it and make what they call 'sacrifice' to the Goddess. The 'sacrifice' makes the grain grow."

Chee wondered, confused.

"The small one," Stoe continued, "of most value is killed. His blood is put on the earth of the first planting."

Breg picked up a small pebble and fondled it in his hand. "Who is a small one of most value?"

Stoe looked into Breg's eyes and told them, "For us, *you* are the small one of most value."

"You would *kill* me?" Breg asked Stoe.

They all waited for Stoe's answer. He smiled at Breg. "We do not plant seeds."

Chee was relieved. She would not want that empty feeling again.

Vrev looked uneasy. He fumbled with small twigs where they sat.

"The others do not believe the right things," he shook his head, puzzled. "They say a new child comes from saying words and making dances to their Fertility Goddess," he explained.

"That's not the way it is," Uria corrected. "I have had a child. Dena has a child. . . ."

"And *we* do not do those things," Chee interrupted. "It is the *Child Spirit*. Oolar told me that. The Child Spirit knows which bodies can feed a child. Oolar *told* me," she insisted.

They nodded in agreement with her. All except Stoe. "But they know things *we* do not know," he said firmly. They listened.

"They have grain to eat when they want it . . ." he added.

"And they don't have to go hunting for it . . ." Uria reminded them. "When it rains they have grain in their women's house. Shael told me."

"But small ones come from the Child Spirit," Chee insisted again. "Their Fertility Goddess may make their grain grow, but nobody made of earth had anything to do with Dena getting a small one."

"Still," Dena said, "it would be good to have grain grow where we want it. When we go back to the Cold Place many suns we are hungry from not finding food." She put her child's mouth to her breast and listened to it. They had been in the Warm Place for three moons. It was a good time for the Child Spirit to have come.

Here in the Warm Place, before the sun was too hot, there were plenty of grain seeds for gathering and there were small animals that were easy for Stoe and Vrev to kill. When it came time for the grain stalks to turn from green to yellow, the seeds were easy to gather, but three moons later, when the stalks would become brittle and the seeds would be blown away, Chee knew that Stoe would start to watch the sky. He would say, as Toan had said, "Sun every day now. No clouds. No cool. Only hot." Then he would listen for a wind to cool them, but there would be no wind. Only hot, dry sun.

Then they would be glad for their sleeping place in the shallow caves. Their food would be harder to get because when the hot sun came, the animals would leave for the higher mountains of the Cold Place.

When they first arrived at the Warm Place, Chee and Breg could find juicy, full berries, and nuts that had fallen from the trees, and they could splash water in the Quiet Stream. But as the hot sun came there were no more berries, or those they had not eaten were dried up like little hard pebbles, and there was no more water to splash in the Quiet Stream.

Their food was harder to find. Overturning rocks produced few bugs, for even bugs searched out cooler places.

Finding a lazy lizard brought a happy shout, and all would descend on the finder. Dena and Uria set out each sun-up before the heat came, to find roots they could eat.

Stoe and Vrev took turns at night, visiting their women in the other place and they came back to tell with envy about the grain.

"They smash it with rocks," Vrev told Dena and Uria, Like this." He placed small dirt rocks on one large hot rock and rolled another rock back and forth over the small rocks until they were fine dust.

"How do they eat that?" Uria asked.

"They mix it with water they have stored in earth jars. Then they put it on leaves and put it on the side of the fire."

"You have eaten it?" Dena asked.

"Yes. It is better than an empty stomach," he laughed.

"Tomorrow I will go find Shael," Uria announced. "I will ask them to show me how they make the grain grow where they want it to grow."

In this Hot Time Stoe and Vrev went further away each day in search of animals. When Dena and Uria left each sun-up to find roots, Chee and Breg followed behind, searching under rocks and fallen tree branches. Dena's child, strapped to Dena's bosom with vine rope, knew no hunger. When it stirred from its peaceful sleep, Dena put its mouth on her nipple, while she searched for certain roots growing along the ground. Looking for food lasted until the sun was straight up over the sky. After that it was too hot and they walked back to their place going a different way to find what they could. Each day's sun brought stronger heat.

When they first came from the Cold Place, their bodies moved quickly, they did not sleep in the sun time, they found food easily and they laughed and chattered often. Now, as the heat became stronger it took their energy, it dried up their food, and it quieted their laughter. Chee felt it must be getting near the time to go back to the Cold Place where they would stay many moons again until the Cold Time told them it was time to move back.

Then she and Breg, and even Dena's child, could once again splash in the Quiet Stream. Then there would be berries again, and nuts on the trees, and Breg would be big enough to kill the animals with Stoe and Vrev.

When Uria came back from Shael's people she had much to tell.

"They have an earth-carrying-thing to keep water. It is water from the Quiet Stream. There is no more water at the Quiet Stream, but *they* have water. *We* have to go to the water hole. But *they* have it at the women's house." She shook her head as almost not to believe what she had seen.

"And the grain?" Dena reminded her.

"They put it under the ground. Shael's sister showed me. Like this." With a twig she scratched a hole in the earth, put a handful of small pebbles into the hole, covered it with earth. Then she dug another hole and repeated what she had done. They looked at her for more explanation.

"When they plant in the rain time they do not carry water to the seeds," Uria said.

Dena was confused. "Do they, *sometime,* carry water to the seeds?" she asked.

"Yes. When they plant in the hot time."

"Do they plant many times?" Stoe asked.

"Yes," Uria said. "The women all have digging sticks for making grain grow. It is better, they say, than going out each day to look for food. And they have much grain stored in carrying things in the Women's House. They said they have to save it because they cannot plant anymore until the rains come."

"Do they *know* when the rains come?" Breg asked. "How can they *know* when the rains will come?"

"*They* know. They say it will be four moons from now. Then they say it will rain. Sometimes much, sometimes not much, for four moons. When four moons end, they plant, then they do what they call 'pray.' If no rain, they plant, they pray to Fertility Goddess, and then if no rain, they 'sacrifice' their strongest child, like Breg . . . a boy child."

"What does that mean? What do they do?" Dena asked.

"And why . . ." Breg wanted to know, "why a boy?"

"They say it is a 'sacrifice' only if the people give to the Goddess what is most valuable. They say it is no 'sacrifice' to give up a girl because nobody wants a girl," Uria explained.

"What do they do?" Chee asked.

"They put their earth Fertility Goddess piece on the planting. Then they dance and pray. Then they all go to the mountain cliff at the end of the Quiet Stream and they take their best boy who is not yet a man, and the Priestess tells the men to throw him off the cliff. When the big black birds come and circle the sky above his broken body, all the people go back and tell the Fertility Goddess."

"And then the grain grows in straight rows?" Breg asked.

"It always has, they said," Uria explained.

"Do *we* have to plant seeds," Chee asked Stoe.

"Do you get hungry?" he asked her.

Uria explained, "They said there could be no planting for many moons."

"We will be gone in two moons," Stoe said.

And in two moons it was time to follow the animals into the mountains of the Cold Place. Stoe and Vrev led the way with Uria, Dena, Breg, and Chee following in line.

Uria had asked Shael to come with her to the Cold Place, but he had told her it was their way to stay with their own, in their Men's House, and to be near to advise their sisters. Uria could not stay with Shael for she could not leave her own people. They needed her.

As for Chee, her stomach had been hungry for many moons. She was happy to be leaving the Warm Place as she had been, many moons ago, to leave the Cold Place.

When they started out she asked Stoe if he thought they would find Oolar.

Stoe's answer was brisk—a simple "No."

Hopeful, she asked Vrev, "Do you think when we cross the river we will find Oolar?"

Vrev told her, "Oolar has gone to the Spirit World. Do not ask unwise questions."

Chee walked along, the last in the line, wondering how anyone could know what happened to old Oolar. She had thoughts of him many times and had empty feelings when she remembered how they left him on the bank of the river. Maybe he was in the Spirit World but she would look for him anyway.

On this side of the river there was no danger

from others and it had been so hot that there were no animals around to attack them, so Stoe led them at a steady, unhurried pace until the sun set each night. Then they had time to look for roots or lizards or any nuts that had been overlooked by small animals.

Stoe moved them on each day to get them out of the heat they all knew would get stronger with each new sun. It was a long moon's walk to the river and once there Dena, with her child tied to her back, made it across without Uria's help. Once again Chee and Breg climbed up on the strong backs of Stoe and Vrev and were carried across the wide river, much shallower now than when they crossed before. Chee looked at the slow ripples of water over the rocks and knew that Oolar could have crossed the river at this time. She looked toward the other side long before they touched dry earth.

Stoe had warned them that when they reached the other side they would be in the area of the people of danger.

"Have any of our people ever *seen* any of the people of danger?" Breg had asked, when he was climbing on Stoe's back.

"One time when we got to the other side they were waiting for us. That was many, many moons ago. Chee was tied to her mother's back and . . ."

"Did everyone fight?" Breg asked.

"Yes, we all fought. There were more of us then." Stoe explained.

"I know," Breg said. "Then we had Oolar and Toan, and Chee's mother and . . . my mother," he added. "What happened when we all fought?"

"That was it. We fought! They had tree branches and poles. There were more of them than us. We fought for awhile and then we ran. Toan was strong. He stayed behind and fought with the big ones. When it was over and we had all run away, I saw Uria carrying Chee and running. She told me Chee had fallen off her mother when her mother was grabbed. We ran on but Chee's mother never came to us. They got her. We heard her noises."

"Was that when *my* mother got killed?" Breg asked.

"No. Your mother was killed when she was finding food. We thought at first it was from other people of danger." Stoe was half way across the river, striding on the shallow rocks. "Your mother was killed by a big animal."

"How do you know?"

"Because we *killed* that animal and opened his stomach. That's how we know."

Breg could say no more. He had been a very small one then and had no memory of his mother. All women were his mothers, just as they were Chee's mothers. They all took turns comforting and caring for the two small ones.

After the long swim across the river, the small group sloshed its way up on the other side onto the dry earth, gathering together near a large tree trunk to stay hidden from view of the dangerous ones. Maybe this time, too, they would be lucky. The last two crossings had been without any sight of the others. Stoe told them hurriedly they would have to get to the foot of the mountain before the sun went away. They must run faster than when they went through these trees before.

"If any one of us is attacked, the rest must run on. We are not enough of us to fight. Now, let us go," Stoe said and they set off in their usual order, with Chee the last in line.

They ran through the trees trying to be silent and trying to not break branches which might alert others. Stoe was hoping that since they had not been attacked on the river's edge, and had not had any fights for many crossings, maybe the people of danger had moved on to another place. Maybe they moved each hot or cold time just as their own group did.

It was hard for Chee to run so fast through a great many trees and fallen logs and broken branches and not fall down. Yet she knew she must not get far behind, that she must reach the safe place where no people of danger had ever been.

The twigs hit her legs and the taller branches lashed across her face. She could see Breg up ahead and she could hear Dena. She heard no one else behind her or around her though she imagined the dangerous ones were everywhere.

It was a long run and the sun was settling down for the night. They must get out of the danger area and up to the beginning of the mountain before the dark came.

And all through this place she thought of Oolar. This was the place where she was going to look for him. But how could she look for him when she was running and if she called to him it might bring the people of danger. She stifled a cry. What if he were near here and didn't know they were here?

When she felt her legs would quit running, she began to slow down, but then her fear of getting left behind made her run faster again. And her stomach began to hurt. They had not eaten since the sun rose far on the other side of the river. All they could find were pods in stalks dried from the heat and wind. It would be good to get to the Cold Place where the animals had gone to get away from the heat. It had been many suns since they had killed an animal.

They arrived at the beginning of the mountain, panting from lack of breath. Breg's leg was cut from a tree branch, Dena's child was crying and eating. Uria told Chee to go with her to gather twigs, while Stoe and Vrev, still breathing in short puffs were putting loose tree branches in a pile. Vrev twirled a stick into the wood fire circle and the brittle leaves caught a spark and sent a flame from leaf to leaf and then to the twigs and to the branches. No animal would sneak up on them tonight. With empty stomachs they fell asleep while Breg and Vrev took the first turn to keep the fire going.

The next day, without taking time to look for food, they started up the mountain. The thoughts of an animal kill on the other side moved their feet quickly up the rocks. Dena's child rocked back and forth on her mother's back as she swayed climbing from one boulder to the next. The climb was easier going to the

Cold Place because on the long side of the mountain they would be going down hill.

They each slipped through the passageway at the top and began the long downward move, careful to put their feet on firm rocks.

When they reached the valley they ran in the direction of Toan's burial mound. They searched over the wide area fearful that the melting snow had made mud of it and washed it away. But Uria found a rise in the earth and they knew it was their mound.

"The earth is not as we left it," she said, pointing to the tall grain on the mound.

"It's grain," Dena said. "There's no other grain like that here."

Vrev broke off a handful of stalks and pulled the grain loose in his hand. He showed it to them. "This is the grain that grows over by the Yellow Cliff. It's grain I put in Toan's hand when we put him in his last sleep position."

They all looked at the grain in Vrev's hand, then at the stalks growing on the mound, and then at each other. "We have planted seeds," Stoe said. "Toan, from his Spirit World, has shown us how."

"Then we can do it again," Uria announced.

"And we'll never be hungry," Breg laughed, and the rest smiled, except Stoe.

"Remember," Dena told them quietly, "what else was in Toan's hand when we put him in the earth?"

Nobody could remember.

"Blood," Dena said.

They nodded, remembering. Their smiles disappeared.

43

"Maybe it is as they said," Stoe thought out loud. "The people by the Quiet Stream told us, to make the grain grow, people must make sacrifice."

"We did not make sacrifice," Vrev reminded Stoe.

"Toan," Stoe said. "Toan was our sacrifice. It was his blood."

"Toan has given us food," Dena said, pulling a handful of grain into her hands.

"No," Stoe said. "It was the Fertility Goddess."

They looked at Stoe and at each other and then Chee said, "But we don't have a Fertility Goddess."

Stoe looked toward the sky. "The Goddess is here. She makes the grain grow. And it must be as the others said, the Fertility Goddess gives us small ones, for it is here that Dena first knew she would have a small one. . . ."

Chee interrupted, "That was because of the *Child* Spirit."

"No, I do not think so anymore," Dena said. "These two things in this place tell me the Fertility Goddess is here. Here she makes grain grow from one of our own and here she puts into my body a small one." She waved her hands over the patch of grain on the raised earth mound.

Then Uria told them, "We shall find a rock and shape a body from it with another rock. We will have our Fertility Goddess and we will place her on Toan's mound. "Tomorrow," Uria added, "we will go to the water hole and mix water with earth to make carry-things as the people from the Quiet Stream made. Then when we put this seed under ground we will carry water to put on the earth, as I saw them do."

"It will be the same as water from the sky?" Chee asked.

"Yes," Uria answered.

"And we won't be hungry again?" Breg asked.

"Not if the Fertility Goddess helps us," Stoe said.

"I'm hungry now," Chee complained, and they all remembered their long-empty stomachs as they wandered off in search of food, leaving the grain on the ground to be used as the seeds for their first planting.

It was Uria who found a rock about the size of her hand that she said would be right for their Fertility Goddess. "It is the same size as what the others had where their grain was growing. We can chip it down on the sides with another rock . . ." she suggested.

"And smooth it too, with rocks . . ." Vrev added. "Their Fertility Goddess did not look like a rock."

"Ours won't either," Uria said proudly.

So they chipped and rubbed at the rock to make it the shape of a female body, bulging at the stomach as Dena had recently bulged, with overhanging breasts, large hips to support her full body, short legs, and flat feet to keep her figure in a standing position.

Their figure had bulky shoulders, fat upper arms, and lower arms that curved peacefully onto her belly. They had chipped away to

45

shape her hair with ripples falling around her ears and neck, as they themselves had. But her face, blurred by dents of the rocks that had pounded it, suggested a half smile as one who had a secret they were not going to share.

They were proud of their Goddess. It was the most important thing in their lives. Their first possession. They held it by turns, as they had shaped it by turns. Except for the wood fire-circle that they had shaped out of a tree branch, they had never made anything before.

When they agreed that it was as fine as it could be, they carried it to the burial mound. Dena, with her child on her bosom, held the Goddess in her two hands stretched out before her, and the others followed. It was she who had most recently had the same shape as the Goddess, so it was she who should honor Her.

Uria followed behind Dena in line. Stoe and Vrev walked behind her. Breg followed after Vrev, and Chee was at the end of the line. The small procession, carrying their precious creation, was silent. Their steps were unhurried because they wished to impress their Goddess with the seriousness of their actions.

This was no casual walk, nor was it a search for food, no escape from danger, from cold, or from heat. This was a walk for a new purpose. This was what the others had called "worship." As they had carefully rubbed the stones on the larger stone that Dena found, and had seen the figure emerge to resemble a woman about to give them another small one, they had each felt Her presence come from the rock and they beheld it as though the Goddess had formed Herself. It was as though She had come to them and said, "I am here to make your group grow large with new small ones and to make your grain grow where none has grown before."

The slow, silent march ended at Toan's burial mound. Uria scraped a flat place in the earth and Dena slowly and carefully set their Goddess down on the earth and then stepped back from the mound. The group was silent, looking at their Goddess with adoration.

"Now," Uria said, "we will plant the grain and it will grow in rows. And her name . . . her name will be Illinini." They all looked at her.

"How do you know that?" Dena asked.

"It came to me in my dream time. I saw her. She told me."

"Illinini," they said softly, trying out the name in their mouths.

"Illinini . . . Illinini."

They felt blessed. Dena, Uria, and Chee mumbled her name as they scratched into the earth, stretching out from Toan's burial ground, dropping seeds into the ground. Stoe and Vrev walked into the mountains with their hunting poles looking for animals to kill.

As one moon followed another they were all busy in their own way. The men went off each day to hunt animals and the women made carry-things of dirt mixed with water which they dried hard in the sunshine. They would use these to carry water to their grain.

When Stoe and Vrev brought back an animal slung over Stoe's shoulder, felled by the hunting pole with a sharp rock in its point, the women stripped off the skin, as they had always done, and hung it on a tree to dry. When they were eating the moist meat, Uria looked at the animal skin and told Dena of her idea.

"We could carry water in the skin, if we could tie it together."

Dena agreed. "And it would not be so heavy," she added.

Several suns later they shook the skin free of small bugs and tried to shape it into a carrything. There was no way the vine rope would hold it closed so it could hold water. Uria took a small stick and poked a hole in one end, pushing vines through the hole in the stick. Then she tried to poke the stick through the animal skin but the stick broke. She found a bone from the animal, same size as the stick and she used a sharp rock to grind a small hole in the thick end of the bone. She pushed a long vine rope through the hole and then pushed the bone into two pieces of skin she held together.

She called out to Dena, "Now we can make a water carrier out of animal skin."

"We can make *many* water carriers," Dena exclaimed.

It was not as it had been on the last time they were at the Cold Place. Stoe and Vrev went daily to search for animals, as always, and when they returned they rested, as always. The women skinned the animals and tore the meat into hunks for roasting. They hung the skins to dry. The skins they did not use for carriers, they sewed into coverings for their feet for the colder time that was coming.

48

Now that they could sew the animal skins, they could shape them to fit their bodies, instead of tying the skins around themselves with vine ropes.

Dena's child's first walking skin had holes torn out for his arms. They laughed when they saw him waddling like a small half-animal creature.

"The She animal with four legs will suckle him," Stoe laughed and Dena became frightened.

"No. He will be with *me*," she declared. "No She animal with four legs will suckle our small ones."

Each day the women and children carried water with their animal skin carriers to pour on the earth where the grain lay underground. The water hole level was always the same though they had taken water out for one moon. It was not like the water at the Warm Place where the Quiet Stream became shallower with each moon until it was a trickle and then nothing but dry rocks.

Uria carried many heavy skins of water to the grain field and lay down in the shade often to make the pain in her back and stomach go away. Since she left the Warm Place many moons ago she had not had any moon blood. She thought if her moon blood would flow from her it would hurt her stomach at first, but then maybe her moon blood would take away the pains in her back. Yet she carried the water loads and worked to make the earth around the sprouting grain loose with her digging stick.

It was when she was bending over, close to the dirt, she first felt movement in her stomach. She dug in the earth again, set the Goddess straight on the earth, and felt the movement again. Then she recognized the feeling. It was the same feeling she had when the Child Spirit had visited her and given her the small one many moons ago.

Water came to her eyes as she remembered the child, Sel. The movement happened again. She knelt in the dirt by Illinini, the Fertility Goddess, and called aloud to Dena who came to her running, pulling her child by the hand, followed by Chee and Breg.

"It is another small one," Uria yelled at them as they came to her. "I'm going to have another small one." Her smile greeted theirs. They hugged her and patted her and she held them in return. Dena's child climbed on her and she nuzzled him, eager to get the feel of a small one again.

"It is Illinini," she smiled. "She made our grain grow and she has given us another small one."

"If we stay here, we will soon be many," Dena laughed.

"And we will never be hungry," Breg told them.

"And never too hot from the Warm Place again," Chee said.

When the men returned, the women and children ran to them. Though the men had no animals for eating, their happiness at the gift from the Goddess made up for their bad day. Besides, the women were making grain cakes to fill with colored roots to cook over the fire.

They had all they could ever want. Their grain was growing, there were animals to kill, and animal hides for body covering and water carriers. And now with the news of the new one they were pleased with their Goddess and with themselves. They talked about how they would not want to leave here.

"We have what we want here," Dena told them. "And we would not want to displease our Goddess."

"If we leave, She may not let us grow grain in the Warm Place," Vrev said, devouring one of the grain cakes in one swallow.

"And She may not give us another small one," Uria said, smiling and putting her hands on her stomach.

The moons went by, with each sun making them more certain that the next sun would be as good as the last. Dena and Uria made earthern tops for their earthern carriers, put the extra grain into the carriers and set them far into the deep cave at the beginning of the mountain. They knew that in this Cold Place water from the sky could turn to snowy earth-cover and no wild roots, or berries, or grain could then be found. Deciding to stay in the Cold Place with their Goddess they would hide food from themselves until they could no longer find any when the Cold Place turned white.

If they could have enough grain they could stay. They could put water in the carriers and hide that too, to use when they could not melt the ice.

"There are many reasons to stay here," Stoe told them. "The animals that come to the Cold Place when we are not here are as big as many of me, and their foot marks in the snow make them easy to find."

"They will be dangerous," Chee thought.

"Am I big enough to hunt when the white earth comes?" Breg asked.

"You are yet a small one. When your head reaches my shoulder, you will be big enough to hunt with us."

Unlike anything they had ever done before, they set up the inside of the cave with grain and water for the Cold Time that was coming. Dena and Uria watched their grain coming to the end of its growth, hoping the cold would stay away until the seeds were ripe enough to pull from the stalks.

When the cold winds came to stay, they had food to eat and water to drink and when the earth was covered with its cold white blanket, they brought the snow into the cave and melted it over their fire to save their stored water. They were learning to save for coming days. This was a new thing for them.

When Stoe and Vrev wanted more grain

cakes than were cooked for them, they were told they had to wait until the next sun.

"In our other days we ate until we could not eat anymore," Stoe complained.

"Yes," Dena agreed, "and we had empty stomachs at many sun downs."

"My stomach is empty now," Stoe complained again.

"Then go out and follow the animal tracks in the snow. It will be good to fill our stomachs with an animal kill," Dena told them.

"I am happy you cannot save animal meat. *That* is what we can eat until our stomachs won't take anymore," Stoe said, gathering his heavy animal skin to tie over his light weight animal skin covering. Vrev joined Stoe as he went out of the warmth of the smokey cave, leaving the women and children sewing animal hides together to put over the entrance to the cave for the time when the wind would blow hard.

Uria, her stomach grown large with her child, moved slowly and clumsily in their small place. Her time for waiting would soon be over. She knew the pains she had had when she pushed Sel from her body were the pains she had been having this sun. When they hurt her more she would walk into the snow and find a fallen tree to sit on and she would push the child from her belly. She would try to make no sound. Then she would carry the small one back to their cave in her arms. That was the picture in her mind, and that was the way her child met its life outside of Uria's stomach.

Dena knew why Uria left the cave and she

would go to find her if she heard a cry. But there was only silence. Breg and Chee threw small dry twigs on the fire and worked at softening the leather of the animal hides. They chewed on the hide and they rubbed one piece of hide against another to get out the stiffness so Dena could sew on it. Dena's child wandered around the cave, sometimes falling down into his mother's lap, or holding a piece of animal skin and trying to chew it with his three teeth. Chee and Breg were laughing at him when Uria walked into the cave holding her child inside her animal fur. Dena reached up for the child as Uria sank to the floor next to the fire and pulled her legs up to her body. Dena examined the new child and saw that it would be as Stoe and Vrev, and as her own child. She covered him in animal skin so no air could reach him except where she could see his small nose.

Chee and Breg went to stand in the door of the cave and Dena called them back. "It is too cold there. Come back into the warm."

"We are looking at the blood that Uria dripped into the cave. It's out there too. A row of it that comes into the cave," Breg said.

Uria, who had heard their talk of her blood, remembered Shael's fear of Dena's blood when she had helped separate Dena's body from Dena's new child. She rolled over and asked them, "Go out into the snow and cover the blood with snow. In the cave, wipe away the blood with an animal skin. It is a thing of fear for men."

"I'm a man and I'm not afraid of it. It's only red spots in the snow," Breg explained.

"To *big* men, it is a thing of fear. The men in the Warm Place told Stoe and Vrev they must not see woman's blood or they will lose their strength," Uria said.

Chee and Breg stood at the entrance unsure of what to do. Dena said, "Stoe and Vrev did not believe the ways of the others."

"They do now, Dena," Uria told her. "See how they believe about the Fertility Goddess. And is it not true that Illinini brings small ones and makes the grain grow?"

"Yes, they *do* believe in our Goddess, but how do we know they will believe as the others about women's blood?" Dena asked.

"Because if it is right to believe the Fertility Goddess brings food and small ones then that would make it right for them to believe that woman's blood will bring bad things," Uria explained.

Still Chee and Breg moved neither back into the cave nor out into the snow. Uria saw the small bundle of animal skin move and she beckoned to Dena to bring her the new small one. Uria carefully unwrapped the animal skin and held her child up for an examination and then she tucked him inside her own animal skin to get his first food from her body.

When she was settled once again, Dena asked her, "Uria, do *you* believe woman's blood will cause evil to men?"

"No," Uria laughed. "But I don't want the men entering my body when I have my moon blood, or, as now, when I have pushed my child out of my body. It would give me pains again. I don't want those pains again."

"Then go and cover the blood with snow," Dena directed the children. "Stay together. Do not go far. Then come back here and get dried by the fire."

They ran out of the cave into the snow, picked up handsful of snow and threw them on the spots of blood.

"I do not want a man to enter my body yet," Dena told Uria. "As long as my child takes his food from my body," she continued, "no man will enter my body. It would not be good. My milk would dry up and my child would go to the Last Sleep Place. Chee's mother told me not to take a man until my child is walking."

"Yes. That is why Sel had been walking many moons before a man entered my body," Uria said.

The children returned with red faces from the cold air. They were short of breath, cold, and happy to have had a short time out of their cave. Dena wiped away the blood spots on the hard earthen floor. Then all but Uria worked at their animal skin, softening and sewing. And after the sun went away, Stoe and Vrev returned, once again with no animal. It was Breg who changed their unhappiness into joy when he told them the good news. "Uria has a small one. She went out into the snow and came back with it."

Stoe and Vrev were startled.

"The Fertility Goddess is *good* to us here," Vrev said.

56

"Uria, what do we have?" Stoe peeled off Uria's covering to see the small one. "Ah, it will be a hunter," he said happily.

Vrev gave a shout and turned his back on the rest, looking back into the cave. He moved many earthen carriers until he found what he was looking for. It was the small rock figure of their Fertility Goddess. They had not wanted to leave her out in the snow.

Vrev ran his hand slowly over the Goddess, Illinini, and then put Her in Stoe's outstretched hand. He, too, smoothed his hands over Her round body and then passed Her on to Dena. After they had all stroked Her plump figure, Vrev returned Her to the safe place they had chosen for Her. "She has been good to us," Stoe said.

"And we must have been good to Her," Dena agreed, "or She would not have given us grain and a new small one."

They celebrated by mixing ground grain with a little water and baking grain pats over the fire to eat with dried small bugs that Dena had hidden away.

They slept well that night, disturbed only occasionally by the small one's cry, asking his mother for a new position to lie in, or more warm food to fill his small stomach. The fire burned low in the cave, only high enough to keep the animals out. Tomorrow they would gather more wood to dry in their cave, and tomorrow they were sure Stoe and Vrev would kill a big animal.

But the big animals avoided them that Cold Time. At times they killed a little animal, and that was when they feasted, filling their stomachs until they could put no more in their mouths.

Dena watched over the grain supply, wanting to make it last until the Cold Time was over. Though they were eating very little she was worried because the grain was getting low in the carriers.

When the cold wind did not blow the snow over the animal tracks, Stoe and Vrev went out of the warm cave on their searches. Only a few times in the whole Cold Time they brought back a kill that filled their stomachs and restored their good feelings.

As the grain level in their carriers dropped lower with each day's eating, the squabbles in the cave increased. When the men came back with no animal, and Dena mixed the small portion of grain with water to make grain cakes, they ate hungrily and quickly. Then they let the fire die down, but not out, and fell into a long night's sleep.

In their cave it was easy to worry and to wonder if the Warm Time would ever come again. When Uria reminded them that they had been there four moons, because she had had her moon blood four times, they were surprised.

"How many moons is a Cold Time?" Breg asked Uria.

"Six sticks Cold Time, six sticks Warm Time. This Cold Time is a longer one because this time we did not go to the Warm Place."

"Will we never go to the Warm Place again?" Breg remembered splashing in the Quiet Stream.

"Our Fertility Goddess is good to us here," Dena said. "She makes our grain grow here."

"And," Uria nuzzled her small one, "here She puts small ones in our bodies."

"That's right." Dena thought out loud, "We never had a small one enter our bodies in the Warm Place."

"And here Illinini makes grain grow on Toan's mound," Chee smiled.

"We must save some grain seed," Dena advised, "to put into the earth when the Warm Time comes."

Chee lifted the cover of the last carrier that still contained grain. "I hope the Warm Time comes soon."

Dena separated seeds from one carrier to place in another. "This is for planting, not eating," she told the others. "If we do not have enough to plant, our Goddess cannot help us grow any grain."

They agreed, yet they looked hungrily at the grain carrier holding the grain they could not eat.

It was a long Cold Time but eventually it blended into a warming up of the snow, then a melting, and gradually into a time of warmer air and light rains instead of heavy storms.

Chee and Breg climbed the rocks to explore and to find insects and small reptiles coming out of their winter hiding. Dena and Uria tied their small ones to their backs and left the cave to search each day for fresh, juicy shoots. Under their feet they felt the earth warming up and they looked for strong digging sticks to loosen the soil for the time when the earth would be right for planting.

When Stoe and Uria took digging sticks and began to help in getting the soil ready, Dena told them, "The Fertility Goddess is a woman. She makes the ground fertile for our grain. She makes our bodies fertile for our children. It is not man's work. Women do not kill animals. Men do not grow grain." Stoe and Vrev put down their digging sticks and walked away.

Each day Dena and Uria picked the soil up in their hands and on the day it crumbled easily, they decided it was time for planting. They loosened the soil once again and carefully put their hoarded seeds into the earth in rows that extended from Toan's grave over to the beginning of the mountain.

When the field was planted, they brought their Fertility Goddess out of its Cold Time place in their cave and placed Her at the head of Toan's mound. Dena followed her, holding her child's hand. Then Chee took Dena's child's other hand. Soon they formed a circle including Breg, Stoe and Vrev. Uria began a sing-song chanting not removing her eyes from the Goddess. The others joined her chant. Round and round they shuffled and chanted, their animal skin garments flapping against their legs. It was as though they couldn't stop. When Dena's child began to cry with fatigue, Dena dropped her hand from Uria's and tied her child on her back, continuing the shuffle in honor of their Goddess who would make their grain grow.

And they knew She would respond to their pleadings when a light rain began to fall on their newly planted earth. She had heard their chant and She rewarded them with the fertility of moisture their seeds needed to take hold in the dirt.

With the first drops of rain, they stopped their shuffling and their chanting and shouted their praises to their Goddess. They adored Her and were pleased with themselves for having been wise enough to know how to please Her.

Now they could stay in the Cold Place and never have to move to the Warm Place and be afraid of the people of danger, nor would they have to suffer in the heat of the Warm Place. Now they knew how to grow grain rather than search for it. They knew how to store grain to last through the snow-covered winter, and they knew how to please their Goddess so She could provide them with Fertility to grow grain and increase their group with small ones. They had all the proof that told them they would never need to have empty stomachs ever again.

The light rain that fell on planting day was the last to fall for three moons. They carried water in their carriers from the water hole to their grain field, but it was not enough. Though they all worked at hauling and pouring the water, the rows of grain only broke through the earth and there they stopped. By the time they had finished watering one end of the field, the other end was so dry the earth had cracked.

They started over again, bringing the water in their earthen carriers and at the same time watching the sky for clouds that would bring a relieving shower.

They shuffled and chanted around the Fertility Goddess, but that made no difference to the weather. Their Goddess must not be listening to them.

They depended on the roots and insects they could find for their food supply as Stoe and Vrev had made only one animal kill since the planting. They could see the animals and they aimed their throwing pole, but the animals shook off the pain of the pole's blow, running out of sight into the craggy mountains. They wondered what they had done to anger their Goddess.

"Maybe it is time that we do what the others did when *their* crops didn't grow," Stoe said.

None needed to ask what he meant. They had all thought about it ever since they gave up hope that rain would come. If they were to please their Goddess how would they do it? They all knew what must be done, or they would all go to the Last Sleep Place from empty stomachs. When Chee and Breg were asleep, the big people talked about it.

"Where shall our sacrifice be made?" was one of the questions Vrev asked.

"The highest cliff that we can see from the mound," Stoe told him.

"Where the Goddess can see the sacrifice," Dena added.

They nodded.

Another question that must be answered was, "Who would be sacrificed to Illinini?" and Vrev asked that question also.

Stoe told them, as he had told them at the Warm Place, that it should be the most valuable small one. "Because," he said, "if the one is not valuable, to kill him would be no sacrifice."

"Him?" asked Dena. "Must it be a boy?"

"Breg is the most valuable small one because he is going to be a hunter," Stoe said.

"Chee is our most valuable small one because she will *have* a small one some day."

"Who is to decide?" Uria asked.

"What would please the Fertility Goddess most?" Stoe asked. "We must please *Her.*"

"She, who is the Goddess of Fertility of the body of women, would not be pleased if we sacrificed a small one who would one day have a body She could make large with a child," Dena said.

"Then it is agreed," Stoe asked, "if we sacrifice Breg it is because he is our most valuable small one who will not have a body the Fertility Goddess can one day make large with a child?"

One by one they nodded.

"When?" Uria asked, holding her tiny boy

close to her body. When, she wondered, would it be Dena's child's turn, or her own child's?

"At the sun's beginning," Stoe said.

"How?" Vrev wondered.

"We will dance and chant," Dena told them, "as we did when we pleased the Goddess the first time. Breg will not know. Stoe, you shall pick him up and throw him off the cliff. We shall dance and chant until the large, black birds come to him."

They agreed and walked back to their cave where Chee and Breg had fallen asleep tumbled together as they must have played.

The big ones did not sleep as peacefully. Pictures of tomorrow foreshadowed the sun-up. They woke unhappily to hear Breg and Chee outside the cave in babbling talk about berries, and about trying to step on fish in the Quiet Stream. They laughed and talked, but the big ones inside the cave neither laughed nor did they talk. They rose off the earthen floor, tightened their animal skins on their shoulders, and went outside, leading the way to the cliff overlooking Toan's burial mound.

"There aren't any lizards up here," Breg told them. "Why are we going up here?"

"There are Igualos and Tolados with the soft skins. I'll show you soon," Vrev lied.

"Some day," Breg boasted, "I'll come up here by myself and have a feast!"

"Some day soon," Dena promised, "you'll be a good hunter." The big ones agreed with her because they knew she meant that Breg would be a good hunter in the Spirit World.

Uria, with her baby tied to the front of her

body, suckling sleepily at her bosom, climbed up the rocks. From a distance it would have appeared, with the animal skin coverings and their moving on their hands and feet, that a pack of markhors were making the climb. The height and difficulty of pulling themselves up over the rocks meant that they did not speak while they climbed over the last ledge, one by one, each in turn extending their help to the one behind them.

It was the first time they had been on top of the cliff because it was in the opposite direction of their route each time when they left the Cold Place.

"This will be *it!*" Dena said.

"Yes," Stoe and Vrev agreed.

"This will be the place where we make all our sacrifices," Dena started when Breg interrupted.

"What's a sacrifice? I can't remember . . . you talked about a sacrifice when we were at the Warm Place."

"It's a . . ." she began. "It's a . . . a time when we *offer* something to our Goddess."

"Look!" Chee said. "Over there. I can see far down there to Toan's mound."

"If you had the eyes of a big-winged black bird you could see our Goddess," Stoe said. "Right where she stands looking up at us here."

"Is She looking at us?" Breg asked. He waved his arms to the mound, back and forth. "Can She see me waving?"

"Yes," Stoe said. "She can see our new, strong hunter."

"I'm not a hunter yet," Breg laughed, and the clouds that were gathering seemed to join the important talk. The black clouds from the Warm Place were moving toward the white clouds from their Cold Place as though they too would be part of the coming ceremony. Even the wind that had grown stronger as they had climbed higher, was adding its part to the occasion.

"Breg, come over here and see what I see on *this* side," Chee called to him. He ran to her. The big ones huddled together, their plans muffled from the children by the increasing noise of the wind. When Breg and Chee ran back to them it was to join the big ones in a shuffling, circular dance at the edge of the cliff. Each time Chee moved too close to the edge it made her dizzy and she tried to remember every time she made the circle to stay away from the edge.

The dance went round and round and the chanting rose from a low mumbling to a loud calling to the Fertility Goddess below. Dena's voice rose and fell with the noise of the wind.

"Look, our Goddess," Dena chanted.
"Look at us above you,
Illinini,
We who love you,
Offer you our best,
To receive your favor.
Let us know you see us,
Let us know you favor us again.
Make our earth and our woman's bodies
   fertile,

Oh Goddess of our Mother Earth,
Look at us above you,
We who love you,
Offer you our best,
To receive your favor.
Let us know you see us,
Let us know you favor us again,
Make our earth and our woman's bodies
    fertile,
Oh Goddess of our Mother Earth,
Look at us above you,
Illinini,
We who love you,
Offer you our best,
To receive your favor."

As they danced and chanted round and round in dizzying hardly conscious movements, the wind blew the black clouds and the white clouds closer together.

The babies who had at the first of the dancing whimpered because their food supply was bouncing away from them, began to cry aloud as the monotony of the shuffle prevented them from satisfying their hunger.

The chant grew louder as each person mimicked Dena's words with more sureness. The cries of the babies joined each new beginning of the chant, and the wind grew stronger. Then the black clouds and the white clouds crashed into each other sending a flash of light from the top of the mountain down through the dark valley to the burial mound and the Fertility Goddess.

They all stood rigid, silent. The babies did

not cry. Their Goddess had spoken to all of them. She had seen and approved. Stoe picked up Breg, as he had always done when they crossed the river. Breg felt his hands being torn from around Stoe's neck, something Stoe had never done when they crossed the river. Not understanding, Breg looked from the mixed-up black and white clouds to Stoe's face. He felt himself flung far out over the cliff.

Did his body falling through the air make the terrible noise that they heard, or was it the noise of his body breaking when it was received by the earth? Those far above could not see where his body lay, but they knew from the large, full drops of water falling from the clouds above that they and their Goddess, Il-linini, were one again. Their fertile earth would grow their grain and their woman's bodies would be fertile. Now they knew how.

2

The Great Transition

Though Chee lived on for many Warm Times and Cold Times she never lost the picture of Breg's small body falling into the valley. She didn't know why she thought of Old Oolar at the same time she thought of Breg. They were in the Spirit World but they were in her head too.

As the Warm and Cold Times passed, Chee's body grew taller and it swelled. And in a regular rhythm it issued forth her moon blood. Later in her short life the Child Spirit entered her body several times. Her children, and her children's children grew up, replenished their group, and died. This cycle was repeated through the milleniums.

Chee's descendents became known as the Berker Clan and about 5000 B.C. resettled in the area near what was later to be the ancient city of Gandhara, south of Kabal in the foothills of the Himalaya Mountains. Here, at the end of the long, thick, dark grove of trees, one of Chee's descendents, a small boy called Nargab, emerged into the clan's compound where there was yet daylight, proud that he had given the cattle a long day of feeding and yet had made it back before the sunlight turned to darkness. He watched the younger children run the cattle into the cattle-hold.

The women came out from their huts to watch through the dust thrown about by the cattle's hoofs. It was Kolar who ran over to Nargab to ask him why the milkless calf did not return.

"What did you *do* with it?" She was angry.

Nargab's pride turned to confusion. He shook his head. His mother, Ashinda went to him. "Do not anger the Fertility Goddess or we will have evil among us," she warned him kindly. "Go and get the calf."

"I . . . I don't know . . . It was with the rest when we entered the trees. . . ." Nargab stammered, looking at everyone looking at him. The men came from their Men's House, stood behind the women, watching. They were curious but they would not interfere, for grain and cattle were women's work. It was women who were related to the Fertility Goddess. Men could not advise because advice came from the Goddess Illinini through those whom she made fertile when she wished to increase their clan.

"You must go back and bring the calf," Ashinda urged her son.

It would be dark in the trees now and the night spirits would make him fearful. Kolar herself had told him cattle will not be moved at night. What was he to do?

He looked at Kolar and at all the eyes on him and he had bad feelings. He thought the food in his stomach was going to come up into his mouth.

Then Kolar changed her voice. She who was the wise one told him, "The calf will come to its mother here when it gets hungry." She took a twine rope and went into the cattle-hold.

"Here," she said, extending the rope to Nargab. "When I bring the mother out, tie her to that tree. She will be unhappy and will call to her calf. You will be unhappy and will call her to her calf. You will sleep out here tonight. When the calf comes to its mother, you will herd it into the cattle-hold."

Relieved that he did not have to go back into the dark forest, Nargab happily agreed to Kolar's scheme to capture the calf. He could see that it would be possible for him to regain his lost position of a trusted one if he could only stay awake and do as Kolar said. He tried to persuade himself that it would not be difficult. It would not be frightening, he said to himself, as he slumped to lean against a tree trunk. He watched the daylight dim to dusk, and then into darkness. He would not be fearful, he would concentrate on the calf.

But if the calf never came back, what then?

If the mother didn't make noise, what then? He had heard Kolar telling the women not to take out any of the calf's mother's milk until the calf came back. "If she is in pain from her full bag she will call to her calf." The women knew that Kolar was right.

Just as Nargab had felt the dreamworld coming toward him, the cow's long, lamenting noise brought Nargab to recognize where he was. The loud, mournful sound continued on and on, and Nargab listened for the sound of cracking twigs, imagining he heard the calf joined with its mother. But there was no other sound. Between the mother's cries there was only silence. All the others in the clan must have gone into the dreamworld because no one came out of their huts. All was quiet around him except for the cow's noise. Was this the Fertility Goddesses' way of punishing him because he had wanted to save the calf? Always before, a calf that would never make milk was killed. Nargab turned his head away when calves were killed.

He had pleaded to save this one. But maybe he had done a wrong. The calf was gone and his people would look at him with side glances. He knew that's what they did when someone had done wrong. Would that mean he could not join the men on the hunt when he was bigger?

Water started to come into his eyes as he thought about the evil possibilities in his future. He wiped his eyes with the backs of his hands and when he opened them he saw a man's figure at the end of the trees near the first of the women's huts. The moon's light did not reveal to him who the figure was. Nargab strained to see. Was it one of his mother's brothers who had come to help him? When the moon's light moved from behind the tree he could see clearly. Nargab pulled back his breath and put his hand over his mouth to quiet his noise. It was a man from the Renk clan.

He had seen one of the Renk clan only once before when his mother and the children were gathering berries in the mountains before the cold winds came. The women had heard men talking, had silenced all the children while they crept silently past the band of talking, resting Renk hunting men. They had been told to walk without breaking twigs and to look straight ahead, but Nargab looked through the thicket of tall bushes at the men who never knew that there were other people near them. Nargab saw frightening strangers, men with animal skins on their shoulders. They had the same kind of heads as his mother's brothers had, but these were fearsome. Each man had what looked like an animal tail coming out of his head.

When his mother and the children finally reached their own huts they told the men of their danger.

"We were close so we could hear them make strange words," Ashinda said.

"If any one of them had turned his head they would have seen us . . ."

"They had tails growing out of their heads," Nargab told the men who laughed at him.

"They *did*," Nargab insisted. "They had caps like yours," he pointed to Kesch, who took his hat off and looked at it, shaking his short hair, "but it had a hole in the back where the tail grows out." Then the man laughed louder because they knew, as they explained, it was not a tail that grew out, but hair, grown long and wound together and tied at the end with twine.

"When we hunted in the high mountains we were attacked by those Renks," his mother's brother explained. "There were more Renks than Berkers. Ghabber was our only brother who was bigger than a Renk. He threatened to cut off their Bodie, that's what they call the 'tail,' if the other Renks didn't release us. They dropped us and ran. If they lose their hair, their Goddess takes away their running speed for the hunt."

Even now in the night's darkness, Nargab could see the tail on the Renk and it frightened him. There he stood, that Renk in the moonlight, on the other side of the cattle-hold, and near the women's huts, his bow over his shoulder, his Bodie down to his hips. Nargab wanted to warn someone. The Renk had ignored the cow's calling and just stood there, waiting.

If Nargab yelled, would his yell be heard? Would everyone think it was the cow, or the calf? No, he would not yell. Instead he would aim at the Renk with his bow and arrow. And when he showed the dead Renk to the others in the morning, they would respect him again, even if the calf did not come back.

Nargab took a good aim on the man standing in the moonlight. But if his arrow did not hit where Nargab wanted it to go, the Renk would have time to aim an arrow at Nargab. Just as Nargab quietly pulled the carved bow back to his small shoulder, he saw a woman's figure next to the Renk's.

"It's Belka," he whispered to himself in great surprise, lowering his bow to his side. Belka came out of her hut and took the Renk by the hand. Nargab saw her lead him straight into her hut where she slept with her mother, her sister, and brothers. Once again on this long day, Nargab was confused. Was not the Renk an enemy?

His own mother, Ashinda, had brought the strange man, Aryites, into her hut at night and he had known there were other men from other clans, but never had she brought a Renk. Now he was frightened to know that one of these of the enemy clan was with one of their women. He had been warned about Renks and he feared them. He could not comprehend.

He was tired. The cow's pleading noise made him want to yell at her to stop. Nargab had had no food and was told not to take the cow's milk and now there was a Renk in one of their huts. He wanted to cry, but was fearful of making noise. He was muddled in his mind and could not think what he should do. He tried to put himself in Kolar's place. What would she tell him if she were here? She who always knew what to do, she would know now.

Nargab did not realize that the cow had quit calling, and that the noise he heard was that of the calf who had come back to fill its empty stomach. He forgot about the Renk and remembered that Kolar had told him to lead the milk- cow into the cattle-hold with the calf running behind. Once there, he pulled the tree trunk into place to secure the animals in the cattle-hold. Now he could run to his hut and go into the dreamworld without having to keep himself awake. His bad feelings had left him. His people would not look at him with side glances. He ran from the hold over the huts, rounded the first one where Maku and her family slept, and started past Shinda's hut when he ran hard into the upright body of the Renk. The Renk held Nargab's arm so he wouldn't fall on the rocks. Muddled and confused again, Nargab stepped back from the Renk. When he was steady on his feet, he felt himself released.

The Renk stood in front of the opening of Shinda's hut, looking at Nargab. Nargab slowly backed away. Then the Renk did a strange thing—he smiled. After a time, Nargab smiled back at the Renk. Then they both went in opposite directions, Nargab to his hut and the Renk into the forest to begin his long run through the night to join his brothers at the Men's House of his totem ram clan.

The next day Belka saw Nargab watching her when she returned with the women from the planting and growing area. Instead of joining in the spirit of play with the rest of the children, Nargab followed Belka to the riverlet where she washed herself. He sat on the river bank and waited for her to see him.

"Well, what is it you want?" she asked. "Why do you stare at me?"

He made his announcement. "I last night saw the Renk. Did he come to see you or your mother?"

Belka laughed. "My mother did not wake up. That is a good one, that Renk. He is a ram." She splashed water on herself and also on Nargab.

"A ram?" Nargab laughed. "A ram with a tail in his head." They both laughed.

"If you were a man, the Renk would be your cousin," Belka told him.

"I will not be a man for . . ."

"Many more moons."

"Then I will hunt."

"But when you grow up you must not kill this man of the ram clan. The Renks are rams, remember that when you are a man."

"Can a leopard kill a ram?" Nargab asked, hoping.

"It could, if the ram didn't tear it apart with its horns." Belka came out of the water, shaking herself and putting her arms in the holes of her fur covering.

"Belka," Nargab asked, "do the Renk boys herd cattle?"

"No," she began, walking the path back to the huts with Nargab behind her, "the Renks herd goats, those wild things that make strange noises."

"How can they herd *wild* things?" Nargab ran to keep up with her.

"The ones they're herding are not wild. Long

ago women brought the wild goat babies into their village where they grow wheat. They raised the baby goats and took the wildness out of them."

"Did the Renk tell you that?"

She laughed and swung her wet hair away from her eyes. "He is not the first Renk I have known."

"He *isn't?*" There had been those frightening Renks here before?

They joined the other women and children who were eating grain and milk cakes in front of a large fire. The men ate meat from the wild male wolf in their Men's House. The women had skinned the wolf, saving its soft fur for garments. Then they pared the meat into separate portions. Berker women and children did not eat wild animal meat. The only meat they ate was from the milkless cattle.

When Ashinda brought the meat to the men's house, she waited at a distance outside for the men to come to get the meat. It was a taboo for women to go in the men's house and it was taboo for men and women to eat together. It was said that the Goddess Illinini forbid it.

After she had delivered the meat, Ashinda walked to the cattle-hold to see what was disturbing the cows. She saw that the one making long, pleading noises was the cow whose calf they had killed long ago. She had been dry of milk for many moons. Kolar was stretching her neck to see if all the cattle were in the hold.

"What is it?" Ashinda asked Kolar.

"It is mostly from the dry one," Kolar answered. "She is disturbing the others. Let us take her to the other hold. The milkless cow is good for the restless ones. After the milkless one has been with this noisy one, it will get quiet," she explained.

But there was no quiet until after the big milkless one had rushed at the incoming cow and almost knocked it over in the dirt. After closing the entrance of the cattle hold, Kolar saw that the women and children watched from a safe distance. It was a dance the two cattle did together. They ended their pawing and mounting like they were stuck together. When they pulled themselves apart the milkless one slumped to the ground and seemed to want to sleep. The milk cow munched on the grass the children had thrown to her.

The men had come out of their hut to look and to sit in the evening coolness. They had seen the action of the milkless cow before and knew it would end the same. Cattle was women's work. It did not concern them.

But it did concern the women. They watched the same motions that they had seen before, but this time Kolar said something she had long thought about.

"I am beginning to believe that the Goddess Illinini gives us more in our herd through the milkless cow. After we have put a milk cow in here, it is *that* cow that has the next calf."

The women murmured together. Was Kolar speaking evil against Illinini? It made them restless. Illinini gave them what they needed. She made their grain grow. If Kolar spoke unknowns about Illinini would the grain wilt and die? Illinini caused the children to swell in their mother's stomachs. It would be dangerous to anger Illinini for She might not put any more children in the bodies of the women. With no more children, the Berker clan would go to the dream of their ancestors forever.

Illinini, they told each other, gave them new calves. To say that She gave the calves first to the *milkless* cows, who *then* gave them to the cows was a bad thing to put into sound. They withdrew from Kolar, the woman who knew about cattle. The children withdrew from her too, leaving her alone, watching the munching cow.

"That cow," she pronounced, turning to the women, wondering why they were looking at her from the corners of their eyes, "that cow will be the next one to have a calf."

What was she doing, the women wondered, telling them what Illinini would do? The women whispered together, but she ignored them. They would not talk with her tonight. They must go into their own huts to consider this. No Berker clan member ever spoke of what Illinini would do. That would be to take away the power of the Fertility goddess.

Kolar stayed with the cow a little longer and then led it back to the cattle- hold with the rest of the cattle. Let the women talk! With time they would know she was right.

Chidpura, who had gone from the Men's House most of the night, had spent much time in the hut of Murda, who welcomed him with pats and groans as she had welcomed him for many moons. Chidpura of the Brykda clan, returned at the necessary times to the clan of his mother and sisters. Though he might spend every night slipping into Murda's hut, he could never become a Berker.

Many moons ago, when he had seen short, fat Murda in the forest he had frightened her. All people are enemies away from their clan village, and though Murda was afraid of the stranger she knew he would not kill her.

If the stranger had shot his bow and arrow at her, Murda knew, he would have brought out woman's blood and his life would be cursed forever.

Murda had been told by her mothers, at an age when all daughters are given the knowledge of their mother's ancestors, that it was the women, many times ago, who had told men not to touch them at their blood times. To have a man enter their bodies at their moon blood, or after a woman had brought a child to earthlife, was not good for a woman's body. That is what they had told the men. To make the men believe them, the women had said to the men that a fierce evil would come to men if the men saw women's blood.

"Woman's blood is a mystery to men," Murda remembered her mother telling her. "Our moon blood is part of our bodies. We do not fear it. But men who have no moon blood and do not bring life to earth, do not understand. And the mystery of it makes men afraid. Their fear has been good for us. That keeps men away from us when it is best for us."

Then, Murda remembered, men thought the

curse of the power of women's blood meant that their blood at any time would harm them.

A lesser curse, but still a curse, Murda knew, would be on a man if he were *near* a woman during her moon blood period. Even if he didn't *know* she had her moon blood, he would be cursed.

Murda was frightened that day in the forest when she first met Chidpura. She called upon the Goddess Illinini to put into the stranger's mind thoughts that if he hurt her and brought forth her blood he would bring a curse on himself. There in the forest that day Murda stood very still on the path watching the stranger who did not move. He was bigger than the men in her clan and he had something shiny hanging from one ear. He saw her looking at this and he smiled. Then she, too, smiled.

He put his bow on the ground between them, reached over his shoulder for the animal skin holder with his arrows and put them on the ground. They stood facing each other smiling, and then they laughed.

He touched Murda's arm and then her face and she did the same with him. They moved closer to each other putting their cheeks together. Accepted, they lay down on the leafy ground and Chidpura of the Brykda clan entered the body of Murda of the Berker clan.

Many nights after that, Chidpura traveled through the mountain pass to Murda's hut, where he entered her body and then went into the dreamworld before returning through the pass to his own clan. But when Murda's mother accepted Chidpura as her daughter's mate, Chidpura could then sleep in the Men's House with the other Berker clansmen. By being Murda's mate, Chidpura no longer needed to make the nightly run back to his own clan.

Chidpura hunted with the Berker men, ate with the Berker men, and when he was not at Murda's hut in the night, he slept in the Men's House. But when his mother or his sisters in his own clan needed him to perform *their* Feast of the Plantings or *their* Feast of the Gatherings he received that message from one of his own Brykda clan brothers who lurked in the forest nearby waiting to sight Chidpura.

"On the next sun down," his brother would call to him, "the wild pigs will be roasted. Your mothers, sisters and brothers will be waiting." Chidpura would wave his reply.

Murda would not expect him then that night, nor would he remain in the Berker clan anytime when his own clan needed him. A man belonged to his mother's clan, no matter what woman he slept with. He would return to his mother's clan at times for other reasons. A birth or a burial also required his presence.

Murda's clan would not ask Chidpura to enter in their Berker ceremonies because a man's spirit and ceremonial life belonged to his mother's and sisters' clan.

Murda's brother, Hon, slept often away from the Berker clan in the hut of a Renk woman. He returned home to the Berkers when Murda sent that message with her other brother who stalked deep into the upper mountains to sight Hon. He would return to his Berker clan when the women needed him for ceremonies, or when he wanted to be with the Berker men again. Then later he would be drawn to his Renk woman, to stay at the Men's House in the Renk clan under the totem ram, until nightfall and to creep into the Renk's woman's hut at dark.

When the boy, Nargab, had seen the Renk invited into Belka's hut, he was frightened. But after Belka and Nargab talked about what he would do when *he* was a man, he had no more fear of this Renk. But he was still confused.

"The Renks come here. The Brykdas come here. Our Berker men go to the Renks, and some of our men go to the Brykdas. I was told we were all enemies. . . ."

"We *are*," Belka said seriously. "The Brykdas and the Renks, their men will kill our men in the forest and ours will kill them and they will eat each other except if they are brothers-in-law." Then she had warned him. "Don't ever think they are not your enemy."

Nargab wondered aloud how any of the men knew who was brother-in-law and who was enemy. Belka pondered how to answer his serious questions.

"If a man and a woman mate, the man is a brother-in-law to all the brothers of the woman."

"Yes, but what about the men who are not brothers?"

"Then they are cousins."

"Those enemies are not enemies? They are kin?"

"Yes."

84

"Then all the men in the forest and in the mountains will be kin. Who will we fight? Who will we kill? Who will we eat to gain the strength of their spirits?"

"Not all are kin, my little brother," Belka said to Nargab, as all girls and boys called each other brothers and sisters. "The forest and the mountains have many enemies. Be careful."

"If I see an enemy, when I have the herd out on the grass, do I aim my bow and arrow as I have always done?" Nargab asked.

"Aim, but do not pull your bow. Look carefully. If you recognize him, put your bow on the ground and he will do the same, for he will know that you are a cross-cousin."

Nargab thought about what Belka said. It would be difficult to put his weapon on the ground in the presence of a possible enemy, but he would remember what she said.

For six suns the Berker men of the leopard clan returned to the Men's House at sun down with no animals and the strain was beginning to be heard in their criticism of each other.

"You tell the animals we are coming by the big-feet-noise you make," Allsonde said to his younger brother Hoken, hanging his bow in the corner of the Men's House as he lowered his big body onto the dirt floor.

"And you," accused Hoken, "you need to ask Illinini for the sharp eyes of a new-born. You aim at a bear and hit a tree." Allsonde grumbled because he had lost two arrows today. His eyes did not see the forest as he used to see it. He was wise, but he was not the hunter he had been.

The other men shuffled into the Men's House, hanging their weapons on the wall of the mud and brick building and then stretching themselves on their sleeping places. It was yet daylight. Not time to go to the dreamworld. They would rest, then rise again. The women would bring their food this night again without meat. They would eat the grain cakes and drink berry juice or cows' milk, but without meat they would not feel themselves ready for tomorrow's hunt.

"A man must have meat to eat, to hunt meat," Allsonde said in disgust, pulling apart the grain cakes the women had brought.

"When we bring back the bear that lives in the cliff we will have meat again," Chidpura, the Brykda, said, relishing his grain cake as he imagined it was a hunk of raw, red, bear meat.

"If we don't get meat soon we will be eating woman's food during all the snow time," Allsonde said.

The next sun down when they came back again without an animal they grumbled at each other, ate the grain cakes, and complained of not feeling strong enough to hunt the next day. "Is it we are not getting animal kills because one of our brothers has touched a woman in her moon blood?" Allsonde asked.

No one answered. "Or has one of our brothers eaten food prepared by a woman who was having her moon blood?" he asked.

No one answered. No man would bring such a curse to the hunting party.

Allsonde knew that no man, not a Berker, or a Renk, or a Brykda would break the ancient taboo and bring harm to the men in the clan. Blood was a part of woman's life, mystifying, cursed, sacred and powerful. It would take a man a lifetime of purifying to overcome such dangers.

"Or," Allsonde continued, "since Shinda's young one came at the last moon, has anyone been near her?"

They all knew what Allsonde meant. A woman who had a baby must not be entered by a man until the child no longer sucked milk from her mother's body. No man would break that taboo for fear of the weakness he would receive in his own body. The Renk, who had been Shinda's mate, would mate with another while the baby was suckling. He would mate either with a Berker girl or with a girl in another clan.

The Renk, Kaal, shook his head. "Since the Goddess Illinini gave Shinda a child, I have not seen her. My mate now is Maku, daughter of Chalian. . . ." Many had been the mate of Maku. Illinini did not give Maku a child. She

87

said she did not want to have a child and she prevented it by never looking at the moon. Those who wanted a child would look at the moon each night it could be seen. Shinda sat outside her hut to look at the moon for many moons before Illinini gave her a child.

A child would help Shinda work the grain and a child could herd the cattle. Shinda hoped Illinini would give her many children. But when she pushed her child out of her body in the forest by herself, she wondered why Illinini gave her all the pain in her body. She carried the newborn under her fur covering back into her hut and fell asleep with the infant suckling weakly at her breast. Kaal had been warned at the entrance to Shinda's hut by other woman that he must not enter. He went away wondering whether he should return to his Renk clan, when the other woman, Maku, had beckoned to him. He would not miss the evening visits with Shinda, for now he would visit Maku.

"No," Kaal told the men, searching for answers to their lack of animals, "I did not break the taboo of being with a childbirth woman. I did not enter Shinda's hut."

"Then what is it?" Allsonde persisted.

"Maybe we have killed all the animals," Allsonde's brother, Hoken, said.

"No," Allsonde growled, "you saw that bear."

"So did the other clans," Hoken told him.

"Maybe we are now too many people," Chidpura, the Brykda, suggested. "We Renks and you Berkers do not kill newborn female children anymore. We let them live because the women say we have enough food to feed them. Women have woman food. But men must have meat. What of the meat from the milkless cow? There is one . . . young yet, but he is to be killed at the Feast of the Planting."

"We should have more milkless cows," Allsonde said.

Hoken sat up on his fur-covered floor space. "The women," he told them, "are saying that Kolar says there is a cow about to have a calf and she *knew* it was going to have a calf."

The other men were not interested in Hoken's information. Hoken was young. Only three moons ago when he reached his manheight, he moved to the Men's House. The men would be more interested if his older brother, Allsonde, had spoken the words.

"She *knows*," he persisted. "If she *knows*, can she make it happen?"

Still the men looked disinterested. What did his information have to do with their recent failures to kill animals?

"Do you think," he continued, "if Kolar can cause cows to have calves, she could add calves to our herd and if there are no animals in the forest, we will not be hungry for meat?"

"You mean," Chidpura asked, "we could *grow* our meat animals here?"

"Yes," Hoken answered, pleased to have someone listen to him. "Let us watch the cow that Kolar said would have a calf. If it does have a calf, then we will know Kolar has a power that will help us."

The men moved their heads up and down,

skeptical but drawn into what he was saying. They would watch that milk cow with interest.

And they did. But when many moons passed and there was no calf from the cow Kolar had predicted, the men lost their interest in the cattle and became even more determined to find the animals that were escaping from them in their forest hunts. Believing their failure to be somehow related to power beyond them, they took an oath that no man should enter any woman until the next animal was killed.

"The women take our strength. They take the liquid strength from our own bodies," Allsonde claimed. "If we are to be successful again in the animal kills we must avoid women . . . *all* women, at *all* times."

The older men shook their heads up and down. The younger men looked at the dirt floor. There was a silence. It was the silence of an oath.

"Berkers have been good hunters," Allsonde boasted, "soon we will be good hunters again."

There was only silence. Allsonde continued, "Is it that the Brykdas and Renks in their clan hunts are killing all the animals?"

"The Renks are not finding many animals . . ." The Renk informed the others. Then Chidpura moved his head up and down and added, "And my brothers tell me the Brykdas are not getting enough to eat. They are eating woman food, all the time, grain cakes, nuts, fruits, tubers. They say they do not feel like men anymore." These things the Renk and the Brykda told were serious.

"Can all clans be suffering from the curse of women?" Allsonde pondered.

"Maybe we have killed all the animals," Hoken suggested again.

"We should move," Allsonde announced.

"The women would not move," one of the old men advised. "They have many fields of grain and clay storage crocks to put extra grain in when the cold comes."

"And milk to drink, all the moons," another added.

"And a milkless cow to kill when we *do* want meat," another said.

"And to increase their grain, or their herd, or their families, they have only to plead to Illinini."

"They would not leave, here, now. They would tell us to go . . . they do not need us . . ." Hoken said.

At the end of each long quandary the men would decide to carry through with their oath and to go into the forest every day to hunt. One day, soon, they knew, they would kill the great bear and then they would know their strength had returned to them.

A large, red fox was the first kill after the oath. The men rejoiced, returned to the clan triumphant, roasted the animal over a slow burning fire after the women skinned it. They savored the few mouthfuls allotted to each man. It was a beginning, they said. Tomorrow and the next day they would return to the forest and bring back other animals that would prove their strength had returned.

91

Each day a different boy took the herd to a different grassy field, as each day the women took their digging sticks out into their grain fields to loosen the soil around the new grain shoots. Women with babies strapped them to their bodies while they worked, and nursed them from time to time.

The children who were no longer nursing were left at the huts in the care of one of the mothers. It was she who would laugh with them, fondle them, feed them, and protect them from falling or from wandering too far from the huts. At sun's end they would await all of the mothers, returning tired and dusty from the fields.

The herd would be secure in the cattle-hold, the food of grain cakes and nuts would be given to the mother who had cared for the children. The women and children would amuse themselves, making whistles of leaves, or telling the ancient ancestral stories.

Women who had delivered the grain cakes each night to the Men's House were required by the men to leave the cakes at the end of the womens' huts since the men had taken their oath. When the women were out of sight, one of the men retrieved the food. The women had not seen any of the men for many sundowns.

When Shinda's hut needed rebuilding the women tore off the old mud-stuck branches and replaced them with new mud. At another time the men would have helped, but Shinda feared the water from the sky would be coming in the next moon and she did not want to wait until the men were more friendly.

Nargab's turn at cattle herding fell on the day that the new calf was born. He had led the herd first to the green grass near the river and then moved them up to the drier grass so their stomachs would not give them pain from too much fresh grass. That was what Kolar said made them sick, when she had to stick their sides with a long-sharp rock-sharpened obsidian stone to let the air out of the cows' sides.

The cow that Kolar had said was going to have a calf had been developing a fat stomach. The women watched her fattening sides and praised the Goddess Illinini. When Kolar was asked by the other women how she knew *that* cow would have a calf, Kolar told them it was because Illinini put the seeds of the calf first in the milkless cow.

"Then," she explained further, "Illinini takes the seed from the milkless cow and puts it in the cow, and in eight moons Illinini gives us a calf."

Nargab brought the herd home early because he feared what was happening and wanted the calf to be born where Kolar would be around to help. The women stood in a circle watching Kolar pull the calf out of the cow's loins. Finally out into the air, the calf lay at its mother's feet dazed for a few moments and then it wobbled up to stand, for the first time, on its own legs. The mother cow, too, stood up and waited for the new calf to find its milk under her body.

Kolar announced that it was not going to be a milk cow and the women accepted that with nods. "And now we know *how* to get more calves," Kolar told the women as she watched the new, moist calf drinking its mother's warm milk.

"We can have many," Belka said.

"And we can have much meat, not only at Feast time," Ashinda said.

"But when," Belka asked, "do you put a cow in with the milkless cow? Will Illinini put the seed in the cow each time?"

"I don't know," Kolar admitted, patting the side of the mother cow. "We'll see," she said. "We'll see. But this calf is a blessing. This calf brings Illinini's message of wisdom. She has told us how we may increase our herd. We must show Her our appreciation."

Yes, the women agreed. Such a gift must be rewarded.

The women gathered dirt from the red soil area and made a hand-sized figure of a fully developed, big breasted, large-hipped woman. When they were satisfied with her figure, with her hair hanging in two divided sections over her ears, with large eyes, straight nose and full lips, they put her into a heat section over their fire in the same place they put their new dirt bowls to fire them and make them hard and eventually to form into hard pottery. They let their statue of their Illinini cool slowly so she wouldn't crack, and then they took her from the firing place and admired her.

"She who has given us so much should have Her own hut," Ashinda said, holding the figure in her hand as others stood around her to admire the small statue.

"Then let us do it," Kolar agreed. And the

women set about bringing in sticks, and soil, and carrying water in their pottery jugs to mix with soil, to make into bricks.

"She should have a better hut than any of us," Shinda, who was a good builder, said. "We will make special weavings on Her hut."

The men, who had watched the birth of the calf from a distance and had seen the women firing up to bake their pottery figure, now watched the activity of the building of a new house. They heard of its purpose and they discussed it.

"We should help them," Allsonde told the men. "They are building a house of the Goddess. Illinini is good to Berkers. We should help?"

"And our oath?" Hoken asked.

"We have followed our oath for one moon. During our oath we have killed one fox, many rabbits and squirrels. We have not been hungry. We have killed meat. Our oath had been fulfilled," Allsonde said.

The men smiled at each other and waited for Allsonde to rise. He was not finished. "We will help the women build the house of the Goddess and we will give praise to Her for the grain, the calves, and the children who increase our clan." Then he rose and the others followed him out of the Men's House, past the tree that separated their house from the womens', and up to the building operations.

The women stopped their work to welcome the men. Then they moved their hands over the men's bodies, rubbed their own bodies on the men's. The children ran to the men and were picked up and held closely. Several couples retreated from the group.

And then the work started again and the mud brick hut area was filled with the noise of talk, laughter, twigs being broken to size, water being poured, and the patting and pounding of materials into the shape of a mud hut.

There was no working in the fields on this day, and no taking the cattle to the grass. The children brought dry grass to the cattle and then ran back to join in the building. The men did not think of hunting. Everyone worked in this dedication to Illinini.

When the hut was finished they cleaned away the space around it and went inside to place the figure of their Goddess. Their big decision had to be made. Where to put the statue? Ashinda held it in her hands while they all looked around inside the hut. Should She stand? Hang? Lie on the floor? They agreed that they should look up to Her when they entered the Goddess house and so they made a ledge directly facing the entrance and placed Her there. Then they shuffled backwards, looking at Her. She was small, no larger than anyone's hand, but Her presence affected all of them. Her large eyes looked out at the Berkers gathered in front of Her.

Kolar extended her arms to the statue and spoke in a low tone to tell Her of the thanks they offered. "We do not know how to say what we feel now. We hope you can feel our feelings as we cannot say them. Illinini, our Goddess, we thank you and we praise you. This is your home. We will keep it clean. We will come here to show you the grain, the calves, and the children you give to us." Should she say more? She wondered. Should someone else say more? "We praise Illinini," she said.

"We praise Illinini," Ashinda repeated, extending her arms forward.

"We praise Illinini," Belka repeated, her arms toward the statue.

"We praise Illinini," one of the men, Allsonde, repeated, lifting his arms in Her direction.

"We praise Illinini," many voices repeated, quietly.

"We praise Illinini," more voices repeated, louder.

"We praise Illinini," everyone repeated, chanting the praise over and over again, extending their arms in Illinini's direction as they moved backwards out of the hut, out into the last part of the day's sun, tired from their physical work and proud of their spiritual commitment.

Illinini rewarded the Berkers with the fertility of the grain. It grew abundantly and the women gathered it for keeping in the storage hut for the cold moons they felt coming upon them. There would be no more planting until the cold snow period would be past them once again. But they had much grain that should give them food for the cold period.

The cows would survive the cold period too as they had survived each snow time. When it became so cold that the frozen water did not melt in day time, each woman brought a cow into her hut. It was crowded in their huts but they could not let the cows and calves stay outside where they might go to their dreamworld standing up stiff and cold as two had done at the last Cold Time.

Only the milkless cow was taken into a hut where no person stayed. There it was tied to an old tree stump. The milkless cow was not a friend to people, Kolar explained, and was best left by itself.

One calf was being fattened for eating at the Feast of the Planting, when the Cold Time would be over, while the other new calf was still being fed from its mother's milk bag.

As the cold winds came off the mountains, and the air changed from clear and dry to clear and damp, both the women and the men repaired their fur coverings or they sewed new body coverings from the hides they had stretched and softened. The women repaired their houses, covering up the holes with mud, rocks, and twigs to keep out the wet of the rain or snow.

The Cold Time was a period of long rest, of talk and of sitting around the fires in the huts.

The Men's House was filled with the smoke of warming fires and of talk of past hunts, past glories, and future hunts with many large animal kills.

The four Renks in the Men's House, the two Brykdas besides Chidpura, and all the Berkers had for many moons been considering a great Warm Time attack on the animals.

"If *all* the Renk men and *all* the Brykdas, and all of us Berkers join together to run the animals we could get them," Allsonde suggested.

"Would Renks hunt with Berkers?" Hoken asked the Renk, Welo.

"Renks are hungry for meat," Welo answered.

"Would Brykdas hunt with Berkers?" Hoken asked Chidpura.

"Our clan is hungry also," Chidpura answered. "We know there are bears in the forest, yet they escape us."

Allsonde appointed himself the leader of this plan. The Berkers had always listened to him. "Will you talk to your men," he asked the Renks and Brykdas. "And we will set our attack on these bears when they come out of their caves if others will join us."

When the Renks and Brykdas returned to the Berker Men's House to tell the Berkers they would be joined in the hunt, they were filled with good feelings. They began to sketch an attack plan in the dirt on the floor. The Renk clan would come from the top area of the hunting grounds of the forest, the Brykdas would come from the middle part, and the Berkers would close in on the bottom and head up around and close in from the back.

The dirt drawing showed that if the Brykdas continued their attack past the circle where the bears would be ambushed, they would run into the Berkers who would be closing in on the bears from the far side of the circle. The circle in the dirt represented a large meadow at the end of the forest that butted up against the foot of a steep hill. The bears would be encircled there.

The Berkers would divide their men, half of them winding back over the hill and the other half coming up from the bottom part of the drawing. There would be no place where the bears could go. It would be a good plan and they had the rest of the Cold Time to perfect it.

"But can we be sure the Renks won't kill *us*?" Allsonde cautioned when he was alone with his own clan. "Or the Brykdas?" He moved his shoulders uncomfortably. "This is a dangerous thing we do. Maybe it is more dangerous than wise?"

"Why would they kill us?" his younger brother, Hoken, asked. "Those clans need meat. When we hunt as separate clans we are too few to make a big kill. They need us. They would not kill those they need."

"And we need them," Allsonde consoled himself. And so they proceeded to develop their plan, Allsonde convinced that there were enough brothers-in-law among Renks, Brykdas and Berkers to make the feelings good among them all.

100

"The bears are our targets, not other clansmen," Hoken advised. "We will work together. The Renks and Brykdas have taken our plan back to their clan. It is agreed. We have only now to wait until the Cold Time is past and the water runs in the river again."

Allsonde grunted his assent and told his clansmen, "We will rest. We will gather our strength through the rest of this no-sun time, and then when it is time we will go out into the forest, many strong, swift men, and we will kill many big bears. Ah-ha," he laughed. "The skins will line our walls, lay on our floors, cover our backs, and make blankets for the women and children." He laughed again at the whole picture he saw in his inner eyes. It made the Cold Time pass faster.

While the men dreamed of the big animal kill, the women dreamed of the new pottery they would make when the ground was not covered by snow. And they talked of increasing the cattle herd because their own clan had increased by three children in the last Warm Time. With more children they would need more milk and the men always wanted more meat to eat.

They knew of the ancient stories that told of ancestral mothers killing their newborn babies when they pushed them from their bodies because there was not enough food in the group. At those times, it was said, newborn girls could not live because they only grew up to have babies and that made the food problem worse. Boys grew up to be hunters, to get food, so they were valuable. And they had heard the ancestral story of the most valuable young clan members sacrifice. But those tales were not of this time.

The Berkers had no sacrifice because they had good grain crops and Illinini gave them as many girls as boys and the food to feed them. The Berkers would not destroy children, not only because boys were valuable as future hunters but because girls and women were treated with a special awe by the men. Everyone knew that females were a part of Illinini's supernatural world.

The men looked at the girls and the women and wondered about the supernatural spirits that inhabited the female bodies that issued blood when not wounded. And men did not have bodies that grew other bodies inside them. A female was a creature partly of the world of Illinini and partly of the earthly world. It would not be good, men knew, to harm a female, or to make her angry.

A female walked and worked on earth, but was from a spirit world. And when the women told the men to stay away from them during their moon blood, or after a child came, saying the men would be cursed, the men did not question this. To break the taboo placed by Illinini on men not to touch women's issued blood would be to take the man's spirit out of him and to weaken him the rest of his life. It would be better that such a man would be dead. And so, when a man did unknowingly enter his mate's body at her moon blood time and when he returned to the Men's House and saw woman's blood on his own body, knowing he was cursed, he ran into the forest and offered himself to the hyenas. He did not return.

Because neither males nor females were killed in infancy in the Berker clan, their population increased, but so did the wealth in grain and cattle. As Kolar explained to the women on those long Cold Time days, "The next cow to get restless will be put in the hut with the milkless one and in eight moons we will have another calf. The Goddess Illinini will do it. She will give us more food."

This time the women did not move away from her when she told of the happening. They were no longer afraid of her saying it because nothing bad had happened from her saying it the last time. And the new calf was growing fast.

Nargab argued again with Kolar, wanting to keep the calf instead of planning to kill and eat it when it grew to be a big milkless cow. But Kolar insisted, "We do not keep cows that do not give us milk. We will kill this one because it will give us meat. We need that. Our men need it for strength to hunt."

Though in this Cold Time it seemed the soft white snow would never quit falling from the sky, or that the wind would never stop blowing through the cracks in their huts, after many moons, the snow did quit falling, and the wind blew less. There were more days for the clan to spend outside the huts, and new shoots on old bushes at the rim of the forest surrounding the huts changed the grey and white colors of the Cold Time to green.

Nargab was the first, proud, young herder to bring the cattle to the snow-cleared grassy area to enjoy their fresh grass of the beginning of the Warm Time. It was a time for both cattle and people to stretch their muscles. The women walked to their fields and watched the snow melt off the mound where they would pierce the dirt with their digging sticks and later plant new grain. Planting would be soon, now. The feeling was in the air, in the way the tall trees moved gradually from one side to another, instead of bending as they did under the strong winds of the Cold Time.

The men assembled their obsidian pointed arrows on the dirt floor of the Men's House. Lowie, the Berker who spent more nights in the Men's House of the Brykdas then in his own clan's Men's House, had put himself in charge of the hunting weapons. A young man, swift in running and accurate with his arrows, Lowie knew the importance of having arrows that would not only hit their mark but would also bring the animal down on the ground, either on the spot where he was hit or close by.

"It is no good to wound a big animal and have him carry our arrow off into the forest never to be seen again," he told the men gathered before him on the earth floor. "This arrow," Lowie explained, rounding the chipped obsidian with his finger so they all could see, "is too blunt. It will hurt a large bear, but you can see it will not go in deep enough. A bear has a thicker hide than the little fox and the wolves we have been killing. A bear can carry this arrowhead in his side until he rubs it out of his hide. Now this one," Lowie said, showing them an obsidian arrowhead he had chipped and had used for instant kill on his hunts when he went out with the Brykdas, "this one is the way our arrowheads should look for our Great Bear Kill. Here are many pieces of obsidian from the Olhar Mountains. Let us make arrowheads that will kill."

"And the others, the Brykdas?" Allsonde asked.

"They, too, are making new, sharper, longer arrowheads for the Great Bear Kill," Lowie answered.

"And the Renks?" Allsonde asked, looking at the Renks in the group.

"We, too, will make good arrows," Arytites said. "Our men will travel to the Olhar Mountains for this good black rock," he said, holding a piece in his hand, smoothing its glass-like surface with his finger.

When the time of thinking and dreaming about the Kill had gone with the Cold Time, and as the earth warmed up, there was more preparation work to do. All of the men of the three clans would need to be better equipped than they had ever been before. For this was to be a massive human round-up and Kill on the largest animals of the forest. They must go into such a plan with the best equipment and with all their strength.

Once again they took the oath against sleeping in women's huts. No woman would steal the liquid from their bodies that gave them the strength for this great hunt.

From a distance the men watched the

women when they brought the cattle out of their huts for the last time and put them in their cattle-hold for the Warm Time, placing new fallen trees where old ones had rolled away, and bracing the upright trees that held the lengthwise tree trunks in position. Once secure, the cattle back in the hold, the women secured the separate hold for the milkless cow.

The men laughed when it seemed that the milkless cow was going to chase the women, kicking and thumping the hard earth. But Kolar came out of her hut to persuade it with an old fox fur, waving the fur in the milkless cow's face until she had it safely in the hold again. Then all the women cheered. The men admired Kolar's work and repeated the women's cheer, from the safe distance of the large tree marking the outside area of the Men's House. The women turned to look at the men and they laughed together.

Then Kolar told Maku to bring the other milkless cow that had stayed in Shinda's hut. When it was brought into a new hold, the milk cow ran at the milkless cow who appeared dazed at first. Then it abruptly turned in a circle. The women thought that this time the milk cow wanted to get its front legs on top of the milkless cow, but if that was her intention, the milkless cow knocked her around and chased her in the circle of the new hold until the milk cow stopped, backed up and waited for the milkless cow to put half of its great body on top of hers. The men and the women had been watching as the long part of the milkless cow's body that hung down from its stomach became longer and fatter. *This* is what they watched go into the milk cow's body.

"That is what Illinini uses to put a calf in the cow," Kolar explained. "We can have as many calves as we want," she said. "All we do is bring a cow here and in eight moons we have a calf."

"Then," Ashinda added, "we have more milk."

"And more meat for the men if the calves are milkless," Belka said.

"And we will have a great herd," Kolar announced.

But Ashinda worried, "Are we not interfering with Illinini's work?"

"I think," Kolar said, "we are assisting her. We will go to the House of the Goddess and ask her. She will let us know in Her way."

The men returned to their Men's House to confer on another matter. They had seen the two animals' action, as they had seen it before, and the men had seen similar action of other animals, two foxes, and smaller animals, like rabbits, go through the same action.

"There are women animals and men animals," Hoken pointed out. "We do not eat woman animals we kill by mistake, because we do not want that blood in us. The woman animal gets her young from Illinini . . ." he said, trying to put into words what was forming in his mind. "We do not want to anger the Goddess Illinini. Illinini gives us many animals to kill for meat. . . ."

"The hanging thing from the milkless cow's

body . . ." Hon interrupted Hoken, "we all have a hanging thing." The men agreed. "No woman animal has a hanging thing," Hon said, and the men agreed again.

"Then it may be," Hoken said as though talking to himself, "then it may be that the hanging thing of the man animal that the milkless cow puts in the woman is the man animal putting the calf in the milk cow. . . ."

"And that may be," Hon agreed. "It may be as Kolar says, Illinini puts the new calf in the milkless cow first to *then* put in the milk cow."

"Yes," Allsonde agreed. "I believe that is so. Each time Kolar puts a milk cow in with that animal, in eight moons the milk cow gives us a calf."

"The hanging thing in *our* bodies," Lowies said, "could it be that Illinini puts new children in our bodies first and . . ." but they would not let him finish alone.

"When we enter a woman. . . ."

"Our hanging thing puts a new. . . ."

"*We* are the ones. . . ."

They all spoke at once. Their idea made them reckless.

"It is *not* the women. . . ."

"They are *not* special. *WE* are special, we are. . . ."

"*WE* have the power . . ."

Only Allsonde was cautious. "We must think about this," he said. "To say such things is to violate the honor we have for Illinini. She may do us great harm."

His words were quieting. He was wise. The men thought of what he said. Their talk ceased, but their thoughts soon flew again in the dream parts of their minds. The thoughts began to come out into words again.

"When it takes eight moons for Illinini's calf to come to our clan, after we enter a woman, how many moons . . . ?" Hoken asked.

"Belka has been putting a stick by her sleeping place, with each moon that she has not had her moon blood. Her stomach grows large," Welo, the Renk, offered.

"How many sticks?" Hoken asked. Welo held up both hands curling two fingers into the palm of one hand.

Chidpura, the Brykda, told of Murda's stomach and the sticks she kept by her sleeping place and held up one hand and one finger of his other hand. "Her stomach is not as large as Belka's."

"You are a milkless cow," Hoken told him. Chidpura reached for his bow. Was this a challenge? Hoken placed a restraining hand on Chidpura's tense arm.

"No, my cousin," Hoken told him. "I mean you are as that animal. . . . Welo, the Renk here too, you are both . . . How do I say . . . you put Illinini's child in your women."

Both men looked at Hoken, unbelieving. The others were puzzled. Hoken's words and their own thoughts confused them. They had known, always, the power that was given to women and not to men, the power to bring life to earth that men could not do.

Women had the power to make other bodies inside their own. They had the power to make seeds in the earth grow into grain. And they had the power to make calves grow in the stomach of milk cows. Would they dare question that power? If the women did not *have* the power, if it was now untrue that Illinini gave them the power, what then? Who *had* such power? What of themselves? What should they think?

"Is it not better we do not think these things?" Allsonde said. "We have been content. We hunt and that is all. That is good. What is this new thought you have brought into our house?" he asked his brother Hoken.

"It is a thought that turns my head in circles," Hoken said. "But you, Allsonde, at first you considered it, and now. . . ."

"Now it frightens me," Allsonde answered.

"I see that," Hoken said. "Why does it frighten you?"

"It may mean new things if what you indicate is true."

"And?"

"The way we live is good. Is it not natural that women who have the power to make life should not also have other powers. Hunting is enough for me."

"But if the women don't really have that power," young Hon said, "then *we* should have it."

"How?" Allsonde asked.

"Well . . ." Hon stammered, "the cattle . . . if it is not woman's fertility power that causes calves, then . . ." he thought, "the calves . . . they do not belong to women."

"The grain . . . ," Hon began.

"Yes," Hoken tried, "I see. When the women

110

control the grain and . . . control the herd . . . well, then they control who has a calf and . . ."

"And control the grain supply," Hon added.

"And give it out to us at each sun down." Lowie said.

"Hmmmm," Allsonde thought. "You want more grain?"

They all agreed that they did not.

"What is it you want?" Allsonde asked.

"If it is that if the women do not have supernatural power . . ." Hoken ventured, "then *we* have the power to have the milkless cow put a calf in a milk cow and . . ."

"*We* have the power to make the seeds of grain grow . . ." Hon said.

"And then *we*, with *our* bodies," Lowie said, "put the new children into the bodies of women."

Were they repeating themselves to convince themselves? All but Allsonde were happy with these thoughts.

"It is dangerous thinking," he cautioned one more time. "We should go to the House of the Goddess to get direction in this. Yes we should go." He rose from the dirt floor. "Who will come with me?" He waited. He moved toward the door.

Not yet convinced of their new thoughts, or not yet ready to break with the old tradition of consulting the Goddess, they would need direction. They all rose slowly and followed Allsonde out the door of the Men's House and walked toward the House of the Goddess. They waited as the women came and went from the religious sanctuary. It was always understood that men entered the House of the Goddess only after the women did not wish to enter anymore for the day.

The last group of women to leave followed Kolar out of the House of the Goddess, chatting. With the women out of their view, the men entered, waited, and then looked to Allsonde to talk to the small, red figurine on the ledge in the mud and brick hut. They would leave it up to Her. Allsonde told Illinini to let them know by Her sign if the men should understand that the special power of women was really a power that belonged to men.

"We know about the parts of the bodies of men animals and the parts of our own bodies. Should we believe that this is where the power lies, to put new animals in woman animal bodies and new children in women's bodies? We know when women take our liquid from these parts, they take our strength. It makes us want to go into the dreamworld. Do they take our power? Illinini, we are confused, we need a . . . a sign from you. Do men, too, have power over cattle and power in the grain field?"

Then he had a new thought. "In the next half moon we start on our Great Animal Kill. Give us a sign that tells us what we need to know. We praise Illinini."

"We praise Illinini," the others repeated.

"We praise Illinini," Allsonde said alone.

"We praise Illinini," the others chanted as they all backed out the door of the hut, arms extended toward the small figurine.

It was dark in the Men's House the morning of the Great Bear Kill for the sun had not yet risen. The Renks and Brykdas had returned to their own clans, the plan of the attack in their heads. Each clan would do its part. Three clans could succeed together where each had failed all alone.

Spirits were high, voices were tense, and men were making nervous steps here and there getting ready. They would wear only one fur covering over their bodies now that the air had warmed and the snow had disappeared. Each man had as many long, sharp chipped obsidian arrows in his animal skin case over his shoulder as he had fingers on both hands. Their bows had been tested many times for strength and tension. They were ready.

The agreement with the Renks and Brykdas was that each clan would leave for the Great Kill when the sun's light could be first seen. It was a time of nervous waiting. All were watching the sky.

The dark grey changed to a lighter grey, and a single cloud at the edge of the earth caught the first rays of the sun that had yet to appear. The pink cloud announced the sun's arrival.

The men stood outside at the edge of their Men's House in silence, facing the sunrise. The women stood at the separating tree to watch the men wait, and to hope they would be safe. The clan's energy had been centered on the excitement of the Great Hunt. Boys who were not yet men lamented that they could not go on the Great Bear Kill.

"Next time," Hon promised his little brother Saku.

"There was never a 'next time' before," Saku said, holding on to his older brother's arm.

"We will do this again," Hon promised. "If we bring home many bear skins to cover you, you know we will do this again. This is the first Great Bear Kill, but it will be the first of many," he said. His young brother smiled at him with pride and envy. Could there be anything greater than going out to a Kill?

Often Saku and the other young brothers had watched the hunters leave at sunrise and had ached with the desire to run with them.

"I am glad I will be a man," Saku had told Nargab when they were splashing in the river water one day in the last Warm Time. "I would not want to be a woman, for then I could not be a hunter."

"Or a herder," Nargab said.

"Aw, that's not as important," Saku said. "Women herd the cattle. It's the hunt . . . that's what I want. I'll take my bow and arrow and," Saku pulled his imaginary bow back to full tension and let the imaginary arrow fly straight into the side of a waiting imaginary wolf. "Kill!" he shouted.

"Yes," agreed Nargab who loved the cattle. "Going on a Kill is the most valuable thing." He too would soon join the hunters, because he had always wanted to, because it was expected that it would be the most important thing, but he would not tell the men that he would rather stay with the peaceful cattle. The

114

men would not understand and they would laugh at him.

Now Nargab looked at the men watching the sky grow light and he wondered about their next days. He knew they planned to run silently through the forest until nightfall and then at the next sun to run until each clan saw the sun at the top of the sky. Then they were to run with voices yelling to push the animals ahead of them into the circle on the dirt map that the men had drawn for the boys to see in the earth by their own huts.

"The boys must know," Allsonde said, "so *next* Warm Time when they join us on our next Great Kill they will have the feeling in their spirits." The boys lined up at the separating tree, ready to depart in spirit when the first sliver of the sun edged over the top of their mountain.

A yell accompanied the change of light. The men turned their backs on the sun and ran in a slow trot to the forest and disappeared, one by one, fur coverings and arrow holders bouncing as they ran. It would be a long run and they must hold down their desire to beat the other clans to the Great Kill. If one clan arrived before the others, all of the men might be killed. The only way to insure a large Kill was if each clan did what they said they were going to do.

As the Berkers had questioned whether they could trust Renks and Brykdas, so Renks and Brykdas, in their own clans, questioned whether or not they could trust Berkers.

"We will have to trust them," each clan had agreed about the others.

"We cannot do this Great Kill by ourselves."

"But we are enemies," it was argued.

"For *this*, we are not enemies. When this is over, then we can be enemies again." And so it went in each clan, until this day at the sun's arrival when the forest was filled with the silent, running feet of three enemy clans moving in the same direction to come together at the conclusion of an attack that had been many moons in the planning.

The men knew their forest. It was the place where they spent most of their time. It gave them the purpose for their existence. The action of carrying a wild sheep, or wild pig out of the forest and back to the women's huts for skinning and preparation was action that said without words, "We have done our work. Our work makes us what we are—strong, swift men, greater than the animals of the forest that would kill our clan if we did not kill the animals. Killing animals brings pride."

That is why the success of the Great Animal Kill was necessary. The lack of animal kills in the three clans was not only sapping the strength for lack of meat to eat, but it was also sapping the reason for existence from the men. If they could not kill animals, what then?

They knew they would be successful this day. There had been bears spotted deep in the forest, already out of their caves. They would scare them into an ambush. A bear would fight one or two men, but would run from many.

When there were many men, the bears would run ahead of the men and into the waiting sounds of the Berkers who would come up the shorter way and surprise the bears from behind.

The padding of many feet sent all animals scurrying into hiding places, up trees, or ahead of the men. All men ran at a distance from each other where they could not see each other but knew of the others' presence. The movement of the net of men through the forest was as a strange wind that did not vary. It affected all animal life in its silent, persistent rhythm. When at nightfall it stopped, the forest life seemed to stop. There was a strange, tense silence—a temporary rest.

The men built small campfires in a line, cutting the forest in two. They slept in turns, ate little, drank water from their animal skin containers, and hardly talked. The excitement of the past moons was beginning to change to fear. The animals that the men had encircled in their planning at their Men's House, were in their heads; the animals they would encircle at the next sun were out there in the woods. There was a fearful restlessness in the forest that night, among both men and animals.

At sunrise the three clans started out again. They could not see the animals but they could hear them crashing down smaller bushes ahead of them. On this second day the men kept up a continuous, low yelling noise, and the forest creatures sent out their own noises.

As the Renks and the Brykdas moved in

closer to the meadow, the Berkers came up the short mountain behind the meadow, and from that height they could see their prey before the other two clans could see the animals. The meadow filled with frenzied creatures running in different directions.

Two gazelles made steps up the mountain toward the Berkers, sniffed the air, caught the Berker scent, descended and ran in the opposite direction toward the lower part of the meadow until they caught the Renk scent. The noise from all three clans had reached the animals' ears. Many bears hovered near the mountain, looking up to make an attack, turned back and growled into the sky. The Berkers thought they heard the other clans, but they were not to attack until all clans could hear each other. All clans had to be in position.

Hoken counted as many bears in the distant meadow as he had fingers on two hands and his eyes shone with the victory that was to be theirs. When he was sure he heard the yelling of the Renks, he held up one arm for his clansmen to see. When Allsonde, far to the other side of Hoken on the mountain, heard the yelling of the Brykdas, Allsonde held up *his* arm for all to see, and that was the signal for the Berkers to fire their arrows into the animals in the meadow below.

The Berkers let go with arrow after arrow and saw animals fall injured or dead. Those that did not fall ran to the lower or upper side of the meadow where they were met by Renk or Brykda arrows. There was no escape. The noise now was loud and confusing. Different animals sent out their own warning or death cries, while the yelling clans came closer together.

Three bears, one with an arrow hanging from its back, attempted to climb the mountain. Hon and Lowie had left a hole in the Berker line and the animals had seen an opening. Angered and desperate, the animals attempted to make their escape from the slaughter below them. The injured bear lumbered up the mountain behind the other two. Hon and Lowie aimed their arrows into the animals that had fallen to the ground to ensure their death and the clan's safety, when they saw two escaping from their man-made net. Hoken saw what was happening on Hon's side of the mountain and called to him. When Hon turned he had time only to reach for his arrow. The smaller of the two bears had sighted Hon and rushed him, knocking him down. Behind the one bear, Hon could see another and he knew he was helpless.

The large paw pinned Hon's chest to the ground and Hon looked into the huge red mouth above his face when, growling a strangled death sound, the animal rolled off of his body and on to the side of the mountain. Hon scrambled to his feet, reaching for his arrow, saw the second bear poised to jump at him when it, too, screamed into the air and fell to the ground.

Hon watched both animals, writhing limply on the ground. He had not fit his arrow into his bow. Ahead of him, Lowie smiled, his bow empty. It was *he* who had brought down the two bears. Hon raised his arm to show his thanks when he saw another bear limp up behind Lowie. Hon waved and pointed in warning at the bear behind Lowie, but Lowie, not looking behind him, waved back, thinking that Hon's signal was to thank Lowie.

Hon raised his bow and Lowie saw that Hon was serious and was aiming in his direction. The injured bear wrapped itself around Lowie, grabbed Lowie's shoulder in its mouth and dragged him up the mountain. Hon shot his arrow at the bear and hit it in the lower part of its leg, but the bear limped on. Hon shot another arrow—his last—into the bear's side. It growled and fell, rolling over the limp body of Lowie as Hon ran to his friend.

When Hon reached Lowie he could see that the earthlife had left him. Lowie's eyes looked up at the sky but did not see. His shoulder was gone and his arm was thrown over on the earth, palm side up. Hon saw that both Lowie and the bear who killed him had gone to their dreamworld. With dark feelings Hon removed Lowie's arrows, picked up his bow, and walked down the mountain to the dying animals and to the shouting, laughing clansmen.

Renk, Brykda, and Berker clansmen circled their Kill. The Great Bear Hunt had been successful. Renks ran into Berkers, who had never seen each other before and at first recognizing the Renk Bodie, the Berkers stiffened for combat, before they realized where they were and what a Great Hunt they had completed together. In mock fun they put their bows and arrows on the ground in front of themselves, laughed at each other and then picked them up to continue looking at the spoils of their victory.

As they circled and mused and cried out their joy, the men of the three clans felt the warm blood of pride flow back into their spirits. Allsonde, the Berker, met Kaal the Renk, and Chidpura the Brykda, to decide how the carcasses should be divided. But first, they would have a feast this sundown, and then they would keep the fires going to protect themselves on this night.

"And when the sun rises we will skin what we cannot carry and we will bring the skin back to our clans. Now we will eat all we can," Allsonde said.

That sun down, as they licked their fingers of the moist bits of cooked bear meat, Allsonde announced, "Illinini has given us a sign."

The other Berker men looked at him, puzzled as they sat around their fire in the midst of bleeding carcasses. "Illinini has told us what we wanted to know," he said.

The men, involved in the Great Kill, had put aside other thoughts. Allsonde reminded them of pictures in their minds. "The House of the Goddess? Remember when we asked Illinini about our power? We believed Illinini gave women power to make new life." The men shook their heads that they remembered. "Then we thought about the milkless cow, and the new calves, and we had something in our minds that said *we* might be the ones Illinini gives power to."

"*You*," Hoken reminded Allsonde, "you were not so believing at that time."

Allsonde agreed quickly. "I thought it was wrong to believe such things. I thought great harm would come to us." He spread his arms out in front of him, indicating the Great Kill. "Does it look like great harm?"

They laughed.

"Lowie was harmed," Hon said quietly and the men stopped laughing.

"That was Illinini's way of telling us to walk with great care," Allsonde said. "We can be *too* brave and we can all go to the Spirit World."

"Lowie was the only one," another said. "A Brykda has a bad leg, and a Renk has not come back from a sleep he was knocked into, but that is all."

"Then you see, we *were* given a sign," Allsonde said again. "Our Goddess has told us *we* are full of power. By putting into our dreams this Great Bear Hunt, and by giving us this great victory, Illinini tells us in the best way she can, that *we* have the power. *We* are the ones who put the children in the women's stomachs, as that milkless cow puts the calf in the milk cow."

The men were silent, skeptical, and cautious. Was all this *really* a sign? Should they believe it? Should they not wait? What of the sticks Belka had been putting by her sleeping place, counting the moons until her child's birth? What of Murda's sticks? They wondered why Allsonde, who had been cautious before, was the one now who was so sure of the sign. The men asked him that question.

"Because," he answered, "I am the one who asked Illinini and Illinini has given us Her answer. One does not turn one's back on such an answer. Just *look* at what She has laid before us," he said, sweeping his arms toward the slaughtered bears. "Our Goddess has told us. It is up to us to follow through on Her sign."

Their return to the clan was welcomed by chattering women and children. Many animals had to be left behind, the men told the women. Even with all the men carrying carcasses, each clan taking its share, there were many left behind all over the meadow for the large black birds that soared overhead when the men left. Tired, bloody, and proud, the men brought their prizes home and dropped them at the women's feet.

"These are for skinning," Allsonde told the women. "Then we will eat what we can. We will keep the fires going tonight to keep away animals from the forest who want to come in to our huts and enjoy meat. We will leave a carcass for the leopards at the edge of the forest." Allsonde held his back erect and walked with his bloodied fur garment dragging behind him.

The dust rose in the turmoil of dropping the animals, the women shuffling around and choosing the ones they would skin. Insects swarmed. Children ran from animal to animal.

The women who had been preparing the soil for seeding and making plans for the Feast of the Planting wondered if now that they had all the meat that would keep from spoiling for several sundowns, would it be necessary to kill the calf for eating?

"There are times when we have no meat," Hoken explained. "It would be better to save the calf until our bear meat is gone." Nargab listened to this decision, happy that the calf would be spared for this time.

When night came and the women were in their huts, Belka waited for her Renk, Welo. It was a good meeting together after many nights apart.

"Your stomach is now grown large," the Renk said. "I did not know you were going to bring a child to life."

"You have been gone many sundowns," Belka reminded him, "so how could you know?"

"I could not come to you and have you drain my strength when I needed it for the Great Animal Kill."

"And when my child comes you cannot come again for many moons."

"I know. I will return to my clan. When your child no longer feeds from your body, send your brother to tell me."

Belka shrugged. Maybe by then there would be another man from another clan who would want to visit her in her hut. If not, she would send word.

"How many sticks do you count now?" Welo asked.

"Why do you ask? That is woman's talk." But she counted out as many sticks as she had fingers, except for one finger.

"How many sticks does it take to make a calf?" the Renk wondered out loud.

"What do you say?" Belka asked.

"You put a stick there for each moon you do not have moon blood and when you don't have moon blood a child grows in your stomach?"

"Yes."

"And a calf . . . if we put a stick . . . no . . . I don't know." It was something he would talk about with the men. He left Belka's hut to discuss his thoughts with the men in the Men's House.

"If we put a stick in a place every moon after a milk cow has been with the milkless cow until there is a calf, we will know how many moons it takes to make a calf in a cow's stomach," the Renk, Welo, explained. He would tell his own clan this discovery and they could see how it went with their sheep.

"Now that we know the secret of the power," Allsonde said, "let us put the right cattle together to increase the herd. We do not need the wisdom of Kolar. We now have our own."

"We will make our own meat and not have to go out on long, empty hunts again," Hon said.

"We will start at sunrise," Allsonde told them. "We will tell the women what we know."

They agreed. At the next sun they would begin.

Their approach was timid. Men were not accustomed to work at the cattle-hold. They saw the women carrying baskets they had woven out of the leaves of the forest. The baskets were full of droppings from the cows in the cattle-hold. It took two women to carry a full basket to the grain field. There they spread the droppings on the ground and others worked the droppings into the earth to make the grain grow tall after the planting.

The men watched the women carry their heavy loads, for this was women's work. Some women carried the droppings while some of the women dug in the soil. When the cattle were led out to the green grass, the men went to herd the cattle with the boys this time. When Allsonde, the appointed spokesman for the men, told the women they would help with the cattle, the women were surprised.

"What is it you would do?" Kolar asked, one hand on her hip and the other on the tree by the cattle-hold.

"We will help the cows get large with calves," Allsonde said, as the men standing near him grinned.

"And how will you do *that?*" Kolar asked. Other women stopped their work and stood near to listen.

"We will put the milk cows in with the other, there," Allsonde said, pointing to the one creature who had no milk bag. "*That,*" Allsonde pointed under the animal's stomach. *That* is what puts the calves into the milk cows. It is *not* your woman power!"

Kolar stepped back. The other women withdrew.

Belka whispered to Ashinda. "Allsonde is saying something Kolar said many moons ago. It was not good what she said then."

Hoken moved forward. "We *know*," he told Kolar and the other women, "it is *not* Illinini . . ." There was a gasp of breath in unison by the women.

"Do not speak ill of Illinini here," Ashinda said.

"Do not dare to speak of the power of the Goddess Illinini," Murda added. "Illinini hears. She will punish."

"No," Allsonde said firmly. "Illinini will not punish. Illinini has given us a *sign*."

"A sign?" Kolar asked.

"A sign." He thought briefly. "We will not reveal the sign, for she gave it only to men. The sign given to us by Illinini told us of *our* power, *not* the power of women. The sign told us something else," he said hesitating. Should he say this now, he wondered. He had not shared this thought with the other Berker men. It was a thought so strong that Allsonde knew that it was true. Yes, he would say it. Now *was* the time.

"What is this 'something else'?" Murda asked.

"The Goddess Illinini is not what you think," he said. All who had assembled drew in their breath, astonished at the risk Allsonde was taking in questioning their Goddess.

"What do you say?" Belka asked.

"Illinini," Allsonde said calmly, "is *not* a woman. The power she made known to us has given me the sign. Illinini is not a Goddess. Illinini is a God."

"No . . ." the women screamed. "No!"

"That is not true," Belka said.

"Illinini is our Goddess. She is good to women . . . she brings us young ones . . . and makes our grain grow." The men had been silent, considering this terrible and yet great knowledge from Allsonde.

Allsonde ignored the women's protests.

"We will move cows into the hold of this big one," Allsonde indicated, pointing to the one, large, lone animal. Allsonde took control. His knowledge gave him that right.

"*You* will?" Kolar asked. She stood firmly between Allsonde and the cattle-hold of restless milk cows ready to be led out to the grassy side of the hill. "These cows are not to do with as *you* will."

Allsonde considered the dilemma.

"*We* will take the herd out," Kolar told Allsonde. "There is no milk cow to be put with that one today. When the time is for that, I will do it, or Belka, or Shinda. Cattle are women's work. A man cannot help the Goddess, Illinini, put the spirit of the newborn in the cow. New life is women's work. . . ."

As Kolar talked, the men drifted together and then away. There would be another sun time. They would decide at another time. It was good for now that they had given the women their thoughts, their knowledge. It was good that they now knew about Illinini.

They would go now to the House of Illinini,

their God, and thank Him for the Great Animal Kill and for his Sign.

When Welo the Renk returned to the Berker men's house he had an unusual wish. He smiled and offered, "My sister, Drialle, to you Hon, for one milk cow. We Renks have only a few cattle. The cow you will give me will make me a good man among Renks."

"One cow is worth more than one mate," Hon said. "One cow gives milk for many Warm Times and many Cold Times. And she gives us calves to eat. What can a woman ever give that would be as much as that?"

"A woman brings newborns," Welo said.

"Newborns eat our food," Hon answered.

"Newborns grow big and work in the fields and make more food. We do not have a grain field as great as yours, but we will," Welo told the listening Berkers, "because our children work in the fields."

"Your women bring girls and boys into the fields?" Allsonde asked.

"Yes. Our fields are greater now."

"*Our* women do not let even girls enter the fields until they have had their first moon blood. They say only women can make seeds grow. It is women's work," Allsonde explained.

"In the last Warm Time Renk boys planted seeds," Welo said. The men waited to hear more. "And the seeds came out of the ground into grain."

The Berkers mumbled to each other. "And the grain was good grain," Welo continued. The Berkers mumbled again. "And no evil fell on us."

The Berkers listened and thought. Now they looked at Hon and they all wondered. Allsonde asked Hon, "You want Drialle?"

Hon shook his head up and down.

Allsonde told Welo, "Pick your cow. Go to the herd on the field, take your cow to your clan. Then return with Drialle. We will build her a hut near the separating tree. It will be ready when you return."

Now there were more than thoughts to consider. There were twigs and rocks to gather for the new hut and Berker women to consult on water content of the mud to make into solid mud bricks. There was movement and talk, and confrontation with women who could not at first comprehend about a strange clan woman coming to live in their compound. This had never happened before and the women complained, not so much about Drialle as about the cow the men were taking from them.

"Cattle are women's work," Kolar scolded when she heard that Welo had taken one of their cows.

"No . . ." Allsonde said. "Cattle belong to men."

"What?" she yelled. "We have worked the cattle all these moons and now when they are of value for something you want, you say they 'belong to men.' That is not so."

"Yes. It is so. The God Illinini gave us the sign. It is He who tells us animals are for men."

"The cattle were not 'for men' when they were cold or dying or not making milk," Kolar shook her head. "The cattle are for all of us, but they are women's work. Men do not know how to. . . ."

"Men know," Allsonde announced and turned his back to her and walked to the men who were building a new hut with the advice of Shinda and the help of Belka who carried and mixed earth in spite of her own large bulging stomach.

When Drialle arrived with her brother, Welo, the Berkers stood at the edge of their grounds to stare. The men stood next to their Men's House, in an irregular line to the new hut. Hon stood nearest to the new hut.

The Berker women stood three deep with their children across from the men. They looked at the stranger, at her fur covering like their own, the bone bracelets at her ankles which they did not have, and at her hair that was hacked off short over her eyes and ears and gathered into a large thick Bodie at the back of her head.

They could see she was like themselves and yet she was different. They who had been enemies with the Renks through their many moons, would now see one living on their grounds. It was a long moment there, where the forest and the strange Renk woman and the Berker grounds came together.

131

Ashinda broke the silence among the women. "She is a big grown one. She will be a good worker in our field."

The women nodded.

"Will her work value one cow giving milk?" Kolar asked unsmiling.

"We will see," Ashinda replied.

The men shuffled. Welo moved his sister in front of him. She stood there looking at the ground. Allsonde motioned to Hon, who walked the long distance in front of the line of Berker men up to Drialle. Hon took her hand and led her back over the distance in front of the men. Head down, watching only her feet, once looking back at her brother, Drialle moved behind Hon who led her into the new hut and dropped the bear skin flap over the entrance.

The women and men moved their separate ways, the strange relationship beginning to form some meaning in their minds.

Later, in the shade of the Men's House, the men, joined by Hon, mused over their transaction.

"It must be now," Allsonde announced, "that no one but Hon will enter Drialle's body. This way we will know that it is Hon who puts the child in her."

"And the child," Hon smiled, "will be mine."

The men, seated against the walls, looked at him and thought about what he had just said. Not one of these men had ever claimed a child before.

"Children do not belong to men," Hoken said.

"They have always belonged to women," Allsonde added. There had been so many new changes since Illinini's sign, they should use caution. They should not take too much.

"But," Hon explained, "was not that because we did not know about *our* power? Was not that because we believed it was only women who caused the newborns?"

They all agreed.

"Now we have knowledge," Hon continued. "We put the newborn in women. They could not bring children here without our power. Is that not so?"

They all considered again and agreed.

"So the children," he ventured again slowly, "belong to men."

No one objected to what he said.

"With the children we will get more women, or more cattle. . . ." Hon continued.

"Wait," Allsonde interrupted. "You go too fast. You now have a mate and already you own many children." The men laughed, but Hon did not.

"You do not see," he said. "Illinini has given us a great sign and I read His sign."

Allsonde shifted his position. Would Hon now have a bigger voice than his own? He listened to Hon's explanation.

"If no one else enters Drialle's body and in nine sticks there is a newborn, then we will know. Is that not true?"

They murmured their agreement.

"And the newborn will be mine," Hon continued. "If it is a boy I will raise him to herd the cattle as well as Nargab. Then I will get

133

him a mate from the Brykdas or Renks. I will exchange a cow. We know how to have more cattle and we will have mates for our boys."

"And if Drialle has a newborn girl?" Hoken asked.

"Then I will exchange her when her time comes. She can go and become a mate of a Renk, just as Drialle has come to our clan and I will receive a cow in exchange."

"The cow, then will be yours?" Hoken asked.

"As the newborn girl is mine, then what she brings will be mine," Hon explained.

The men were silent for a long time reflecting on this new idea. Then Allsonde considered aloud, "These new ways of talking and thinking may not be Illinini's wishes. What we have had in our clan has been for all. The children belonged to all the women. The cattle belonged to all. Now you speak of getting cattle that would be only yours."

"You, too, could do the same. Your child could be traded with . . ."

"*My* child! I have no child," Allsonde said.

The men looked at him until he realized the significance of their staring.

"Or maybe," he said, "maybe I do. Yes . . . I see now . . . All of the newborns from our women among the Renks and Brykdas . . . Yes, I see . . . but we are not the only men who mate with those women. . . ."

"No," Hon said, "that is true. Now you see why it is that we must bring our mates here to be sure we are the only ones they take into their bodies. That way we will know the newborns belong to us."

134

The men fell silent again, considering Hon's suggestion.

"But how," Allsonde asked, "can we be sure we are the only mates? It has never been this way before."

"We will need to watch the women all the time. I will not let another man lie with Drialle. I will tell her I will beat her or send her home and take *two* cattle back if she has another man. For the child must be mine. I must know that."

"And when we go to the Spirit World," Allsonde said, "our children . . . our men children, will have our cattle. That way," he laughed, "we will not die." The men laughed with him and they all felt good about their new ways of thinking.

For the women there was not much joy. Drialle's coming caused a restlessness among them. Would there be, they asked each other, more strangers coming to live in the Berker huts? If one woman had come, wouldn't the men use the cattle to get more women? They looked at their cattle wondering about these large, silent animals that had brought them food, drink, and hides. What would they mean to them now that the men were herding them and mating them with the milkless ones?

Nargab stroked his calf who nuzzled up to him through the log fencing, knowing that the Feast of the Planting was not far away and that his calf did not have long to live. Kolar seemed to appear from nowhere and unexpectedly put her arm on Nargab's shoulder. There was a sense of an ending in the air.

That afternoon the women had watched Belka walk off into the forest looking for the private place for her pain in delivering a newborn from the Child Spirit. No man would claim *her* child, she had told the women just as she had told the men. This child was hers and if it should be a female, *she* would never trade it for cattle. The Goddess Illinini would be good to women, Belka knew. She did not believe, as the men and as some women were beginning to believe, that Illinini was a God and not a Goddess.

Many moons after Drialle came to live among the Berkers, Allsonde and other men told the young Berker boys that the boys were to go through a ceremony in the large ceremonial house the men had built deep in the forest away from the village, and especially away from the women. The Ancestral Spirits, they said, must not be heard or seen by women.

The men gathered the boys together at the entrance of their village Men's House and made their announcement. The women also had gathered to be with their children and to hear the strange news.

"The God, Illinini, has said that all boys,

when they are at the door of manhood, must be rid of their mother's blood," Allsonde said. "It is the blood of woman that takes away a man's power to kill animals or catch fish."

Kolar scoffed. "That is why you do not come near us when we are in our moon cycle."

"It is more," Allsonde said.

"Yes," Kolar said. "When the Child Spirit. . . ."

"No," Allsonde interrupted. "It is the blood of woman in our boys. That is what makes us weak. That is what we must let fall and bury."

Kolar stepped forward. "What is this you are saying?" she demanded. "Our blood is *sacred*. All of you there," she indicated with a sweep of her arm toward the men, "you, all of you have your mother's blood."

"Yes," Hon said. "And now we know it is because we did not get rid of our mother's blood that we were weak. Illinini has told us. Our next Berker men will not be weak as we were."

"In what way," Kolar persisted, "have you been weak? You have brought meat from the forest, you have helped us clear the land, you have helped us build our houses. What is this you speak of?"

There was a shuffling of feet among the men and a glancing from one to the other. After a time Allsonde spoke.

"We have been weak because we did not know before this time that the children were of our making. We have been weak because we let women own the cattle, and we let women plant seeds and dig the soil, and the grain became theirs. . . ." His voice seemed to disap-

137

pear. It was a new beginning for the men and it was difficult for them to say the same things in front of the women that they said so boldly to themselves in the Men's House.

Now it was the women's turn to shuffle and to mumble and to decide without saying who should do their speaking. Kolar looked to Ashinda, to Belka holding her child, to Murda and to Shinda. Then Ashinda spoke. "Since men have replaced the Child Spirit in our clan and have made our Goddess your *God,* you have made us your captives."

The women nodded. Ashinda continued. "You watch over our girl children as we used to watch over our cattle. And when we ask you why you do this you tell us it is so our daughters will bring more cattle to Berkers when you, our men, trade our daughters to the Brykdas or Renks."

"And that is as it will be," Allsonde said firmly. "The God, Illinini, has told us that a girl must be fresh from her first moon blood and never have had a man in her body before she is mated."

"Illinini . . ." Kolar scoffed. "You use the name of Illinini in ways we do not like." Kolar would not concede to the men their claim on the Goddess. She persisted. "Illinini would not make women as captives or say that our daughters cannot do this or that. . . ."

"Be careful," Allsonde warned, "of what you say of the God Illinini. We have been weak before, but the Ceremony of Manhood will make men of the Berker boys. As Elders we will see that there will be no more womanish men in this clan." He turned and walked back to the Men's House with the others following him.

For a long time the women had been aware of the men's work and their goings and comings into the forest in activities that had nothing to do with hunting. Murda's older daughter, Helia, not yet a woman, had accidentally come upon the men's ceremonial house in the building stages. The work stopped and her brother, Gabber, told her to go away or she would be visited by evil. He had seen that she was starting her moon blood. He knew that this must be her first time. He yelled at her to run home to their mother.

Not aware of why her brother was so frightened, Helia ran anyway and told Murda what had happened. Gabber left his work on the ceremonial house and began the building of a small hut outside the village. This is where Helia would be sent for the first month of her new womanhood.

The men had insisted that females in their first moon blood must be isolated. No man should see such a female. The first moon blood to issue from a young woman's body carried with it the power of destruction. This was part of the total power that women had had over men and men must be protected from its sight. Just seeing a girl in her new moon blood could, the men said, destroy a man's hunting skill, cause a man to never have children, spoil his fishing, and even make his mind leave him.

When the women objected to this new treatment of their daughters, all the men would say was that it was the wish of their God Illinini that men remain pure. A man who saw a young girl in her first moon blood, or who mated with his wife at her moon blood time, or who let his wife touch his hunting tools, or prepare his food during her moon blood, was rendered powerless, if not worse.

Frightened that he might be changed for the rest of his life for having seen his sister's moon blood, Gabber worked furiously to erect the hut where his sister would live for the next moon. Getting Helia into the hut immediately was Gabber's only hope. He erected the tree poles, ran to gather large limbs to use as walls and roof and then sent word back to his mother, Murda, to bring Helia to the hut immediately.

Gabber retreated back to his work in the ceremonial house, but only after he had been held over an open fire by the other Berker men. His skin was warmed almost to the point of burning before he was released, and all were satisfied that the evil of having seen the power of woman's blood was destroyed by the heat of the fire.

Murda brought Helia to the hut because she had been told by Gabber's messenger that Helia would have to be killed if she were not isolated and out of view of any male. Kolar wanted Murda to defy the men, but Murda would not risk the danger that threatened Helia.

Murda and the other women brought food to Helia and warm fur to cover her in the cold nights, but they had been forbidden to stay with her lest the power of the first moon blood be communicated from them to the men.

Helia's pain and loneliness were shared with no one. She shed her childhood in solitude. No other Berker or other clan girl, then or later, experiencing the transformation of her body, was able to share the event with another human being.

For the boys it was different. The ceremonial house and all the preparations made by the men to celebrate the occasion of manhood, proclaimed the honor of this stage in a male's life.

Women were not permitted to see the men working on their ceremonial house. "Women, here, will bring evil to us," Women were told when they approached in curiosity. The women were learning not to question as they had questioned long ago.

When the men took over the women's work of the cattle and the grain fields, men's voices became stronger and firmer toward the women, and men sometimes beat the women if they did not do as the men wished. The women remembered that this had not been so before the Great Bear Hunt.

When the men's preparations for the Ceremony of Manhood were completed they called for the women to assemble, to hear of the ceremonies for their sons. The women, whose anger would have been quelled in the past by a simple refusal to let their sons take part in the men's ceremonies, now in fear of what their sons might endure if the women refused, put down their anger, and turned their sons over to the men.

"In the name of Illinini," Ashinda asked, no longer using the word 'Goddess,' "you will not harm our boy children?" she asked.

Allsonde, who had been standing at the entrance of the Men's House at the edge of the village, straightened himself and raised his chin. "Would we harm the future Berker men?" he asked. "Our wish is to make them strong and wise. That is all."

"And how long will this take?" Kolar asked.

"One moon," Hon answered. "And when the Ceremony of Manhood is over, the boys who will then be men will live in the Men's House and will not be permitted to return to their mother's huts."

The women and boys shook their heads in protest. "But our boys have not yet reached their man-height. They are not men as you were when *you* moved to the Men's House. They are boys. It will be a long time before they are ready to mate . . ." Ashinda pleaded.

"It is better that we take them and make men of them before they become too woman-ish with too much living with women," Hon said. "We do not want them to be as we were, believing in the Child Spirit instead of believing in the power that we get from the God, Illinini when He revealed this to us on the Great Hunt. We will take them, those whose bodies are about to change."

"Only the weak will be permitted to return to live with their mothers, and boys who cry will not become men," Hon continued.

The boys looked at each other and then to their mothers.

"And if they are weak and return to their mothers," Allsonde said, "they will not have the scars of manhood on their chest. They will not be allowed to hunt, and they will not be allowed to mate. They will never claim children, cattle, or grain as their own."

And so the terms were set. The women and boys ambled back to the center of the village, and the men retreated into their Men's House. Each boy would wait and question; each Elder would plan his part in the performance; each mother would wonder.

The boys talked and worried together until the day the Elders came to each hut and took them away. Their mothers and younger brothers and sisters stood at their huts watching the men and boys walk through the village and into the forest.

Each of the seven Elders held a boy by the hand. They had been kind when they took them from their mothers and they were kind walking through the forest. The path was well worn and there was no difficulty. The boys were both fearful and curious. They dreaded and welcomed the unknown that was about to happen. If they had been given the chance to run back home, their curiosity would have prevented it.

When they neared the large house that they could see in the distance they heard strange whistling noises coming from inside. They thought that all the other Berker men were in the house until several appeared out of the forest demanding that the boys and their Elders stop where they were. The boys were told to sit

143

on the ground and all the men stood in a circle around them.

"What you hear and see in the next moon you must never tell to any woman," Hon said. Nargab looked around but did not see Allsonde, though he did see Allsonde's younger brother, Hoken. Saku recognized *his* older brother, Hon.

The boys listened and looked into the forest. Then they looked at the house. Hon's voice became angry. "If you do not listen to your Elders you will not know what to do." He waited until they were all looking at him.

"If your Elders learn that you have told the secret of the Ceremony of Manhood to any woman—your mother, your sisters, or later, your wife—you will be killed."

"Killed?" Ashtar, son of Shinda asked.

"Yes. Killed! The secrets of the Ceremony of Manhood must never be told." He waited. No one said anything. The eerie, whistling noise from inside the house grew louder. All the boys looked to the house and all the Elders watched the boys. Then the noise stopped instantly.

"The noise you heard was from the Spirits of our ancestors. They are asking us to make men of our Berker boys. They are asking us to release you from your woman's bondage, to take out your mother's blood," Hon explained.

"How can you take out our mother's blood?" Ashtar asked.

"It will happen. You will see. You have only to be patient, to wait. Do not ask questions. All things are planned. One thing we must know . . . *now* . . . that *you* know you will be killed if you tell any woman, *ever,* what happens in the Ceremony of Manhood."

The boys nodded that they understood.

Then they were told to rise and enter the house. It was black inside and their eyes had to get used to the dark before they would see large figures carved in wood, lined against the walls. The Elders led them around the circle of the house and told them the figures were the Spirits of their ancestors.

"They talk to us through their whistling sounds," Hoken, younger brother of Allsonde, said.

The boys circled the hut, examining the carved figures, taller than any man in the Berker clan, and frightening with their enlarged staring eyes and unsmiling faces. Each figure had been carved from a tree trunk and painted with the colors of the dirt or plants in the forest.

"How did you know what our ancestors looked like?" Saku asked his older brother, Hon. "They are in our minds," Hon explained. "We had only to let them move our hands over the wood as we carved."

He had not finished his explanation when the eerie whistling began again. Everyone turned and looked at a raised section at the end of the long house. Logs had been piled up to make a place where a person could sit. Behind the log was a large, black drawing of a leopard. In the dim light Nargab thought he saw a person sitting on the top of the log pile. The whistling stopped once again as suddenly as it had begun and the boys heard a voice.

145

They recognized it as Allsonde's.

Though they had never seen Allsonde wearing anything except an animal skin cap on his head before, the boys saw that on top of his head there was a band of fur with wood carvings rising upward. Nargab wondered how Allsonde could keep it on his head when he walked because it looked heavy. The Elders brought the boys up to Allsonde, lined them up, and then stepped back. There was a long silence while the boys looked from one to the other, then from Allsonde to the other Elders behind them. Nargab, even though surrounded by all the men in the Berker clan, and all the boys of his years who had been his brothers, felt alone.

"Now we begin," Allsonde announced. "Now the Berker men will make the Berker boys into men. Women make children, but only men can make men." Saku wondered again how that could be done.

"I have been chosen," Allsonde said, "to be the Berker chief. Illinini has chosen me. Through the Spirits of our ancestors He has made it known that the Berker men's blood shall flow into the bodies of the Berker boys."

The boys looked at each other again.

"My blood will flow," he said again, holding out his arm. Hon approached him holding a sharpened obsidian stone in his hand. With Allsonde's hand in Hon's, the younger brother scraped the obsidian stone across Allsonde's wrist and Allsonde's blood spurted out and ran down to the earth. Then each boy was led to

Allsonde, where Hon scraped the stone across the boys' wrists. The blood that ran from their wrists was caught in a pottery vessel, the other men being careful to see that no boy's blood dropped on the floor of the ceremonial house.

The wrist of each boy in turn was laid on Allsonde's wrist. The whistling accompanied the whole ritual. The boys were returned to their position in front of Allsonde, holding their wrists, but not crying.

"You are on your way to becoming men," Allsonde said. "But before we can proceed, we must get the women's blood out of our sacred house."

Hon picked up the pottery vessel and left the house with two other men. All was silent in the house until they returned. "It is done," Hon said. "We have buried the vessel. The Spirit of woman's blood has been removed. Their blood has been buried. It will not defile us."

Relieved, Allsonde told the boys that they would now have the marks of manhood put upon their chests. "You will be the *first* Berker men to be so honored. From now on *your* sons will look at your signs of manhood and will wait for the day when they, too, can become men."

Nargab and Saku looked at each other and with closed mouths they smiled at each other with their eyes. It was a better day than they had thought it would be and the cuts on their wrists were nothing now compared to their feeling of closeness to each other.

"You will lie down, one by one, your back on

my back and my strength will flow into your body as the marks of manhood are made on your chest."

Ashtar remembered when he was smaller he took the yellow dirt and the red dirt and mixed it with water and made marks across his body. It would be a happy thing to have the men know that that had been fun. Perhaps they had done this also when they had been young. He would enjoy this.

"No one Berker boy must see the others at this time," Allsonde said, pointing to Hoken to lead all but one boy outside. Ashtar was the one left.

Allsonde stepped down to the floor and made a table of his body. Ashtar was placed on top and quickly before he knew what they were going to do, the Elder Kesch drew the sharp obsidian stone across his chest, cutting a thin slash from one armpit to the other.

Gabber clapped his hand over Ashtar's mouth to prevent his crying out. Then Hon sprinkled ashes on the cut and patted it with leaves. He was removed from Allsonde's back and led to a dark corner facing into the wall.

A Berker man sat next to Ashtar, his arm around his shaking shoulders. Ashtar knew he must not cry though he could feel the sticky blood creeping down his chest and stomach. He heard another boy led in, and then another, and as each boy finished the ritual, each was led to a separate part of the hut to sit with an Elder.

No boy cried.

After the last boy was raised from Allsonde's

back, all of the boys were reassembled in front of the pile of logs again. Crouched to protect their wounds they looked from one to the other, not at the others' faces, but at their bodies. Though their wounds throbbed they felt good. They were proud of themselves and of each other. They felt a part of each other. They had endured pain together and would never talk about it to any woman. Their bond, now, was to each other.

"You are brave," Allsonde smiled at the boys. The whistling began and ended.

"The Spirits of our ancestors welcome you," Allsonde said and the boys grinned. "But you have yet one more ceremony to prove your manhood. You are the first new men of the Berker clan. Each planting time the Ceremony of Manhood will be repeated and your young brothers will become men as you will become men today."

The boys looked at each other again, wondering what more would happen to them.

Allsonde continued. "Because this is the first Ceremony of Manhood for the Berkers, on all of you there is a great duty. You must be very brave. Your younger brothers must not know what you are going through."

The boys shook their heads in agreement.

"The women and children must know only that you were asked to be brave. What we will now perform is the Great Ceremony. Let us proceed."

Nargab knew that they had been through the worst and maybe now they would be given something—maybe a cow—for being brave. He

149

had done what was expected of him. His mother, Ashinda, would be proud of him. Then it made him sad to think of her. If she were here she would bring him some herbs to help his pain.

"This Great Ceremony of Manhood will be performed together," Allsonde said.

The boys were happy about that news. "When this Great Ceremony is over you will be ready to hear the stories of your ancestors and you will learn the secret of the Spirit whistles. These secrets must not be shared. And only those of you who know these secrets can ever be Elders and lead our people. Illinini has said this. But now we will begin."

"Each of you will lay your back on the stomach of an Elder. He will be your strength," Allsonde told them. "He will hold you through the ceremony."

As Allsonde explained this, Elders lay down on the dirt floor as other Elders led the boys to the center of the Ceremonial House and placed them, chest up, on the stomachs of the men on the floor. The Elders underneath the boys held the arms of the boys while two other Elders, for each boy, knelt on the floor.

One Elder held the penis of the boy, pinning the boy's legs down to the floor, while the other Elder with a chipped-sharpened obsidian stone quickly cut away the loose skin covering the opening at the end of the penis. Each tiny piece of loose skin was collected and placed in a basket made of fresh fern leaves. The blood that ran from the boys, over their Elders' bodies, was wiped away with fur remnants and the boys were left lying on their Elders for sometime while the whistling continued, at times rasping and loud, and at times soft and soothing.

Nargab wanted to cover the terrible pain with his hands, but they were held by his Elder. His wrist hurt, his chest hurt, and now he had a pain worse than anything he had ever known. His blood trickled from his body and scared him. The powdery ashes in his chest wound made him want to scratch. Yet he dared not try to pull his arms away.

He had not cried and he did not know why. He had not heard anyone cry. He thought of his mother again and he longed for her comfort, but he wondered if he could go to her for anything ever again once he had been through this Ceremony of Manhood and had to go live at the Men's House.

Nargab would herd the cattle as he had done when he was a small boy, but he would not be doing it to please the women who were in charge of the cattle then. Now he would herd the cattle because he was a man. Since the Great Bear Hunt when the cattle had been taken over by the men, women no longer told men what to do. It was the other way now and he, Nargab, who had passed his Manhood Ceremony, was one of the men who would tell women what to do.

His sons would know that this secret of the Spirit Whistles must not be learned by women, for if men are to keep secrets they must have others to keep their secrets from and so it was said that if a woman should ever hear the sound of the Spirit Whistles she should go into the forest and die because that would be an easier death than what the Spirits would bring her if she didn't.

And so Nargab, and Saku, and Ashtar, and the other boys were gradually removed from their mothers in many different ways. Their link to the future would now be through their Elders with whom they would live, eat, hunt, plant, and herd cattle. And when they took wives from neighboring clans, their wives would give them children, skin the animals, sew their garments of hides, make their pottery, build their houses, and prepare their food except when their wives had their moon blood. Then the wives must isolate themselves so as not to weaken their husbands. And the wives must never have another man enter their bodies because then what man would know his own children? But there was no reason why a man could not have other women, or other wives.

And always the feeling of closeness would be felt by the boys who had endured the pain of the Ceremony of Manhood together.

3

*Babylonia**

Belka's child grew to womanhood, bore children who also bore children. Azurelea, one of the female descendents of two milleniums of descendents of Belka's first child, was born in the year 584 B.C. in the thriving commercial civilization of Ancient Babylonia.

In the fertile lands of the Tigris-Euphrates Rivers, this high civilization which rose out of the ravages of its conquest, erected luxurious palaces, temples, and commercial buildings, monuments to civilization's entrenchment in the world. Abundant grain, gold, slaves, and wives became the dream of most men and the reality of many. Civilization, the new phenomenon, ushered out the doubt of humanity's

*Customs in this chapter are based on Herodotus, *Histories*. c. 485 B.C.

153

survival as the gods of certainty multiplied. Humans, who as nomads and primitive settlers, were victims of their environment, learned, as civilized beings to victimize it. Belka's civilized Babylonian descendent, Azurelea, had no need to worry about exposure to the elements, a scarce food supply, or tribal enemies. Her father's slaves filled the granaries and bred the animals for food and transportation. His soldiers protected his boundaries from invasion, and his wives provided him with pleasure and progeny.

As her mother personally supervised Azurelea's dressing in preparation for her visit to her father's chambers, Azurelea wondered about all of the elaborate arrangements of her hair and her dress. The favorite daughter of Burabaish, King of Urak, Principality in Babylon, Azurelea knew this day was more important than the other days when she visited her father, but her questions about this day were not satisfactorily answered.

"It is the Day-of-Thy-Birth-Celebration," her mother, Ninaltra, told her the third time that day, handing the slave girl, Kito, a newly made lavender tunic to slip over Azurelea's immature shoulders. As her mother talked, she combed Azurelea's hair, arranging it in a high coiffure, changing the curls in a different fashion than the slave girl had set it only this morning. Her mother perfumed Azurelea's ears and added a shade of blue eye-lid coloring over her daughter's dark and wondering eyes.

"I did not go to my father's rooms when it

was the Day-of-My-Birth-Celebration before," Azurelea told her mother.

"No. That is true. You have a good memory, my dear," her mother said, squeezing Azurelea around the shoulders playfully. "This Day-of-Thy-Birth-Celebration is a festive day for the whole palace."

"But why is *this* day different than my *last* Day-of-My-Birth-Celebration?" Azurelea asked, pulling away from her mother's pinches on her cheeks which her mother hoped would make Azurelea's flesh more radiant and therefore more pleasing to King Burabaish.

"Not so many questions, my daughter. You will learn soon enough." Ninaltra clapped her hands toward the slave. "Kito. Get the sandals with the gold thread. And hurry. We are awaited."

Kito shuffled quickly into another room, returning immediately with two small sandals, laced with gold thread. Azurelea seated herself on the silken tapestry stool, and Kito knelt to place the sandals on her mistress's small feet.

Kito, a grown woman, adored the small Azurelea, having attended to her clothing needs and wishes since the princess's birth. Other slaves waited on Azurelea at meals, nibbling at the palace delicacies which were a special dividend of that post. Other slaves were chosen for their abilities to entertain the princess, and still others were assigned to the cleaning of Azurelea's suite of rooms, set to the east of the main palace corridors so that the first morning sun would shine upon her.

No one except Kito, though, had had the intimate pleasure of dressing Azurelea in her first garments at birth, and in replenishing her outgrown satins and brocades with longer and newer ones. And on *this* day, Kito had the special privilege of dressing the princess on her Day-of-Her-Birth-Celebration that would change Azurelea's life.

The young princess had tried to penetrate her mother's secretiveness, and had asked Kito only yesterday why *this* Day-of-Her-Birth-Celebration was more important than all the others. If Kito had even whispered to Azurelea what she suspected, as all the underground rumors of the palace had suggested, Kito would expect to lose her life. That knowledge to be imparted to the princess on this day was to be spoken to her only by her father, King Burabaish.

Kito thought of the solemnity of this occasion, lacing Azurelea's sandals slowly. She would have liked to tell the princess what was in her heart, but of course no slave would do that. Azurelea's curiosity was unrelenting. She looked into Kito's eyes, trying to read something in her slave's face. Kito returned Azurelea's glance and held it with the power of her being, wanting to tell her adored mistress many things. But both had to be content with silence.

"Come, come," the Queen urged, clapping her hands again, which brought two young men from the outside dressing room. "We are ready," she told the smooth-faced youths. "Tell the King we are coming. Get up my lovely," she told Azurelea. "There, you look beautiful. Beautiful!"

Kito backed away from the royal pair and watched their disappearance down the long mosaic tile corridor until they turned and could no longer be seen. Then she put her hands up to cover her face, to hide the tears that fell, once her mistress could not see her.

"Kito," the soft voice of the slave from the bed chamber spoke, "why do you cry? Is it not a *happy* day?"

"Yes," Kito struggled. "Happy, yes, and sad, yes." She felt the tears falling again and could not speak.

"But why do you cry? I don't understand. It is an important day. The whole palace will rejoice tonight. The King will get drunk and stay drunk for days and that will mean we can *all* have a lighter time of it."

"That's what *you* see . . ." Kito said. "*You* see how it will be for *you. You* see the celebration as something to make everyone have a festive time. Who sees Azurelea?"

"What do you mean? We *all* see Azurelea."

"Not in the way *I* see her," Kito lamented. "I watch her go down that corridor, a young girl . . ." her lips began to tremble. "And she'll come out of her father's room with knowledge that will change her freshness. She will never be the same." Kito cried aloud.

"Don't take on so, Kito. It is the way it should be. But I must go now. I must repair the confusion in this room. When they return I would not want the Queen to scold me again."

Kito removed one of Azurelea's robes thrown

over a high-backed carved chair, folded it lovingly and laid it down, smoothing it on the chair's velvet cushion. She walked to the end of the room to leave by a side entrance, but turned full around to look at the room as if she were memorizing it, to remember it as the way it was before this time.

Azurelea and her mother approached the King's room with different apprehensions. Queen Ninaltra, first wife of Burabaish, wished only to please her husband. She knew that her daughter, Azurelea, was her husband's favorite child and so in this way at least, Ninaltra had pleased her King. Bringing her daughter to him on this important Day-of-Her-Birth-Celebration would also please her King. Since Azurelea's birth, life had been easier for Ninaltra. She thought back on the days before she had a child when the thoughts of old age and childlessness had occupied her mind.

As she had grown older, her wrinkled cheeks and sagging eyelids had made her disconsolate and yet she would tell no one the source of her misery. The slaves would bring her special food. And her husband, when he saw her, would send for the entertainers for her, but no one could give her a present of last year or the years before. In her barrenness the years had dragged past. She felt herself becoming an old and empty vessel.

She remembered that for many years, her reign as first wife and Queen had been happy. Burabaish, when he was not drunk on fig wine, had been kind to Ninaltra, not fretting when she bore him no children.

"Leave that to the others," he told her, when she begged his forgiveness. "The others," were the other wives he married, year after year, who bore him sons as well as daughters.

As was expected, the first son would be the heir to his throne, and the mother of the first son would be elevated in importance. All Kings of Urak, and indeed of all Babylonia before Burabaish, had elevated their first son's mother to the position of Queen, often dethroning an earlier wife. Burabaish did a new thing. He told his first son's mother that Ninaltra would be Queen when her son was King. If she was unhappy with that arrangement she would not have dared to complain for fear of Burabaish's angry retaliation.

When the other palace wives learned that Ninaltra was going to hold her position they reacted with hostility, for it was then obvious that Ninaltra was not only the enviable first wife but she was also the known favorite. If a first son's mother would not displace her, what then would it take?

Though the other wives watched Ninaltra

jealously, and they spoke in her presence of her lack of fertility, she did not let them see her anguish. And then a remarkable thing happened. After twenty-three years of marriage to Burabaish, Ninaltra became pregnant with his child.

She dared not hope for a son; the Gods would have outdone themselves. When she spoke to the Diviners, to determine the sex of her child, they opened up an infant lamb and perceived that its heart died before they removed it from its body, thus prophesying that her child would be a female. Sadly disappointed at this revelation, Ninaltra's only wish was that she be able to carry it through to its birth. When other women were coming to the end of their lives, and attending the marriage of their children, she, Ninaltra, at thirty-seven was going to bring a new child to Burabaish. The birth of a female child, though a disgrace in most homes at that time, was, to Ninaltra better than nothing.

Burabaish, too, was happy. All told, he then had seventeen daughters and twenty-three sons with his many wives, but thoughts of the unborn child of his Queen and first wife brought him joy he had not felt about the other children.

"My bride," he laughed with her when he invited her for a private meal together, "we finally did it, eh?" He shook his head in disbelief. "It took us twenty-three years to do it *right!*" Then he gave Ninaltra a hard slap on the back of her shoulders, and though he often hurt her in this way, she laughed with him.

She saw that the birth of this child was special to Burabaish. He dwelt on the birth date, talked to the Diviners, and even forgave her ahead of time that it was not to be a son. Ninaltra did not know why this child was more important to him than the others, but she was grateful that it was so. She brought offerings to the Goddess Ishtar and thanked Her for being permitted to please her King after so many long, barren, and lonely years.

There were times in Burabaish's drunkenness when he would laugh and tell her, "Well, my old witch, so you're going to present me with a princess after all. What kind of creature will it be that can crawl out of your old loins?" Ninaltra, not showing her sorrow at these remarks would force her mouth to smile lest he know that he had penetrated her sensitivity, a knowledge that would encourage him to strike yet deeper.

Those times had passed, Ninaltra remembered, as she walked down the long corridor with Azurelea. Yet the memories paraded themselves before her. She remembered how large she had grown in her pregnancy, and how at last she was painfully delivered of her girl child. She remembered, too, that Burabaish had named the baby Azurelea because he said it rolled off his tongue like heavy, sweet fig wine.

Unlike many newborn infants, Azurelea ate when she was supposed to, slept peacefully at most other times, and grew up to smile and to please those about her. Her father adored her as though she were his only child. As she grew, he sent for her to come to his rooms often and he frequently required that she come without her mother. And though it would seem that the other children and mothers in the palace should have been jealous of her, they could not help themselves but to love Azurelea because she smiled on everyone. Ninaltra, pleased that she had brought the King great pleasure, luxuriated in the sunshine that fell on her, though second-hand, through her child.

Burabaish's adoration of Azurelea was sometimes almost enough for Ninaltra to forget about her aging face and body. Vicariously *she* was the young Azurelea, enjoying Burabaish's love. Through her daughter she was pleased and she was able to please. Today, Azurelea's hand in hers, she walked smiling into Burabaish's rooms, tall, proud, beautiful, and feeling young. Today was *her* Day-of-Her-Birth too, as the Gods had delivered Azurelea to her on *Her* Day. Today Ninaltra was fifty years old.

Different from her mother's, Azurelea's apprehensions were mixed with curiosity as she entered her father's rooms. Since this was a *different* Day-of-Her-Birth-Celebration, was it something good or something bad? She had tried unsuccessfully to pry from her mother the significance of this day, but she saw that her mother would do nothing to displease her father and apparently it was to be a surprise only her father could give her.

She had also tried to read Kito's face and she thought she saw for a moment a flash of sadness and another message of some kind of danger. It was a foreign feeling Azurelea had when Kito had looked at her strangely back in her palace suite. Then, walking down the corridor, hand in hand with her mother, Azurelea had a strange urge to turn the other way and to run.

She'd run to Kito. Kito would save her from this unknown. Her mother tightened her hand on Azurelea's. Was that accidental? Was it for comfort? For courage? Happiness? Why was there a sensation that her mother was leading her to her father, not to please Azurelea on her Day-of-Her-Birth-Celebration, but because her mother wanted to please her father. For the first time in her short life she had a sense of betrayal.

"But they love me," she assured herself quickly. "What is this fear I have?" She walked on, unable to resolve to do anything different.

Burabaish, his large body resplendent in his white, silk tunic, his gold mesh belt, his sandals decorated with gold leaf paint, and his intricately coiffed hair, awaited his queen, and especially his beloved Azurelea.

His heart beat faster than was good for a

man of his more than fifty years. But let his heart burst if it must! When Azurelea was born, Burabaish had envisioned this day. He had waited all these years. *This* was the daughter from his first wife. *This* was his special treasure, and *this* was the Day-of-Her-Birth-Celebration that he had waited for so long. This was the day of her betrothal. Years ago Ninaltra had agreed that on this date the betrothal would be announced and she had left the choice of a husband for Azurelea up to him.

"You, who have knowledge of the great leaders in our country and elsewhere," Ninaltra had long ago told Burabaish. "You will know the best one to choose for our child." She did not know that Burabaish had made his selection at Azurelea's birth.

Seated in his receiving chair, Burabaish fidgeted as Ninaltra and Azurelea walked toward him. He knew he was soon to hear Ninaltra's screams of protest for his selection of a husband for Azurelea, but he was prepared.

He watched his queen advance in respectful silence, proudly bringing him her most precious jewel. He was confident that she did not know his choice for their child's future mate though rumors had been flowing through the palace for weeks. True, most everyone knew it was to be the day of the betrothal, but no one except Burabaish knew the arrangement. Ninaltra, serene and appearing more confident than she was, presented herself as a person who had come for a reward for a job well done. His observance of Azurelea was not so comforting. He saw that her eyes were wide as in fright and that she glanced repeatedly from her father's face to her mother's. Burabaish would need to calm her. What he had planned would be the best that any maiden could have in Urak and he was impatient to impart his news and to start the palace celebration.

"Come here, my beauty," he asked Azurelea. "Put your hands in mine. There. They are cold. Ninaltra, sit next to me here while we talk to our child."

Ninaltra, flattered at his courtesy, obeyed happily. "There now. We are a joyful family, is it not true my child?"

Azurelea nodded but found no ease. "And," Burabaish continued, "our little threesome, we have an especially happy family among all these others in the palace," and he turned to pat Ninaltra on the knee. "Is it not so, my Queen?"

"Oh, yes. We are . . ." but Ninaltra could find no words. She had not thought of the three of them as a family. Nor had they been much together as a threesome. She remembered only that she delivered Azurelea to Burabaish when he requested it. She was uneasy about Burabaish's references to them as a family. She shifted nervously in her chair.

"Yes, father."

"It is the most important Day-of-Your-Birth-Celebration in your life," he told her.

"It is? But why?" Again she looked to her mother for a clue, but Ninaltra only smiled.

"This is the day of your betrothal," Burabaish announced expansively. Azurelea tried

165

to jerk her hands away, but her father held them and continued. "It is time, Azurelea. You are thirteen years today. It is time."

She looked to her mother again. Why hadn't she herself guessed. She should have known. Other girls in the palace had been betrothed younger than she. Her father had arranged all of the marriages of the girls in the palace, and that was as it should be. Now many of the girls were gone, just as she would be.

Why had she not thought about this for herself? Had she been too busy riding the horses from the palace stables to think that soon she would have the responsibility of being someone's betrothed? Someday, yes. She knew it would happen. Today was too soon. She shook her head.

"Do not shake your head," her father told her. "You will get used to the idea. . . ."

"I am sorry, father," she explained. "The news is so strange to me. I am not ready . . ."

Her mother leaned forward to put her arm around her daughter, but Burabaish indicated to Ninaltra to sit back.

"You will be ready, Azurelea. The wedding will not be for a year."

"A year?" Azurelea asked. The word used to sound like a long time, but today it sounded too soon.

"But . . ." she started to cry. She looked to her mother who shook her head in disapproval.

"What? You cry?" Burabaish asked angrily. "It is the most important day of your life and you cry?" Indeed, he wondered, should he let his temper have its way? He decided he would remain calm. There was still much he had to say.

Azurelea, knowing she had angered her father, sought to soothe him. "I'm . . . it's just that . . . well . . . when I am married I will have to leave you and my mother and all my friends in the palace, and Kito. . . ." She saw that these words, which were true, quelled her father's anger.

"But, my love, that's just it. You see, you won't *have* to leave any of us when you're married."

Ninaltra sat forward on her chair. The lines in her forehead deepened. "What are you . . ." she began, but Burabaish interrupted.

"You may live right here in your *own* palace," he told Azurelea.

She did not understand.

Nor did Ninaltra understand. "What is it you are saying, my husband? Have you not selected a nobleman of Babylonia, as we had agreed, for the husband of our daughter?"

"I have," he smiled, superciliously.

"And is this Babylonian nobleman a man of wealth who will endow Azurelea with the riches she is used to here?"

"Yes, my wife," he grinned. "The Babylonian nobleman is *very* rich."

"And what dowry does he ask of us?" Ninaltra asked.

"Nothing."

"Nothing? I find that hard to believe."

"The nobleman is so grateful to be marrying our beautiful daughter that he asks nothing." Burabaish explained.

"It is unbelievable," Ninaltra said. "He has *seen* Azurelea?" she asked, dreading that the answer might be "yes."

Could that have happened, she asked herself. Whenever Azurelea left the palace she was veiled, as were all females, so that no man except fathers or brothers ever *saw* their faces. And when she was away from the palace, Azurelea was always accompanied by a retinue of slaves.

"Yes," Burabaish said. "He has seen her and has wanted her for his bride. . . ." He stopped.

"My king," Ninaltra said. "I implore you. Tell us who you have chosen for our daughter. Who is this nobleman who could have *seen* her. I will not be disgraced as it is *my* duty that she not be seen. I do not believe there is a man who has seen Azurelea, except those inside the palace, her brothers, you, and the eunuchs."

Burabaish looked scornfully at Ninaltra and told her, "You are a foolish woman. You have no faith in your husband. I have chosen the best man in the world for her. One who loves her. One who will share his kingdom with her . . . will make her his Queen."

"His *kingdom?* He is a *King* then?"

"Yes."

Azurelea looked into her father's face to discern some meaning behind his strange half-smile. Ninaltra recognized his cunning. Why was he being sly, she wondered.

"Father," Azurelea said, "may I ask, at this

168

time . . . Do you . . . can you tell me . . . who *did* you choose for me?"

"Yes. You may ask. And I will tell you. I have chosen . . ." His eyes expanded as he looked into hers and his breathing quickened. "I have chosen," he repeated slowly, "the best man for you." He drew her to him. "Burabaish, King of Urak."

"But that . . ." Azurelea laughed, "that is *you!*" She laughed again, knowing that her father was joking to make her feel better, making her forget the seriousness of this day. Burabaish did not share her laughter. Nor did he release his tight hold around her waist.

"Yes. That is me," he said, unsmiling. "In one year we will be married and you will be my Queen."

"No!" Ninaltra screamed. "That cannot be. You must not be speaking the truth. This is a cruel joke. She is your *child*. *I* am your Queen. No! No! Azurelea . . ." Ninaltra stood up, tripping awkwardly over the hem of her tunic. "Azurelea," she said, trying to pull her stunned daughter away from her husband. "Azurelea. No. This won't be. You shall marry a Babylonian nobleman. . . ."

"Madam," Burabaish yelled. "Sit down!"

Ninaltra, who had begun to sob, stopped. She stood with her arms around Azurelea.

"You are forgetting our agreement," Burabaish reminded Ninaltra. "*I* was the one to choose. Remember? Well, I have chosen. Now *sit down!*" Ninaltra released her daughter and obeyed her husband. Azurelea stood motionless and silent.

169

Everything in the large, cool, stone room was silent. Wife, husband, and daughter looked at the mosaic tile floor. Now, Azurelea thought about the words that had been said. I am to be my father's *wife?* She looked at the torn hem of her mother's tunic and then slowly, and she didn't know why, guiltily, raised her eyes up to see her mother's face. Her mother continued to look at the floor. She knew her mother knew she was looking at her but was refusing to met Azurelea's eyes. Why did she think that her mother was ashamed? Azurelea wanted to tell her mother that *she* didn't want to be Queen.

Burabaish interrupted the long stillness. "This will not be the first time a father is marrying his daughter," he explained, in a bored, business-like tone of voice. "The Egyptians practiced this wise custom to preserve the fortunes of their kingdom and to keep the line of descent pure."

Azurelea looked at her father questioningly.

"*Children,* my daughter," he answered her unasked question. "Yes, we will have *children* and they will have the pure blood that your mother and I have."

"Children," Azurelea whispered.

"No!" Ninaltra cried again. "This cannot. . . ."

"Madam," Burabaish told his wife, "if you do not cease your railing I shall have you removed and closeted until I can be assured that you will not rail against me."

For a short time again the large room was silent. Azurelea wanted to leave, to return to places she knew before this had happened. If Azurelea had had enough of important news and wanted to escape, Burabaish had had enough of seriousness and wanted to get on with the celebration. The worst moments were over, he told himself. The news was out, and now it was time to begin the festivities.

"Can you," he asked Ninaltra, "wipe the sourness from your face and make this announcement to your ladies?"

She shook her head up and down, afraid to speak for fear of crying.

"If you can't," he threatened, "I can closet you until you are ready—or I can eliminate your unhappiness forever. A year from now, at your daughter's wedding . . . well, we'll see then. . . ."

Ninaltra tried to smile, to not hear those last words. "I will tell the news," she said in a whisper.

"And you, my future wife," he asked his daughter, smiling upon her, "how will *you* tell the others of this Day-of-Your-Birth-Celebration?"

Azurelea, who had lived her short life time amongst people she endeavored to please, knew what her father wanted to hear. "I will tell them of my joy," she replied, sadly.

He squeezed her hands and let them go. Then he rose, stretched his back to release the tension of the difficult session and dismissed them.

"I am going to call my Council, now," he said, "to make the announcement. It will be a night of great celebration. Be certain the slaves set the barrels of wine in the dining chambers. Tell them," he added as he turned to walk into his inner chambers, "tell them also, to set extra tapers on the parapets. The lights of Azurelea's betrothal celebration to Burabaish shall be seen from every direction."

Mother and daughter walked slowly from the room, not hand-in-hand as they had entered. Ninaltra, who had walked in with the pride and carriage of a queen, exited in defeat. For her there would be no more happiness. She, who had looked forward to the joy of preparing for her daughter's wedding to a nobleman, could not look forward to Azurelea's marriage except with foreboding. It would be better to be dead.

Azurelea walked away from her father's room confused. She wanted to take her mother's hand, but she felt Ninaltra's isolation and could not intrude on it. She was sad for her mother. It had not occurred to her to feel sadness for herself.

The months that passed went too fast for Azurelea. Preparations for her marriage began immediately after the week-long betrothal celebration ended. Burabaish called in his architects and directed them to bring in new designs for an addition to the palace. "For my virgin bride," he announced to them, "we must have virgin dwelling spaces."

He sent for chefs from Assyria, well known for their mountain herbal concoctions that he knew delighted Azurelea. When they were married she would satisfy her palate at her every desire. The palace weavers were ordered to create the most intricate geometrically designed fabric alternating in silk and satin. The material would be the beginnings of Queen Azurelea's wardrobe. No female in Babylonia would surpass Burabaish's child Queen in costume, food, or dwellings.

Azurelea, aware of these activities, took no part in them. She was not consulted, though her father called her to his chambers regularly to tell her of the details of his planning.

"And do you like this, my child?" he would ask her, holding up some shimmering fabric.

"Oh yes, my father," she would answer. Azurelea had never told anyone that she disliked anything.

Burabaish ordered his master craftsmen to construct all new furnishing for the new rooms, as they were completed. It was, he said, a new life for him and he would not live it among the remnants of the past.

"We will be great, you and I," he told his daughter. "We have only to wait for seven months and then we will be united as rulers with strengths never before known in Babylonia. Your youth and your endurance combined with my experience and my wisdom will keep my kingdom alive long after my soul lives in the Other Kingdom."

"Is that why you are marrying me?" Azurelea asked. It was the first time she had spoken to him of the marriage. When Burabaish hesitated, Azurelea asked, "Are you marrying me because I am young and. . . ."

"Yes, yes, yes," he answered quickly, wanting to dismiss further questions.

"But my mother . . ." she asked, "your Queen. . . ."

"She will be all right," he interrupted. "She will have everything she wants."

Azurelea looked down at the floor. Her mother, she knew, was *not* all right. Ninaltra roamed about the palace, directionless, her eyes glazed, her figure slumped. The days of talking happily with Azurelea had gone with the day of the wedding announcement. Azurelea no longer attempted to cheer Ninaltra.

Burbaish's other wives who had scorned Ninaltra in her reign, now pitied her. She grew frail, refused her slaves' help in selecting wigs to cover her grey hair, and seldom consented to having her body anointed with oils and perfumes. With vacant eyes she watched the daily routines of the palace and, distractedly, the gathering momentum in the wedding preparations. It was as though the spirit of Ninaltra, never strong and ever fearful of her position in the palace, had given up the struggle to sur-

174

vive and had left the body of the old woman who mumbled as she shuffled down the mosaic corridors.

Azurelea, without her mother, spent more time in the company of the daughters of the King's other wives. These half-sisters, too young to be jealous of Azurelea's future position, welcomed her company, gossiping with her and sharing and enlarging on rumors, a pastime of people who have little to do.

Burabaish was aware that Azurelea would be in need of advice about marriage preparations that concerned her, and he did not want to trust this advice to come from Ninaltra. He called Kito to him one day and advised her to take over as select-woman-counselor for his daughter.

"I am honored, my King," she answered, kneeling before him in her simple tunic. "I praise the great Burabaish. You do me great honor. But, forgive me, what of the Queen's rightful place? What of my mistress's mother?"

"Do not refer to Azurelea's mother as Queen," Burabaish said as he rose and strode across the room, knocking over the silver ornaments on his side table. "There has been no Queen in the palace since Azurelea's betrothal day. There will be no Queen in my palace again until Azurelea's marriage day."

"Forgive me, my master," Kito pleaded. "I meant no. . . ."

"That woman in her lunacy would defy me!" He picked up a silver goblet, examined it in his large, manicured hand. "I cannot dispose of her before the wedding. Azurelea would not be a willing bride."

Kito hung her head, fearful of the words she was hearing. She remained silent as Burabaish walked about the large chamber, shouting attacks on Ninaltra. Kito knew he was not talking to her and that she must wait in stillness so as not to disturb the storm that would, uninterrupted, spend itself.

Suddenly Burabaish stopped his pacing and shouted at Kito. "I charge you, Kito, chief select-woman-counselor, to prepare Azurelea in all ways for our marriage."

"I am honored, my King, but . . . I . . ."

"Yes. I know you are going to say that you are only a slave. Yes . . . well . . . a slave, yet you know Azurelea better than her mother, and her mother has lost her wits." He sat in his chair and looked at Kito who had still not lifted her eyes to look at him.

"Yes," he said. "It is not fitting that a Princess be prepared by a slave for this great occasion. *I* do not want to marry a woman who has only a slave to prepare her. Yes . . ." he thought aloud. "Yes, I'll do it this way."

Kito waited.

"Tomorrow you will be free," he told her. "Tomorrow you will live in the freedmen's section of the palace grounds. I will arrange for it . . . tomorrow I will have the Scribe of Seals give you your scroll."

Kito, whose mother had been one of Burabaish's slaves, taken captive in Urak's skir-

176

mish against Kish, had become Burabaish's property at birth. She might also have been Burabaish's offspring, as all female slaves' bodies were owned by their masters. Slaves' children had no identity except as their mother's children.

Kito, whose life had been controlled by the whim of her master, could not comprehend that she had been given her freedom from slavery also by a whim. She could not speak.

"Yes," Burabaish explained, unaware of Kito's turmoil, "you will now, as my subject, *not* as my slave, inform my daughter of the rituals of marriage preparation and performance. No mere slave will be entrusted with this important function. I do not want anything left out. This will be a true marriage in the eyes of the Gods.

"First, prepare Azurelea for the Ritual of the Ceremony of Blood-Letting so that I as her husband do not have the soil of the virgin blood in my bed. Then prepare her for the excursion of the Temple of Ishtar."

This last directive shook Kito back from the contemplation of her own strange and new condition. The ceremony of the Temple of Ishtar evoked visions of action. She saw herself leading a retinue of slaves to assist Azurelea in this difficult performance.

"I will summon you to keep me informed on matters of importance to the wedding. And now, that is all."

"It must be done," Kito explained patiently to Azurelea two months later. For this meeting,

Azurelea had been assisted in her dressing by a *new* slave, while Kito sat in Azurelea's outer suite of rooms awaiting this important pre-nuptial conference.

Azurelea's loss of Kito's company had been sad for her. Next to her mother, Kito had been her closest friend since her birth. Azurelea had shared Kito's sorrow when Burabaish sold Kito's son to a traveling caravan leader. She had dared to speak to her father on Kito's behalf, only, then, to see Kito beaten by another of her father's slaves for allowing Azurelea to have such thoughts as slaves keeping their own children after the age when they were capable of working. Kito had not known of Azurelea's attempted intercession.

For Kito, the pain of the beating was nothing compared to the pain of the tearing away of her child, though she had known of that possibility since her son's birth, as all slaves knew that all children born of slaves belong to masters. And, as Kito and Burabaish knew, Kito's son may have been Burabaish's son. Kito's body had been used by her King on many times when he was bored with his many perfumed, oiled, and over-anxious wives. Slaves and young boys provided the variety necessary in life filled with a succession of self-indulgences.

When Azurelea walked into the room where Kito waited for her, she looked at Kito at first as one looks at a stranger. Kito wore the more elaborate tunic of the freed woman, yet her manner to Azurelea was at first one of defer-ence, though it did not take long for the old relationship to establish itself. Kito soon called Azurelea, "My mistress," and Azurelea spoke to Kito in intimate, loving phrases.

"You are in my bosom," Azurelea said, using an ancient expression reserved for the closest associations.

"And you are in mine," Kito answered, returning Azurelea's embrace. "I am here, as you know, to prepare you for the pre-nuptial ceremonies."

"Yes. My father has told me. But he does not tell me what they are. When I ask him, he says 'the Freedwoman, Kito, will tell you.' "

"Yes." Kito released Azurelea and walked her to a low couch where they both sat. "There are several ceremonies in which you must participate."

Azurelea saw that Kito was reluctant. "I am ready to hear," she told Kito, hoping to ease the discomfort.

Kito, who saw Azurelea as the sweet child, ever willing to please, had difficulty saying what she must. She had an impulse to cry and to ask Azurelea's forgiveness for what she must help her former mistress to endure. The ceremonies for marriage, required of all girls in high class and ruling families, were filled with pain and humiliation. But Kito must explain them to Azurelea, as all advisors for centuries explained them to pre-nuptial girls.

To inform herself, Kito had talked to the medicine practitioners for an understanding on the Ceremony of Blood-Letting, and she had gone to the Temple of Ishtar, standing far

179

in the background as an observer to learn first-hand about the Ceremony dedicated to the Great Goddess Ishtar. As a slave, Kito did not have to endure these ceremonies. Now, as an advisor, and as a representative of the King of Urak, Kito had to explain the ceremonies to Azurelea.

"Before the next month passes," Kito explained, holding Azurelea's hand, "you will go with me to the medicine practitioner."

"But I am not sick," Azurelea smiled. "And besides, why would he not come here?"

"It is the custom as the Goddess wills it. High born pre-nuptial girls belong to the Goddess, not to the King, until they are married."

Azurelea was confused but she would not argue about the Goddess.

Kito straightened the folds in her tunic, not yet used to the excess materials of the costume freedwomen were expected to wear. To her, the garment of the slave gave her body more freedom and was cooler. In these elaborate tucks and stitchings, Kito sweltered in Urak's continuous desert heat. But as she must get used to the cumbersome clothing of her higher status, she must also get used to the position of advisor rather than slave to Azurelea. She told her, "I will bring you to the High Priests of Medicine myself and wait until they have completed their divine duty."

Azurelea nodded, watching Kito's face intently. She waited for more explanation, but Kito was silent, looking into Azurelea's eyes as though to communicate without words. Azurelea did not like the look in Kito's eyes.

"What is it you are trying to tell me?" Azurelea asked.

"You must be prepared to be put in pain," Kito said.

"I have been in pain before," Azurelea said, wanting to put Kito at ease.

"Yes," Kito agreed. "When you had the sting from that poisonous spider, and we thought we would lose you in this life, you had great pain."

Azurelea remembered and hugged Kito who had sat and held her hand in her delirium, when Ninaltra was only able to wail helplessly on the floor by Azurelea's couch. "But the Gods gave you back to us," Kito said.

"Yes," Azurelea agreed. "So you see, I can be brave against pain. Do not worry. If the Gods and Goddesses ordain that I shall go through pain, then I shall. Now," she rose to command the eunuch who stood waiting in the next chamber, "what delicacy shall we. . . ."

"No," Kito interrupted Azurelea. "Not yet, please. . . ."

"Yes?" Azurelea asked, standing motionless.

Kito, who had stood up when Azurelea stood, because she was still a subject in the presence of a princess, tried once more to prepare Azurelea for the ceremony that she did not want to explain. Bringing this knowledge was to Kito the bringing of physical harm to her dear Azurelea.

"You will be hurt," Kito said, looking once more into Azurelea's eyes. This time Azurelea made no effort to put aside whatever it was Kito needed to tell her.

"Not like that spider?" Azurelea asked as

she sat down.

"No."

"I will recover?"

"Yes."

"Then what is so bad?" Azurelea smiled, desiring once again to lighten Kito's duty. Kito did not answer. Azurelea asked, "What is so bad then? I will be hurt and I will recover and I will be the same as I was before I was hurt and. . . ."

"No. That is it," Kito said. "You will not be the same as you were. Your body will not be the body of a child anymore," and she turned from Azurelea, guilty that she must violate the innocent mind of Azurelea by telling her what she must expect.

This was the duty of Azurelea's mother, Kito knew. But she knew, too, that Ninaltra had retreated behind her own wall, away from the reality of the world that was changing her daughter from the free-spirited child to the obedient child-bearing woman, as it had changed Ninaltra from a proud, first-wife Queen to an incoherent, stumbling derelict, unaware of her husband's arrangements for her disposal after the wedding. The palace rumors of Ninaltra's decomposing condition rippled regularly through the corridors and down into the freedmen's section. As Ninaltra's condition worsened, Kito's responsibilities increased. She could not hope that the former queen would be capable of being Azurelea's advisor.

"You will not be the same after the prenuptial Ceremony of Blood-Letting," Kito said.

"Is it not as when one is ill, the priests and medicine practitioners open up the veins and bring forth the sick blood?" Azurelea asked. "That is what my mother told me was done to make my father well long ago." Kito wished that what Azurelea pictured were so. "No," she said sadly, "that is another thing."

"What then?" Azurelea asked, getting impatient.

"It is a Divine Ceremony," Kito explained as she had memorized it. "The Gods have willed it. I will take you there." She stood up quickly.

"You do not wish to tell me now?" Azurelea asked, standing to face Kito.

"I changed my mind. It will be best that you learn of the ceremony further, on the day of its happening," Kito told her.

"I wish to know," Azurelea said.

"My mistress, please do not demand further explanation from me."

"You do not wish to tell me more?"

"You know that if you demand further explanation, then as your subject I must tell you." Kito paused, but Azurelea remained silent. "Please know," Kito continued, "from your slave and one who adores you, it is best that you do not know more at this time." Kito could only hope that Azurelea would spare her from having to explain anything more.

Azurelea hesitated. She could demand to know. She, who was soon to be Queen and could demand anything of anyone except from her husband, had never demanded anything. Happy to be the one who pleased, Azurelea would be a different person should she now demand, even from her former slave, something that held her curiosity.

Kito remembered that Azurelea had not demanded to know what was going to happen on her last Day-Of-Her-Birth-Celebration, though Kito's suspicions were right, then. And true to her childhood habits, Azurelea did not demand to know what would happen on her prenuptial Ceremony of Blood-Letting. What little knowledge she had learned from Kito at this time, Azurelea decided, would have to be enough. She smiled on Kito and embraced her. Kito encircled the small Azurelea in her arms and held her, rocking her back and forth as she had done for many years. She kissed the top of Azurelea's head, slowly releasing her former mistress and then she backed away, bowing, until she was away from Azurelea's outer chamber of her suite of rooms in the palace of Burabaish.

When the day arrived, Azurelea waited for Kito in nervous anticipation. Dressed in simple finery, perfumed and anointed, she was fearful of the unexpected pain, yet excited to learn the secret of the unknown.

She had tried to learn these secrets of the ceremony from her half-sisters, but as they were all younger than she was, they were unaware. Once a girl went through the Ceremony of Blood-Letting, she was removed from her child-friends and prepared then for the Ceremony of the Temple of Ishtar. And when *that* ceremony was completed, the marriage was performed and the girls assumed the duties of womanhood. This was the procedure that Kito had explained to her on their first session.

When Azurelea asked Burabaish's other wives about the secret, being jealous of her because she was going to be Queen and favorite wife, they scoffed at her and told her nothing.

On this important day, as the sun made its first appearance, the horses pulling the royal chariot arrived at the palace's eastern entrance. Her slaves announced the arrival of the chariot, hovering around her, handing her sweets and fruits, but she had no appetite.

Kito's entrance was announced and Azurelea waited for her in the same room where they had last parted. Kito's eyes widened when she saw Azurelea, her hair curled up on top of her head and encircled in a crown-like silver braid.

"You are indeed a woman today," Kito said, bowing to her.

Azurelea embraced her. "Why are you restrained, my dear Kito?"

"Because today you look like a Queen," Kito said, holding Azurelea at arm's length, adoring her.

"Oh Kito," Azurelea said, smiling, as the attendant slaves swathed Azurelea in the lightweight black veil, leaving no part of her body visible except her eyes so that no man's desires would be aroused at the sight of her body. Women, she had been told, must protect men from their baser selves.

"Let us be on our way," Kito said. "The Gods await you," and she preceded Azurelea out of the chamber, down the many corridors, and out into the palace yards. Seven male slaves assisted the two women into the chariot, with one male, the charioteer, standing between the two women.

The palace gates were opened for them by other slaves, and Kito and Azurelea were taken through the city and up to one of the few hills where the Temple of Healing stood.

Azurelea saw how the streets were lined with slaves and subjects, waiting since sunrise to get a glimpse of the princess who was soon to be queen, on her way to the pre-nuptial Ceremony of Blood-Letting. It was a day in their lives that they would remember as vividly as Azurelea would remember.

Five priests stood on the granite steps of the temple with their arms folded, watching the horses of the chariot struggle up the hill. The long-robed, bearded priests, ready to function as human Gods, squinted their eyes into the slanted morning sun to satisfy their curiosity about Burabaish's daughter who was soon to be his queen.

The horses galloped to the temple steps and halted in a massive cloud of dust. Kito and

Azurelea were assisted from the chariot and up the high steps where they were preceded into the temple by the priests. Knowing the limits of her duty, Kito stopped at the entrance of the temple and Azurelea hesitated, looking at Kito questioningly. Kito stood where she was and Azurelea knew that she must enter alone without her.

The five priests walked ahead of Azurelea whose eyes needed to become accustomed to the darkness inside the temple. At the innermost room, the priests stood in a circle around Azurelea, indicating that she stand in the center as they chanted incantations and walked slowly around her. The reverence of the priests humbled her and she was ashamed that she had been curious about something sacred.

In the seriousness of the priest's divinity, Azurelea swayed to the rhythm of their chants and lost herself to their direction. As she swayed to one side and then to the other, two priests still chanting, lifted her and stood her on a low stone table at the end of the room. Azurelea was only barely aware of the two dimly lit candles at each end of the table. The chanting continued unbroken and she was caught in its sounds and contributed her own sounds. The priests who carried her, dropped her veil from her body, but she was not alarmed. She swayed in their arms to the rhythm of their chants. Unveiled, she need not worry that these men would be concerned about seeing her for they were human Gods.

The priests' chanting had words that became more distinct and she repeated the ones she heard without thinking about them. On and on the swaying and chanting continued. The flicker of the candles' lights doubled the figures in the room by the shadowy images. The priests and their shadows moved in tempo to the chants.

Those who held her, moved her body back and forth as others removed her tunic and then she was placed on the low table that had been covered with soft cloth. The chanting told of purity of all their kings and how the priests were endowed with the divine responsibility to ensure that purity would continue. No king must ever touch or see the blood let by the loss of virginity. They would save their king from that fate.

As the chant was repeated over and over and over, each priest lay on top of the naked Azurelea and made up and down motions as he chanted. She felt the warmth of their bodies and the stickiness of their perspiration, and a warm fluid oozing from her own body.

Though the men exercised themselves on top of her, they did not cease their chant, and it was only when she felt a ripping pain that she herself stopped her own chanting. She dared not cry out. Tears rolled down from her eyes onto the top of her ears and into her hair, moist from perspiration and from the heat of the small room where the candles burned up the fresh air.

After the priests had torn a part of her body, Azurelea could not get herself back into the chanting. She wanted very much to cry, but she told herself that she must not. The liquid coming from her body frightened her and she wanted to be at home in the palace with her friend and former slave, Kito.

Would Kito be outside waiting for her? She wanted this Ceremony of Blood-Letting to be over. And then it occurred to her, because she wondered what blood had to do with this ceremony, that maybe the liquid she felt was blood—her own blood. Or could it be the blood of the priests? It must be her own blood because they had hurt her. So this was the pain that Kito had tried to tell her about. No wonder she didn't want to tell her. Then she felt both anger and pity for Kito. If only the priests would stop! If only Kito were near her to help her now!

When the priests moved away from the table, Azurelea saw that there was a woman in the room. In the dim light she thought at first that it was Kito. But she saw that the woman was a priestess, robed in the blue robe of the Temple of Healing. She had entered as the priests began to leave, chanting as they went. The priestess held a flat pottery bowl of water in her hands and toweling over one arm. She bathed Azurelea and stroked her moist hair, chanting the same words the priests had used.

After she dressed Azurelea, the priestess took her out into the sunlight into the waiting arms of Kito. Again Azurelea wanted to cry, to tell Kito all that had happened, but she was changed from the girl who entered the temple, and the change restrained her.

No one had ever told her not to talk of changes in her body, yet she never did. Last year when her breasts had enlarged she had not talked of this. She would not talk of this change that happened today though she knew she would never again be the same young girl who had entered the temple, anxious and curious about the secret of the ceremony.

When she and Kito descended the temple steps, they were the object of the many subjects who had come to stare at them. Swathed in her veil, Azurelea was glad that they could not see her face. She endured the ride back to the palace, holding her head erect as would befit a noble woman, though her body pained her and she felt partly destroyed.

She wanted to talk to Kito about all this, the chanting, the swaying, what the priests did, how they hurt her and yet went on hurting her. They must have known. They must have seen her tears. Did they care? Or was it more important for the priests to complete their religious performance than to stop if they knew she was hurt? Was the hurting, she wondered, part of the religious duty, as for instance at a sacrifice? Maybe it was not considered a completed performance unless they *did* hurt her?

Kito moved over to Azurelea's side of the chariot, ignoring the charioteers' complaints that it would throw the carriage off balance. Holding on to the front of the chariot, as they both did, Kito put one arm around Azurelea who softened and wanted again to cry, but did not.

That night she was bathed in special oils by her slaves on the advice of Kito who told her she would stay the night on the couch in

Azurelea's room if the princess desired Kito's presence.

"Oh, yes," Azurelea told her. "More than anything I want you to stay, but I must get used to your absence. You have told me that you will be leaving the palace. I must become used to that idea. As a freedwoman you can now search for your son. I do not blame you for leaving. I will ask the Goddess Ishtar to help you. Perhaps your son is, as you say, still on the caravan-trading routes that go into Egypt crossing waters into Greece. I will miss you, Kito. And I must condition myself to your absence. In a short time I will be married. Then I cannot have a friend sleeping in my room where my husband sleeps."

"Queen Ninaltra did not. . . ." Kito started.

"I know. My mother had her own rooms, though long ago she told me, when my father and mother were first married, they always slept together, even after my father had many wives. Those, he visited, but always came back to my mother."

Kito said nothing.

"My father has told me I am to be as his first wife. Kito, I wonder what happened to our happy days," she added unexpectedly. Azurelea bathed and dried, and looking more like a child than a woman, wanted yet again to tell everything to Kito. The woman part of her that was awakening, held back the child part that would have cried out in pain and protest. The woman part of her resigned herself. She embraced her former slave and then told her she would see her after the passing of a month when Kito would prepare her for the Temple of Ishtar, the last pre-nuptial ceremony.

The slaves dimmed the candles, helped the princess into her large bed and covered her in satin sheets to spend a sleepless night in wondering about the day, the priests, the pain, and all that it meant about saving her father from the blood of a virgin. She remembered how only that morning she had entered the temple expectant and curious and how she had left the temple pained and frightened, and unwilling to share these feelings with her beloved Kito.

When Kito came to take Azurelea to the Temple of Ishtar, built to honor the great Goddess of Babylonia, people were swarming around the temple grounds. Azurelea and her retinue of slaves arrived at the Temple at the sun's dawn when they believed there would be fewer people, but the people were already there.

Azurelea's charioteer pulled her horses up in front of the Temple behind another chariot. Kito and Azurelea's slaves assisted her from the chariot even as another pulled up behind them and threw a mass of dust in their direction.

Azurelea hesitantly observed the many veiled women ascending the Temple steps, accompanied by their slaves, as she was. Were so many women to be married soon?

Kito had helped her to understand the ritual to be performed at the Ceremony at the Temple, telling her it was the last pre-nuptial preparation she was expected to perform before her marriage.

"Then you will be ready for the great ceremony of your marriage," Kito had said.

Since the Ceremony of Blood-Letting, Azurelea's curiosity was subdued. She had few questions about what would happen at the Temple of Ishtar. But this time Kito forced herself to explain more than she had about the Ceremony of Blood-Letting, because, she told Azurelea, there would be no priests or priestesses to help her.

"You must be willing," Kito said. "You must not refuse any man. It is the way our women of Babylonia help the citizen men to pay their respects, and their money, to the Goddess Ishtar."

"I will be veiled? No one will unveil me?" Azurelea asked.

Kito, who had watched the ritual many days so she could explain it to Azurelea, told her that she would arrive veiled and no one would know who she was, but once inside the Temple, she would remove her veil herself and wait to be chosen.

"You will not have to wait long because you have beauty," Kito assured Azurelea the day before they were to go to the Temple.

Azurelea shuddered. These pre-nuptial ceremonies were frightening. "I saw many girls," Kito said, "who were large of features, or deformed. They waited through every day that I visited the Temple and no one chose them."

"What will happen to them if they are not chosen?" Azurelea asked.

"They can never marry."

"Would that not be good?"

"Oh my mistress. Do not say that. Do not let the King know any thoughts like that. I would fear for you if he knew you had such thoughts."

Azurelea, unsmiling, answered that she had never said those words aloud before and would not say them again.

Azurelea and her slaves entered the inner Temple rooms where they saw unveiled, highborn women standing or sitting against the stone Temple walls, their slaves nearby, chatting, sewing, or weaving as they waited for their mistresses to complete this necessary performance before they could be permitted to marry.

Men wandered among the women, looked at their faces, a sight forbidden at any other time or place. Azurelea and her slaves moved to a corner where they could wait for Azurelea to be chosen. Silk cushions were spread on the stone floor for the princess. Kito helped her remove her veil.

Azurelea, unveiled in public the first time in her life, shivered even in the intense heat of the Temple. She seated herself on the cushions and her slaves stood on either side of her, watching the crowd of people, the women seated or standing and the men roaming through the open Temple rooms, looking at women who offered themselves, and choosing women whose appearance pleased them.

Azurelea, with downcast eyes, unused to the feeling of exposure of being unveiled, saw large sandaled feet pass near where she sat. She raised her head to watch the young man pause in front of the woman next to her. The woman who had been talking with another woman opposite her, stopped talking when she saw the man in front of her. She looked to the stones on the floor and stared, unseeing, at the design. Azurelea watched the man throw his tunic over his shoulder and reach into a leather pouch he wore around his waist. She heard the clinking of coins and saw the man withdraw his hand from the pouch, examine the coins, and toss them into the lap of the woman, saying, "I praise thee, Goddess Ishtar."

The woman waited a moment and then she gathered the coins and put them in a pouch in the folds of her clothing as she rose. Azurelea watched the man accompany the woman, eyes still downcast, into another room in the Temple. Again, and in spite of the heat, Azurelea shivered.

She saw other men come and select women, toss coins at them, and accompany them to the other room. When the women returned not much later, the men did not come back with them. The women quickly gathered their possessions or beckoned to their slaves that they could then leave the Temple.

Several men walked by Azurelea's group, paused and walked on. She dreaded that she would be chosen, hopeful that they would move on, and then she knew that she could not leave until this ceremony was over.

The heavy, dark-browed man who stood near her, looked at her slaves first and then at her. She smelled the wine from his breath and hoped he would move on. Instead he moved closer to her. She pretended not to notice him.

She hoped he would consider her too young, or too small, or too rich. But she despaired that her hopes would turn him from her. She looked at the floor, at his large, dirty toe-nails, the broken sandal strap, and she heard the sound of coins and felt their sudden weight in her lap. "I praise thee, Goddess Ishtar," he said and waited. She had been chosen. She had no choice. Her slaves waited. The stranger waited. She must rise.

She gathered the coins slowly and handed them to Kito who would give them to the priest at the entrance as the other women did. Azurelea rose and followed the man into the Temple room where she had seen the other women led by men who had chosen them.

The room was filled with men and women on the floor, the men either on top of the women or to their sides in what seemed to Azurelea a mass of silent women, tangled clothes, and panting, groaning, sweating men. She thought she was going to sink to the floor, but she lay down and closed her eyes so she would not have to look at him. She remembered the priests at the Ceremony of Blood-Letting.

The man made her body available to himself and left her wet, dirty, and sticky. When he groaned and rolled off of her, she rose and left the room, leaving the Temple with Kito and her slaves as fast as she had seen the other women leave when they had performed the ceremony.

Her father required her presence when she arrived back at the palace, after she had been bathed. He told her he knew she was now ready for her marriage. She sat quietly in his presence, as he talked of his pride in her.

"You have grown up, my beauty. My little princess is soon to be my Queen."

Azurelea smiled only slightly.

"You have performed the rituals without reluctance, without hesitation. Kito has told me all. You will be a good ruler after my death," he told her. "You know what it is to do what is necessary."

Azurelea did not speak.

"What is this?" Burabaish asked. "My happy lark has become a sad swallow?" He reached for her hands and held them. She did not draw them away. She let them lie in her father's hands.

"You will be my bride, you know," Burabaish said to his silent daughter. "You have been purified by the Priests of Healing and I have been spared the danger of your virginal blood, and you have performed the Ceremony of the Temple of Ishtar. You are now ready," he squeezed her hands affectionately.

"Yes, father."

"We will be great rulers."

"Yes."

"Everything is ready now. The rooms, the furniture, your clothes. I am ready and now you are ready."

"Yes."

He rose and pulled her up and held her close to him. She wanted to respond to his affection as she had as his little girl, his child, but she could not as the woman who was to be his wife. She knew that as she had survived the priests in the Temple of Healing, and the stranger in the Temple of Ishtar, she would learn also to respond to the King, not as a child and daughter, but as a woman and wife. For now, though she wanted once more to cry, to bring back the mother she had known, and to tell her slave Kito all about her fears and loneliness, she knew that as she was no longer a child, all those things were gone forever. The joys and happiness that seemed always available had disappeared in the history of herself.

4

The Golden Age of Greece

Two years after the elaborate wedding to Burabaish, Azurelea smuggled her first-born out of the palace into the waiting caravan where Kito's fourteen-year-old son, Malius, accepted the small bundle, handing Azurelea an identical one. Malius bowed to Azurelea in the shadows and then hurried away.

The caravan lumbered out of the city of Babylon, the infant princess rocking back and forth in the arms of Kito. Except for the sorrow of saying goodbye to her sweet Azurelea, Kito was happy. Though she knew she would probably never see Azurelea again, she would raise her mistress's child. She had found her son and had purchased his freedom from the caravan leader, Hagarasium, who kept Malius on as an assistant and paid him wages. Kito knew from her son, Malius, that Hagarasium was a kind man.

Azurelea, scurrying back into the palace, held the bundle close to her breasts. She felt the small body of the slave child move in the womb of blankets. Carefully chosen by Kito for its similarities to Azurelea's week-old infant girl, this slave child would be raised as a princess.

Azurelea knew that Burabaish would never suspect this plot. In his nightly debaucheries, when he alternately threatened to kill their new-born because she was only a girl, exposing her to the elements until she died, or to marry her himself when she was ten years old, his slurring, wine-soaked voice would mean nothing to Azurelea because the child that was theirs would be far from Babylonia, in the care of Kito and her son. She would feel sorrow for the child, but Azurelea would not go mad as her mother had. She would love the slave child as her own princess but in all of Babylonia only she would ever know her secret, and her sorrow.

The caravan with Kito and her son, Malius,

its forty-two camels, its tents, slaves, Babylonian gold, and goats to give milk to the new infant, wound its way out of the city. Laden with oils, spices, and silks, the camels began their long journey skirting the Armenian Taurus Mountains into the dusty desert of Phrygia. It took four days to ferry the entire caravan across the Bosporus before it resumed land travel again on the mainland of Thrace and then wound its way down through the hills of Macedonia and Theassauleia just as the earlier Persians in their conquest of Greece had traveled a few years earlier.

Hagarasium, a student of geographical politics, knew he would not be competing with his oriental countrymen when he traveled to Athens. After the Greeks had driven out Xerxes, the Persian ruler, Hagarasium began making his plans to lead a trading caravan from Babylon to Athens. He was too good a businessman not to know where trade would be best.

Only two years earlier, in 479 B.C., when he had learned about the Greeks retaking their land from the Persians, Hagarasium had outfitted an extensive caravan, adding twenty additional camels. It was then that he gave his slave, Malius, more authority over the other slaves and made him his first assistant.

As Hagarasium's caravan approached Athens he complimented himself on his good sense and on his planning. Thoughts of the good years ahead soothed his tired, travel-worn body.

At the outskirts of Athens he thought about how he would set up his trading stalls. He could already feel the weight of money in his hands and the excitement of the noisy market place. He knew the Greek's desire for new goods from the Orient was insatiable. Here his goods would bring him western silver which he would bring back to the Persian lands to buy more silks, laces, spices, oils, and scents for the Athenian market.

Looking back to scan his caravan, his eyes rested on the freedwoman, Kito, and the bundled child who had hardly left her arms in the two months' journey. They had been no trouble, he mused. He turned back to watch the city as they neared it. Tonight, he sighed, he would sleep in an inn and not in his wind-flapping tent.

Kito, too, was watching the city. She could barely see the wall in the dusk. Malius had told her about the wall. It had been erected quickly by Athenian men, women, and children when they knew the Persians were nearing their city. Seeing that they were outnumbered and that the wall could not keep out the Persians, the Athenians fled into the hills. The Persian King, Xerxes, angered when he had no one to fight, set fire to the city.

In time the Athenians joined with their other countrymen from other city-states and returned to drive out the Persians. And when the fighting was over, the women and children of Athens who had been hiding in the hills returned to join the men and to start building their city again, stone by stone.

Kito uncovered the baby's fur blankets and smiled at her, happy that the infant, only one week old when they started, had endured the journey with no more discomfort than if she'd been in her own palace rooms with many slaves. Looking at her, Kito remembered the last conversation with Azurelea, when she had asked, "What did you name her?" It was when they were making their secret plans months ago.

"We would name her with the Diviners on the first full moon," Azurelea told Kito from her couch where she was recovering from the child's birth. "But," Azurelea whispered, "as my baby will not be here then, I will leave it to you to name her."

"Oh, no, my Queen," Kito protested. "She is yours. . . ."

"No," Azurelea interrupted, "She will be yours. I entrust her to you. You have been my faithful, loving slave and I know you will be as good to her as you were to me. My child is yours. You will save her from her father. The child you bring to me will be my husband's to name." Her eyes drifted off into spaces that Kito would never see.

"It shall be as you wish. I will care for her with my life," Kito promised Azurelea.

And as they traveled from Persia, down into Thrace, through countries Kito never dreamed of seeing, she began to feel that the child's name should not be that of any of Azurelea's ancestors, for fear of possible recognition in the years to come. Her name should be of the countries which would be giving her protection.

She remembered that Hagarasium referred

to this country as the Hellenistic World. She liked the sound. She named the infant daughter of Azurelea and Burabaish, Hellisia. "We have arrived at our new home, Hellisia," she whispered to the baby. "I will promise to make your life as near to that of a princess as is possible for me to do."

Malius set up their tent and then went back to dismantling the caravan. When he had time the next day he moved his mother and Hellisia inside the city into two rooms on a narrow street. Kito worried that the milk Malius had to carry from the goats, tied up outside the city, would spoil from his long walk through the town.

"If it is sour the baby will get sick and die," Kito complained. Malius was careful not to shake the milk gourd as he hurried through the streets. He did not want to arrive home with churned milk.

When Hagarasium came to see how Kito was living he was not pleased with their rooms. He scolded Malius. "Is this the best you can do for your mother?"

"Yes. All the money I have, I paid for the use of these rooms." Malius bowed his head to his employer.

"It is better to live in a tent," Hagarasium said, but Kito had not liked the wind that blew through the tent. During the whole journey she had slept with the infant inside her clothing every night, yet always afraid of crushing her.

"Tomorrow you will have a better place," Hagarasium said. All the next day in the fly-ridden rooms, Kito wondered about Hagarasium's words. At the end of the day Malius walked into the dirt-floored house with the gourd of goat's milk in one hand and many coins in the other.

"We are rich, mother," he smiled. "My employer has given me a big promotion with money in advance and two days not to work so I can find us a better place to live."

"This must be a dream," Kito said.

"It is not a dream," Malius spoke proudly. "Hagarasium says, as business is better than he thought it would be, he will soon be going back to Babylon for more merchandise. He will leave me in charge of all of his stalls in the market place."

"But you are so young."

"Mother, you forget. I am almost fifteen."

"Yes," she smiled and nodded. "You are a man."

And true to his word, Hagarasium left him in charge of his trading stalls. Malius sold the merchandise for the highest prices he could get and secreted the money for his employer, taking only his allotted wages.

When Hagarasium returned after six months with a full caravan of oriental goods, Malius knew they would make a great deal of money selling to the prosperous Athenians. Hagarasium, visiting Kito in her new rooms was pleased. As Malius had spent much of his own money on their rooms, their home imitated the palace style where Kito had lived most of her life. To Hagarasium it was a Persian oasis in Athens.

"I am at home here," he told Kito.

"My home is your home." She bowed to him in the habit of her own servitude. "We are grateful to you," she said lifting Hellisia from the child's chair. "It is the money you pay Malius that has made our home beautiful."

"No," Hagarasium said with authority. "Money alone does not do this. You have a Queen's style."

Kito, flustered, fluffed Hellisia's black curls. He did not know she had been a slave in the palace. Kito said nothing.

Then Hagarasium turned his attention from the wall hangings, the draperies, and the vases to the smiling Hellisia, almost a year old. She reached her arms toward him and he put her on his lap.

"You are a little Persian Princess," he said to Hellisia, affectionately. Kito shuddered.

That night Kito told Malius of the words Hagarasium had spoken. "You have never said anything to him of me, or of Hellisia, have you?"

"Never."

"Then, why. . . ."

"It must be his flattering ways. He could not know. He thinks she is your child and the father is dead."

"He must not know. No one must ever know. King Burabaish would search us out, kill us all. He would take Hellisia back and of course Azurelea would suffer a terrible, tortured death."

"Yes. I know that. He will never know. Only you, I, and Queen Azurelea know what we have done." Malius spoke with a manly firmness. "No one else will ever know."

They spoke of it no more.

Their life was good in Athens. Malius prospered and lavished his earnings and bonuses on his mother and Hellisia. And as a little girl, Hellisia was easily satisfied with simple trinkets or with Kito's simple teachings. She learned to speak the language of her mother's homeland and could write a few words Kito taught her.

"I want to write the words like are on this paper," she told Malius one night, holding a Greek circular she had pulled from his pocket.

"You can't do that," he laughed, taking the paper from her. "It took me many years to learn to write or even read this. See," he showed her, "this is very difficult."

"But you say I am smart. I want to learn. Will you teach me?"

Malius put the paper back in the pocket of his tunic. "No," he said, "but I will get you a tutor."

But when the tutor learned that he was going to teach a girl, he refused his services.

"Nobody teaches girls, except in the household skills, and women teach that," he told Malius. "I teach only boys. What do you think would happen to my name as a master tutor if it were learned that I teach girls?"

Malius did not tell Kito or Hellisia of this. He found another tutor and offered him twice the sum expected and told him no one would know he was teaching a girl.

"A girl? Why would you want to spend all this money teaching a girl? They can do nothing," the young man told Malius.

"I want her to learn to read and write so she can help me in my business," Malius lied. He would never ask Hellisia to work at anything. But if he needed to tell an untruth to please her, he would do so.

"In that case," the tutor said, fingering the money, "I will come once a week in the evening, after it is dark. And I will come only on the condition you do not tell anyone that I am teaching a girl."

"I will agree to that." Malius said.

"It will appear that it is you I am teaching," the man said.

Malius smiled. "And indeed you may be teaching me. My skill is not good. I will also learn."

Hellisia's ability to pick up the words easily and form the sounds that she saw written on the paper surprised her tutor. "Sometimes," he told Malius, "She is so intelligent I forget that she is a girl."

For Malius, and Hellisia, and Kito and for all people in Athens it was a good time. The influx of foreigners from nearby city-states, drawn to all the activity of rebuilding the city after the wars, brought new customers to the market places. After ten years Malius could hardly remember his old life as a slave child in Babylon, but if he had to make a comparison he would have referred to Babylon as slow and unchanging and Athens as vibrating with the fever of a new beginning.

He learned that the ideas and philosophies and the arts of Athens were discussed all around the Mediterranean. He felt a part of the achievements, the architectural magnificence of the Acropolis and the Parthenon, the drama that was played in the public antheneums.

Old-time Athenians came alive to the success of what Athens was doing. They believed the glory would live forever, and more than that, that it must be reserved for Athenians only.

The citizen-fathers recognizing the richness of the developing culture wanted to hoard this heritage for their own people. With all the foreigners coming into Athens, the old-time Athenians feared there would be a foreign weakening of the lineage.

"Athenian citizens," it was proclaimed, "can only be men whose fathers have been born in the city limits of Athens."

"This can include fathers who were born here and who escaped to the mountains when the Persians came," it was declared in the Assembly.

No transient could cast his vote in the Agora—the market place. Nor could a transient's son become a citizen regardless of how many years he might live in Athens. To his sorrow, Hagarasium learned that no matter how rich he might become, he could never be an Athenian citizen, nor could Malius, nor of course, Kito.

No woman could become a citizen. When Malius made inquiries about the possibility of his own citizenship he learned that there were women who were called "citizen-women."

"That means," he explained to his mother, "that their fathers and grandfathers are citizens. The citizen-women can't vote, but citizen-women are the only women that citizen men can marry."

Kito's concern was not for herself but for Hellisia. "What if a citizen man *did* marry a woman who was not a citizen-woman? What would happen?"

"The citizen man would lose his citizenship."

"And is that so bad?" Kito asked.

"Yes," Malius answered, his eyes downcast. "From what I have learned, no man would want to lose his citizenship. They say that Athenian citizenship is more respected than money. They say of those who are not citizens that we are nothing, even if our houses were to be lined with gold."

"And Hellisia? What is to become of her?"

"She cannot marry an Athenian citizen."

"You are saying then," she questioned further, "that Hellisia will not be acceptable for marriage?" She rephrased her question. "She will not be eligible for the best marriage?"

Malius shook his head, wondering about Hellisia. Though she was yet only ten years old he had watched her features change from child to the beginnings of womanhood, and to the coming beauty that would resemble Azurelea. He, who had taken her from the arms of the Queen, had for ten years been Hellisia's protector and would always be. But he could do nothing about the marriage laws that were not good for her. He worried about her future. At the same time his mother worried also about Malius's future. She spoke many times of making arrangements for his marriage, but he could not listen.

When Kito spoke of marriage of Hellisia, Malius felt only emptiness. He could not arrange the picture in his mind of the grown Hellisia leaving the home where he and his mother had protected and loved her. Yet his mother insisted on asking these questions about marriage.

"She is only ten years old," Malius reminded Kito, who didn't need reminding.

"That is no matter," Kito answered. "Marriage arrangements and preparations take time." She remembered often and with melancholy the lengthy preparations for Azurelea's wedding.

"Who will you see about marriage arrangements?" Malius asked her cautiously.

"I must soon talk to Hagarasium. He knows the people. He will talk to his wife."

"Which one? The one in Armenia, or the one in Thrace, or the one here in Athens?"

It was Hagarasium who presented Kito with a scheme to solve the dilemma of Hellisia's marriage arrangements. Seated, oriental style, in Kito's home, smoking the long Persian pipe with the sweet tobacco filling the air, he slowly brought forth his plan. A man who had developed paternal feelings for all three in the house, feelings stronger than those he held for his wives or his own children, Hagarasium had also pondered the question of Hellisia's future. When he had settled himself among the soft pillows and when Hellisia had gone off to her room, he told Kito and Malius what he had in mind.

"For Hellisia to marry well she must marry a citizen. Those men are of the wealthy families. When she marries an Athenian citizen she will live in the best part of the city, in the best of houses, and she will have slaves, clothes, and nothing to worry about for the rest of her life."

"Hellisia cannot marry an Athenian citizen," Malius said not with regret, "for she is

212

not a citizen-woman. Her father," he cast a sideways glance toward Kito, "is dead. In Babylon."

Hagarasium shook his head and then asked, "And what *is* a citizen-woman, Malius?"

"A woman whose father was born in the city of Athens."

"Yes. That is true. And how does anyone here know that Hellisia's father was not born in the city of Athens?"

Kito looked at her son, fearful of what he might reveal. Fortunately, Hagarasium did not wait for an answer. "Who," he asked, "in Athens, knows about her father?"

"No one," Kito answered instantly.

Hagarasium leaned back on his pillows, sucking on his long pipe in short puffs. "Who knows but that Kito's husband was an Athenian?"

Kito and Malius looked at each other.

"All that anyone remembers," Hagarasium said, "except that it's a long time ago and likely nobody noticed to remember, but all that anyone *could* remember would be that Hellisia came into Athens with her mother and brother on an oriental caravan. Who is going to contradict me if I say I picked all of you up in the mountains where you were living outside of Athens?"

Kito looked at her son again, not persuaded that Hagarasium was doing anything more than weaving playful tales. But he had rehearsed the possibility of the story's truth many times and was neither surprised nor disturbed by his listener's doubtful looks.

213

"You had not known of Xerxes defeat, and you were reluctant to return to the city," he said to Kito. They waited to hear more. "Your husband was killed by the Persians."

Kito waited.

"His name," Hagarasium supplied, "was Kopolous."

Kito waited.

"There *was* a citizen named Kopolous who fought with a small group of untrained citizens in a last battle. Two survived and fled to the hills, and of those two, only Kopolous was thought to survive."

"This is *true*?" Malius asked.

"It is true."

Hagarasium sucked slowly on his pipe, smoothed his tunic and told them how he had discovered this information over the past year. With his money and persistence, his inquiries brought him information. Kito knew the story was as yet incomplete. She waited, nervous and anxious. Malius became restless.

"Kopolous was born in Athens and so was his father," Hagarasium said.

"People will know his wife and children." Kito rubbed her forehead and shook her head.

"No," Hagarasium assured her. "He is one of the citizens who died after the war who leaves no friends alive and no relatives. I have checked this out most completely. Because no one knows of his family, I settled on him as the one who should be your husband."

Kito worried, "You are sure he is dead?"

"Oh yes. He died up in the hills," he laughed, "and you were afraid to come out of

214

the hills until I saw you and told you that the Persians had been driven out of Athens."

"But your slaves on that caravan," Kito said, "they know the truth."

Hagarasium laughed again. "My dear, have you ever known a slave who would not say what his owner told him to say?" Kito knew from her own past that slaves said what they were told to say except in the company of other slaves. "And also," Hagarasium reminded her, "no slave has ever been allowed to testify to anything." Kito knew that also.

"It seems to be a good story," she said hesitantly.

"I do not like it," Malius told them, rising from the pillows and walking across the floor.

"It will be the best for both of you." Malius turned to face Hagarasium.

"How do you mean?"

"You, Malius, will be a citizen and Hellisia will be a citizen-woman."

"Still I do not like it," Malius repeated.

"I have only to swear to these facts in the Agora before the archon. I am a man of good reputation. My word and honesty will be accepted," Hagarasium told them.

"But there are so many who came in with us that first time, was it ten years ago?" Malius asked.

"Ha—and where are they? Most were old then, and many have died, and we will not waste our words considering what a slave might say. It is what *I* say that will be listened to."

"Will it not be asked," Kito questioned,

215

"why ten years have gone by and we have not. . . ."

"Yes. I have thought of that. You did not think it was necessary to claim your citizenship."

"Why not?" Malius asked.

"Your mother did not believe it was necessary until she began to make marriage arrangements for Hellisia."

"I do not believe it will be possible to do all this," Malius said.

"If this fails," Kito wondered, "what will they do to us?"

"It will not fail. You are not known by many people. I will present this case in the Agora through my patron citizen, Diophenes."

"You will not be there? We will not be there either?" Kito asked.

"No one debates in the Agora except Athenian citizens," Hagarasium explained. "No foreigners, no slaves, no women." He pulled his tunic away from his sandaled feet and pushed himself up from the pillows. "I will leave you now and when I see you again you will be Athenian citizens."

"How can you know this will happen?" Malius asked.

"Do not doubt me, Malius," he smiled, "I have earned the respect of many. Many are in my debt. Now, I will leave. When I see you again it shall be to discuss a dowry for Hellisia."

A dowry?" Malius said. "She is only ten years old."

"My young man, you have not learned the

marriage ways. It is not too soon . . . but let us not talk of that now . . . I leave you, and I give my thanks for your hospitality."

True to his word again, Hagarasium many weeks later returned to the house of Kito with a parchment in his hand. Kito, Malius, and Hellisia looked to his face expecting him to read, but he handed the paper to Hellisia and asked her to read. Warily she took it in her hands, unrolled it and read aloud.

"This document will vouchsafe that Kito, wife of the Athenian, Kopolous, and Hellisia, the daughter of the Athenian, Kopolous, bear full rights of Athenian citizen-women. Malius, son of the Athenian Kopolous, bears full rights and privileges as an Athenian male citizen."

Kito and Malius leaned over Hellisia's shoulders. "Look at all the names here," Hellisia pointed. "There are so many."

Kito turned to Hagarasium and bowed before him in her old ways as a slave. "You have been good to us, and now this. We are grateful. It will be good for all of us."

"Mother," Hellisia spoke, handing the parchment to Kito, "You have never told me of my father. When I have asked, you have only said that it makes you too sad to talk of him. Can you tell me now?"

Kito said nothing.

"Is it more than I should ask?" Hellisia wanted to know. "I do not mean to change your happiness to unhappiness."

Still Kito said nothing.

"Does Malius know our father? Surely he was old enough. Was he a brave fighter against the Persians?" Her questions brought no response from Kito. Hellisia could read in Kito's face that Kito would reveal nothing. She did not question her further.

"We will not speak of your father," Kito told her, "because it is too painful for me." Kito knew she was speaking the truth. "I do not wish for you to question Malius either, as it will be painful for him too. This is all that I can say and it will have to be enough for you. All you need to know, as the parchment says, is that you are a citizen-woman and we may now begin arrangements to find you a husband."

"So soon?" Malius asked.

"My son, do not worry. We will not marry her at ten years old, but we are already late in seeking a husband and in getting together a dowry."

Hagarasium put his arm around Malius's shoulder. "Now," he said, "as you are an Athenian citizen you may mix with other Athenian citizens. It will be your duty as an older brother to help make a match. There are places your mother cannot go, and even I, as a foreigner, cannot go. So much will depend on you, Malius."

"But Hellisia is so young," Malius persisted.

"And," Hagarasium informed him, "in a few years she should be married. If she is not, it will be said she is imperfect and no one will marry her. Do not concern yourself that she is young. Some children are betrothed in their cradles."

Still Malius's gloom persisted. "The men I

meet," he told them, "will not be ten years old."

"You must understand, in Athens girls are married to men twice their age. Children do not marry children. Young girls marry men who are already established. You are the right age, Malius, to meet men who will also be the right age to be Hellisia's husband. But there is much to be done first."

"Yes?" Malius asked reluctantly.

"You must have a dowry to offer a man," Hagarasium explained.

Kito, who had been listening to Hagarasium's instructions, told Malius that she had been putting aside money for ten years from what he had given her for the household.

"At first it was a little bit, but as you gave me more and more money for the house, I put more away."

"And of course," Hagarasium offered, "We will make it a large dowry to get a man of good fortune."

And so the duty of finding a husband for Hellisia fell on Malius. He should now go into the market place for husband-shopping to buy something he did not want to buy. Of all the young men in Athens, he alone was probably the best negotiator. An experienced bargainer with a precise perception for worth, he could bring buyers and sellers together at the right amount for a good purchase. He knew the merchandising game well and its challenge excited him. But this time he did not want to participate. Yet he could not tell his mother, or Hellisia, or Hagarasium of his reluctance anymore than he had already intimated.

He left the house and the little group of happy people and wandered through the quiet night streets. In an area where the rich lived, he looked in at windows as he passed and he saw men in conversation. These were citizens, he reminded himself, just as he was. He would do as he was told. That was his way. Soon he would go to the Gymnasium, to the Agora, and to the Academy to begin to talk with men and to search out a husband for Hellisia. Hagarasium said he knew of several men that Malius should become acquainted with and Malius would get to know them first.

As he walked the empty, darkened streets he remembered the first nights after they had arrived in Athens. From his hot and busy work day where he competed, argued, and bargained to win, he would return to the serenity of the little home with his mother and Hellisia. It was the first time in his life he had known that there was comfort for him.

When he was a slave of Burabaish in Babylon, he was in turn cuffed playfully, whipped, overworked, ridiculed and used homosexually, as were all the boys. If he had complained he would have been drowned in the Tigris-Euphrates River. It was a good surprise when Hagarasium purchased him from Burabaish at a time when the King was too drunk to know that he had not made a wise transaction, though it was a great sadness to be taken from his mother.

His treatment from Hagarasium was different from his treatment from Burabaish. Hagarasium was kind. And though he was then still a slave, he was not beaten.

When his mother came to him in a little village in Eastern Babylonia where Hagarasium was buying silks that had been carried over a new route from China, he could not believe at first that it was really Kito.

"Have you escaped?" he asked her. She laughed. He was afraid for her. "If you have escaped you will be killed. I will hide you here . . . how did you find me?"

"Not so many questions at once, my son," she had laughed again and then he saw that somehow she was different. "I am no longer a slave," she announced.

"But . . . how. . . ."

"Burabaish gave me my freedom."

"*Gave* you. . . ."

"Yes. It was important that a freedwoman and not a slave help in Azurelea's marriage preparations, and I was truly a fortunate one. Well, that is why I am here. Why I set out to find you."

After they had rejoiced at their reunion she told him of the plan, of the large sum of gold

221

Azurelea had given to Kito in exchange for a slave child and for getting the little princess out of Babylon.

The years that had passed since then had brought Malius more and more happiness. But as he walked the streets now, thinking about finding a husband for Hellisia, he worried that the happy part of his life was coming to an end.

He was saddened that Hellisia would go to someone else, live somewhere else. He did not want to think of that. He would still have a home, and if his mother persisted, he might even have a wife in his home he shared with his mother, but he did not want to picture such a thing.

This citizenship that Hagarasium had brought them had brought with it a heaviness. Malius felt it would be with him always. When he rounded the last city square and walked in the direction of his home, he felt that it had somehow changed everything. Tomorrow he would begin to learn how to act like a citizen.

In the market place he half-heartedly directed the slaves and freedmen under his supervision. When the female slaves from the best homes came to bargain for supplies for their mistresses, he could not hold to his price. One day, he believed, slaves as these would be bargaining to buy goods for their mistress, Hellisia. When he saw a group of citizen-women and slaves on their way to a religious festival, he peered at the citizen-women with curiosity, almost as if he suspected Hellisia were already in their group.

One late afternoon when the narrow streets of the market place were jammed with people and the voices of bargaining were at their loudest, when Malius's quick decisions and orders were imperative, he stopped, motionless, the satin from the bolt in his hands sliding slowly to the street, as he watched a funeral procession pass by. The veiled citizen-women who followed the ox-drawn cart with its coffin, attracted no one but Malius. Under each veil he imagined he saw the grown Hellisia, for he had learned citizen-women were confined to their homes except for religious festivals and funerals. He imagined Hellisia in these processions whenever they passed his market stalls.

He delayed doing anything about finding a husband for Hellisia as long as his conscience would let him. It would not be good if Hagarasium told him again of this duty. He, who had been an obedient slave and a responsive employee would do what he needed to do as an older brother, an Athenian male citizen, to establish Hellisia in the upper class of Athens.

He planned his actions step-by-step, determined to succeed. He would put down his sorrow when he thought of the end of his plan. With a political wisdom he had not known he possessed, he made arrangements to get himself accepted in the Gymnasium where he steamed out his body in the baths after his games and talked with the other citizens and learned their economical and marital situations. He endeared himself to two men who invited him to their home when they learned he was a successful merchant who had a part ownership in more than half the stalls in the market place.

It was to be his first visit inside the home of an Athenian citizen where he must remember that he was one too. He would try to appear at ease. Kito and Hellisia prepared him with their conversation and their selection of the clothes he should wear.

"Remember, you do not remember much of Athens as a boy." Kito reminded him of the story he should tell if he had to. "Your father and you and I fled to the hills when Athens was defeated."

"Yes, mother."

"And we lived there for many years. You do not remember much."

"Yes, mother."

"And then your father died, believing Athens was still occupied by the Persians."

"Yes."

"And when Hagarasium picked us up and brought us here we did not know that long ago citizens had had to declare themselves."

Malius nodded. It was the third time in the past week that Kito had put these words into his mind. Hellisia handed him his best tunic, and the new belt she had woven for him. She smiled at the way he looked and he loved her. "Malius is very clever, Mother," Hellisia said. "He will not say a wrong thing." And when he was ready to go she put her arms around his waist and squeezed him and said, "Do good at this as you do at everything else, my brother."

Malius, joyous at her joy and her confidence in him, would not spoil her delight by stopping to think now of his dilemma. Success at this evening would bring him sadness. He knew there was nothing he could change because he had not set the course. It was not his way to change what had been determined by a superior.

"We have our faith in you, my son," Kito said as he left.

He walked the same streets as he had walked several months before. He looked in at the same windows where citizens gathered for evenings of conversations, and he felt the same heavy sadness.

When Hellisia was fourteen she was married

to Eulonius, a merchant who was thirty years old. She moved into his home where she shared the women's quarters with his five concubines. She seldom saw her husband who spent most of his time with his men friends in town. He permitted Hellisia's mother to visit her once a month.

"He says I may not go out of the house," Hellisia complained to Kito. "I cannot even go shopping. My slaves do that."

"But he has given you many slaves," Kito reminded her as one of the slaves served them sweetcakes and fig tea. Kito waited until the slave left the room before she continued.

"You knew the customs of marriage before you married, my darling."

"Yes. You told me and Malius told me, but I didn't realize it. Do you know what it is like? I am a prisoner." Hellisia stood up.

"No. No. It is only because you were not raised like a daughter of a citizen. You had too much freedom. If you had been raised right. . . ."

"But I was raised right, mother." She went to Kito and put her arms around her. "I long for the days we had."

"Your days will get better."

"I do not think so. Eulonius tells the slaves to take away my reading and my parchment. He says women should not read or write because . . . he says we have smaller brains than men and . . . if we put too much work on our brain it makes our children imbeciles. And I have no one to talk to."

"The other women. . . ?"

"The other women have nothing to say. All day they get themselves dressed up waiting for Eulonius. They have hairdressers pile their hair this way and that way," she said, moving her hair from one side and then to the other. "They know nothing except about powders for cosmetics. Oh, mother . . . sometimes I wish you and Malius did not make it so easy for me to learn. I am the only woman I know who can read and write. Eulonius says no wife of his friends can do such a thing and he does not want his friends to know. He is ashamed of that."

Kito kissed Hellisia on the cheek and then stood up to hold her by the shoulders. "It is the way. It is all the custom. It was . . . it was the way to give you the best life."

Hellisia pulled away from Kito. "How can it be the best life? I was happy at home."

"But not for a life time."

"Yes." She started to cry, her back to Kito. Kito stepped toward her, then stopped.

"You will need to be . . . to be. . . ."

"I miss Malius," Hellisia cried. Kito knew that Malius longed for Hellisia but she said nothing. Malius was no longer the happy man who returned home each night with a smile and a story to tell of the day.

He quizzed Kito when she returned from her visit to Hellisia.

"Is she happy?" he wanted to know.

"As happy as citizen-wives are, I believe," Kito would answer.

"Does she smile?" Kito hesitated.

"There," he said, "your silence tells me I did

227

a terrible thing. I thought Eulonius would be good to her. But I see him always with his men friends in the taverns."

"You know he would not be seen in public with his wife."

"I know that, mother. But I see him with the hetairae, those prostitutes, and also with the boys. I think I did a terrible thing getting him for Hellisia's husband."

"Do not blame yourself, Malius. I think it would be the same for Hellisia with anybody you found for her."

He almost shouted. "But not with *me*." He had blurted it out and then stared wide-eyed at Kito, shocked at what he had said. There was a tense silence. After a while she whispered, "Don't forget, people believe you are her brother. And don't forget, you were born a slave."

"Yes," he agreed quietly. "And she is a princess." He slumped into the pillows on the floor. "And now . . . and now *she* is just like a slave. Eulonius's slave."

"Don't say that, my son," Kito scolded. "She lives like a queen, in a beautiful home, with slaves of her own. . . ."

"What good is it all when she is not happy?"

"And how do you know that?" Kito demanded. "I do not tell you of any unhappiness."

"No, you don't. But it is what you *don't* tell me that speaks to me of her unhappiness."

Silence separated them once more. Kito walked up to Malius and stood in front of him.

228

She spoke softly, sadly. "We must let our souls accept that she is gone."

"No," he cried, shaking his head looking directly up at his mother. "Until I know she is happy my soul cannot stay quiet."

"She is going to have a child."

Malius groaned, sinking back into the pillows. Kito added, "And if it is a boy, Eulonius has promised her. . . ."

"Don't tell me anything more, mother, please. My heart breaks," he cried softly, looking down to the tile floor.

When the midwives delivered Hellisia's child, Eulonius waited outside the room, ready to rejoice if it were a boy. When he heard that it was a boy, but still-born, he walked away.

Hellisia had known the baby was dead for many weeks. The life in her body had not moved, and with that quietness inside she became quieter outside. When Kito had last visited her she returned home upset at the change in Hellisia.

Malius and Hagarasium had been waiting for Kito, anxious for news.

"She is not well. It is as though some spark has . . . has died."

"Maybe we should get her away," Malius wondered.

"Don't think of that," Hagarasium warned. "She is the property of Eulonius."

"But she is unhappy," Malius wailed.

"My dear man," Hagarasium consoled. "You made a contract with Eulonius when you gave Hellisia to him."

"But I have learned," Maslius told Hagarasium, "that the man who gives the bride can dissolve the marriage."

"You are learning Athenian law now?"

"A little."

"Hellisia is treated no worse than other Athenian citizen's wives," Kito advised her son.

Malius was quiet.

"There is nothing to do," Kito said. "Possibly when the baby comes, Hellisia will take on new life."

But when the baby was still-born, Malius did not know how to feel. If it made Hellisia sad, he would be sad. But maybe she didn't care. His mother described her as listless, almost unconcerned. In the weeks that passed after the child's birth, Malius sometimes felt a strange surge of joy, glad that she had not had Eulonius's child.

"She will only have to try again," Hagarasium explained to Malius at the market stall. "That is a wife's purpose, to produce a son."

Hellisia recovered slowly, not caring whether she got out of bed each day. On one of her mother's visits Kito brought Hellisia a basket of pastries Malius had assembled. She left them on the table by Hellisia's bed not knowing that Malius had tucked a parchment into the lining of the basket. After Kito left, Hellisia indolently reaching for a biscuit, detected an edge of the parchment protruding from the lining.

As soon as the slaves were out of the room she emptied the basket of pastries on her bed and tore out the lining. There were words on the parchment in Malius's handwriting. It was poetry. She read quickly. And then she read the parchment over and over again.

The next day she directed her slave to return the basket to her brother, Malius, in the Agora. She said to thank him and to tell him she would enjoy more of the pastries when he had time to gather the ones that he knew she liked. Each week Malius sent a basket of pastries or fruit, and in the lining, a new poem each time. When Kito returned home from a visit to Hellisia she told Malius that Hellisia was improving. "I haven't seen her look so well since she was married."

Malius smiled broadly and Kito noticed that he, too, seemed to be happy lately. Was it that he was over the worst of his missing Hellisia? She felt relieved.

Hellisia bounded out of bed when Kito visited her, dismissed her slaves and put her arms around Kito.

"Dear Hellisia," Kito said, "I am so glad you are happy again."

"Did you bring me something from Malius?" Hellisia asked eagerly.

"Yes . . . always it is a basket for you. What is in this food," she asked, handing her the basket, "that brings color to your cheeks again?"

"Simply good food, mother, and what comes from my brother is always good." She took the basket, looked at it longingly and then placed it carefully on the table by her bed.

"It makes me happy again to see you happy. What has changed Hellisia?"

231

Hellisia smiled.

"Do you have some secret?" Kito laughed.

"Yes . . . yes. I do," Hellisia answered quickly. "I'm going to have another child."

"Another, . . . but it is so soon. . . ."

"Yes. Eulonius said we should not waste time. That we should have many sons."

"But he has children by his concubines."

"They are not his heirs, mother. He can only have a legal heir from me. I am the only one who can give him the son that will keep his family name going."

"And this new baby. . . ." Kito asked, taking Hellisia's hands in hers. "This new baby is giving you this happiness? I don't understand. You were not this way before."

"Oh, I am . . . I am different," Hellisia answered, removing her hands from her mother's and looking at the basket on the table. How she almost wished her mother would leave so she could read Malius's poetry. But Kito could visit her only once a month. She must prolong the visit, not shorten it.

"Come, mother, we can go into the inner courtyard today. Eulonius's slave told my slave Eulonius will not be back before dark. So you and I can get some fresh air for a little while."

They left the room and walked hand in hand through the women's quarters of the large house into the inner courtyard, safe from the eyes of strangers outside the house from which Hellisia was seldom permitted to emerge.

After Kito left, Hellisia emptied the basket and read through the poetry quickly. Then, as she usually did, she read through it again and again, always careful to listen for her slaves' footsteps. She must not be seen disobeying her husband.

After she read Malius's poetry she took out the writing marker he had sent her and wrote a line or two of her own poetry on the backs of the parchment sheets Malius had sent her. Some of her poems came into her imagination as she read his, but most she composed when she was weaving or listening to music. She would repeat the lines over and over in her mind so she would not forget them until she could be by herself and write them down. She had to be careful that the slaves did not see her for Eulonius must never know.

She could endure the punishment, but if she could never again write her poems, or read Malius's poems, Hellisia felt she would die.

Each time she sent the empty basket to Malius, she had tucked the parchment in the lining and sewn the lining closed around the edges of the basket. All of this gave her the joy of her days.

And the joy Hellisia felt shone in the face of the little girl born to her on a night when Eulonius was attending a party in the city.

When the midwife handed her the infant, Hellisia held her, kissed her slowly on the forehead and then put her to her breast.

"What is this?" She soon heard Eulonius speaking to the slaves outside the women's quarters. "A female? I do not want a female." His voice was raw with disgust. "I have not waited all these months for a female. I do not raise females." She heard his footsteps going down the stairs, away from her rooms.

Hellisia brought her small child closer to her own body, nursing her until the slave came to take the baby away.

The next morning Hellisia awoke and asked for her baby. She unlaced her night dress to nurse her.

"I can't bring the baby," her slave said.

"Then get someone who can."

Hellisia finished unlacing her gown.

"No one, please forgive me for telling you this, my lady, but no one can bring your baby."

Hellisia stared at her slave. She saw the slave's tears fall from her cheeks.

Hellisia shook her head.

The slave shook her head in agreement.

"When?" Hellisia asked.

"This morning. They put her outside when they took her from you last night. It did not take long. It was a cold night," she cried. "It was his orders. It is a father's right to say if a child should live."

Long after the birth of the child, Malius, worried that Hellisia had stopped writing her poems to him, received permission from Eulonius to visit her in the main hall of the big house.

As no man ever entered the women's quarters, Hellisia was permitted to visit with Malius in the main house. Female slaves wandered freely between the main sections and the women's quarters, but as a citizen-woman, Hellisia must not be seen by any man except her husband, or the men in her own family. When Eulonius entertained his men friends at home she must not be seen. When she had at first asked Eulonius about being kept in seclusion he told her, "It is to protect the family."

When the subject was first discussed between them, Eulonois and Hellisia were sitting in the dining room after a supper which they seldom shared together. Eulonius ate most of his meals either out at restaurants with his friends, or he entertained them at home when Hellisia must remain in the women's quarters, or he often spent his days and nights with the hetairae, the educated prostitutes of Athens.

The slaves had cleared away the last dishes and Hellisia had told him she did not like being expected to disappear when Eulonius had company. She had asked, "How do you mean, to protect the family?"

"My dear wife," he explained, wiping his chin with his napkin, "when you bear my son who will inherit my wealth, I must be certain he is *my* son."

Hellisia lowered her eyes trying to understand what he had said.

"You do not trust me?" she asked quietly. "No citizen of Athens can leave something as important as the legitimacy of his children up to his *wife. My* son will be a citizen. The lines for Athenian citizens must be *pure.*" He stood up, pushed his chair back from him. A male slave came into the room but Eulonius waved him away. "Foreigners," he continued, "stream into Athens."

"I thought that was good," Hellisia said, wanting to ease the tension she felt between them. "You buy from foreigners, and foreigners bring goods to fill your warehouse."

"Do not talk when I am talking. My dear wife, a citizen-woman does not talk to her husband unless she is asked. Sometimes your ways are like the foreigners."

"Foreigners," Eulonius declared, "would weaken our ancestral lines. For the good of Athenians we must keep our lines strong. We cannot trust something as vital as that to women."

Hellisia dared not ask the questions that were crowding her mind.

Now, here on her visit with Malius, she thought how sad he seemed. And Malius had the same thoughts. He saw that she did not bubble with questions as she used to. After she dutifully answered his questions about her health he asked, "But you do not write poetry to me anymore?"

"No."

"Why?"

"I don't know . . . I am afraid if Eulonius should find out. . . ."

"You are afraid of him?"

Tears filled Hellisia's eyes. She shook her head and could not answer.

"But why? Does he hurt you?"

"No," she cried. "But he exposed my baby so she would die."

Malius took her hand. "But that is the way. You will have other children."

"And if they are girls?" she cried instantly.

Malius put his arm around her shoulders and she leaned against his chest.

"If you would write your poems again it might help . . . you could write away some of your pain. It has helped me. . . ."

"Oh Malius. You make things seem better. But I am afraid if Eulonius should learn about my writing he would make it so I couldn't ever do it again and then I don't know what I would do."

Malius held her close to him. He had never held her before.

"My brother," she said, controlling her tears, moving away from him, "if only we could be as we were. We were happy."

"Yes," he smiled, not letting go of her hand.

"If I could make a dream come true I would come home with you."

Malius dropped her hand and stood up. "Do you want to leave Eulonius?"

"Leave? Is it possible?" Her eyes pinned Malius for an answer.

"Yes. Possible. But I don't know how probable. I could petition . . . I don't know. I have the right as your brother who gave you to Eulonius to petition the Archon. I don't know. I will have to learn what I can do."

"You give me new life. You are an important man now in Athens. How can the Archon deny you? I will not sleep for the joy I will feel if I can come home to you and my mother."

"But," he hesitated, "you would need to remarry. No citizen-woman is respected for long if someone does not marry her."

Hellisia stood up and faced him. "I will not think about that now. What I will think about is coming home. And Malius, then I can write whenever I want. Maybe if you can arrange it, I can be home for my birthday. I'll be sixteen soon."

"I know," he said. "I will go now and learn what I must do."

"Oh my dear brother," she hugged him. "I love you. You bring joy to my life."

When Malius returned home, Kito was not so pleased, and Hagarasium urged Malius to forget his plan for Hellisia's divorce.

"You have no grounds," Hagarasium told him.

"You do not give me enough credit," he told both of them. "I have been studying the laws of Athens and I have learned I do not need grounds to take Hellisia back. I am the one who gave her to Eulonius. I will merely petition the Archon. It should be simple. But Hellisia cannot do it herself. Women cannot petition for their own divorce."

"But why," Hagarasium asked, "why the divorce? She will only need to remarry. It will be the same again. Any citizen-woman has the same life. It is not so bad."

"Her dowry will be returned," Malius said, ignoring Hagarasium. "What is left of it, anyway."

"That was a great dowry," Hagarasium reminded him. "Where has it gone?"

"Eulonius has used some of the principal to build a new warehouse, but what he can't repay he must pay interest on."

"And you, son," Kito asked, "how will you arrange another marriage for her?"

"I have some plans," he smiled and turned away from them. "I have some plans if Hellisia will hear of them."

Malius arranged a meeting with Eulonius at a small tavern. He asked for a table in a quiet corner and waited for Eulonius, a glass of beer in his hand. Nervous, he moved the glass back and forth in front of himself. He must obtain Eulonius's consent to a divorce without a contest. He would be afraid his own background and even Hellisia's might be unearthed if a divorce needed to be argued before the Archon.

Eulonius arrived, his tunic draped casually over his arm. He looked like a prince, Malius thought.

"What am I, compared to Eulonius?" he thought. "He owns three warehouses and more than thirty slaves. I am still just an assistant to Hagarasium." But he greeted Eulonius like an equal and ordered wine for him and more beer for himself.

"What is so important that we must meet,

239

you and I?" Eulonius asked. "My friends are waiting for me at the plays."

"I came to tell you I am taking Hellisia home." He saw Eulonius scowl. Malius continued. "As her brother, it is my right to ask for the return of her dowry in this divorce." Eulonius's face contorted.

"So it's a divorce, is it?" He drank his glass of wine in two gulps.

"All right," he said with a quickness that surprised Malius. "You may take your sister. She is no good to me. She is impertinent and sullen and she produces only still-borns or girls."

Malius closed his eyes for a moment in relief. There would be no contest.

"But," Eulonius was saying, "I will keep her dowry because she has been unfaithful to me. It is the law. A woman sacrifices her dowry if she is an adulteress."

"But she is *not!*"

"And how would *you* know that?"

"What . . . what proof do you have? The Archon would need proof."

"Parchments . . . her slave showed my slave parchments she found in a basket. Love poems, in two handwritings. I told her to sew them back in the basket and we would get more proof. Did you know, Malius, your sister was using you to send your baskets to someone she wrote love poems to?"

Malius was speechless. Eulonius continued. "I would have had the man killed, the man who intruded into my house with his love poems. But the poems stopped. After the last child," he paused, "only the Gods know who the father was . . . she sent no more baskets."

Malius looked deep into his beer glass trying to know what was best to say. Should he tell Eulonius the truth? Even the truth would be a crime against Eulonius for Hellisia had disobeyed her husband. Should he take the case to the Archon? If so, Malius would expose Hellisia to humiliation. She would be called an adulteress even if she weren't.

"The dowry belongs to Hellisia," Malius ventured. "She will need it for a remarriage."

"Ha!" Eulonius scoffed. "There are no remarriages for adulteresses. No citizen would risk such a marriage. Maybe to a slave. Yes . . . let her marry a slave and have many daughters." He pushed his chair away from the table. "You may come for her tomorrow. She may keep the clothes she has, and one slave. But nothing more." He walked out of the tavern.

Malius, alone, sat, shoulders rounded. What had he done? He had started out so bravely . . . even ready to negotiate if he needed to. How could he now tell his mother and Hagarasium that he had impoverished their adored Hellisia. And what of her? What would she think of him?

"My dowry?" she asked the next day when Malius came to get her. They were standing alone in the big hall of the main house where they had met before. "What do I care about my dowry, Malius? I am going home. I will be with my mother and with you." Laughing, she put her arms around his neck and kissed his cheek. He encircled her waist and pulled her next to his body. Their lips met and there they stayed until they heard Eulonius.

"What is this?" he shouted. "You! Malius! So *you* are the adulterer! Her brother! What kind of depravity is this?"

"No," Malius broke from the embrace. "I am *not* her brother!"

"What?" Hellisia and Eulonius asked together.

"No . . ." he started to explain to Eulonius and then changed his mind and turned to Hellisia. "It is . . . I will tell you about it. For now, let's leave."

Hellisia smiled at him the way he remembered her smile from long ago.

"Oh, Malius," she said, running out of the room, ignoring Eulonius, "I must have known all along. Those poems . . . you wrote them to *me*, didn't you? They weren't just poems you copied from scrolls like you said."

Malius didn't answer. He led her out of the house. Once outside he turned to her. "Eulonius said you could take your clothes and one slave. But now you have neither."

"I don't care," she smiled.

"And who will marry you without a dowry?" he asked.

"*You* will. I know you will, Malius. Say you will. I would be so happy."

He held her. "My dearest Hellisia. My dear wife."

5

Medieval France

After Malius and Hellisia were married they lived a contented life with Kito in her home. They did not mingle with the citizen class. Hellisia's royalty was never revealed to her so her four sons never knew they were Persian princes. Malius, who was thirty-three when they married, lived until he was over fifty, a long life for those times.

There was never a day when he didn't tell Hellisia how happy she made him. And though he didn't write poems to her anymore, he told her every night that he loved her. Hellisia's good nature filled the house, and her shining eyes reflected her love for Malius. Whatever pain she had endured with Eulonius was in time erased by the joy she shared with her worshipful Malius.

243

Three of their sons supported Hellisia in her old age and the fourth left Greece in his early manhood for more northern countries. He moved from village to village trading goods further and further north and west until he settled on a sloping, hillside green by a river near what is now Paris. There in Navron he married a sheepherder's daughter who gave birth to their twelve children, though only five lived beyond childhood. The children grew and raised families of their own over the years and through many, many generations.

About the year 800 A.D., most of what is now Europe lay devastated by the wastes of the Black Plague, an epidemic that killed most of the population in every town. There were no people left to administer to the towns' needs, to protect the town walls from invaders, and few with energy enough to plow the fields. There was little food, no trade, very little money. Villagers who had survived the Plague, lived without hope for their future.

Scandinavian Vikings saw the great despair to their south as their opportunity for riches. They swooped down to plunder village after village, filled their sacks with treasures from the churches, ransacked and burned huts and town buildings, killed the men, raped the women, and carried them away to slavery.

During one of these Viking raids on Navron, Marie, a girl of ten years, a distant descendent of Hellisia and Malius, hid herself behind a burned out shed. She had seen her father killed—one of the first.

"Run, Marie," her mother had yelled to her

when her father fell. Marie screamed and ran, not away, but into her mother's arms. She was thrown aside by two large men who knocked her mother to the ground and then pounced on her mother's body.

"Run . . ." she heard her mother's muffled cries. Marie ran behind the shed and cried, knowing she should be quiet. She looked out when she heard horses galloping away. She would run to her mother. But she saw the men riding off with her. She pulled back behind the shed and slumped to the ground.

When the sounds of the raid died down, Marie scurried along the rubble on the outskirts of the village. She heard distant shouts of the Norsemen as they rode off on stolen horses with the screaming women. She heard the closer cries of dying men around her in the dark. She began to run, afraid that one of the moaning men might be a Norseman.

At the edge of town she ran through the fields for a long, long time, until her legs slowed down and finally crumpled under her. When she fell down in the tall grass, too tired to get up, she slept.

At daylight she jumped up, shivering and hungry. She began to run again, not knowing where she was going, only that she had to get far from Navron. Norsemen were sometimes known to return to villages to pick the town bare of anything they might have missed the first time.

Marie's hunger steered her to the edge of the trees. There she looked carefully at the green plants growing and then pulled one from its soft soil, wiped the dirt from the root in the moist grass and nibbled on it, at first hesitantly. Then she gobbled it and pulled up more of the same roots, pulling, cleaning, and eating over and over, before she went on her way again.

When the afternoon sunshine warmed the air she lay down, believing she might be safe for awhile. Thoughts of her mother and her father began to come into her head. She had not had time to think of them when she was running. Tears ran from her eyes and slow sobs accompanied her into her sleep. A whizzing sound awakened her. She heard something fall to the ground nearby.

"No, Louis," she heard someone shout from a distance. She got up and ran. "That's not a deer. It's a child."

Marie ran through the grass, right up to a large deer rolled over on its side, an arrow sticking out of its neck. Its huge eyes stared at her. Rough hands grabbed her shoulders.

"No one from these parts," one man said.

"Must have escaped from Navron," another said. She was turned around and around. She dared not look up. They were going to kill her, she knew it. She saw large feet and legs covered with animal skins and lacings. How long would it be before she was thrown to the ground like her mother. She would soon be as dead as that deer. Yet, she could understand their words so maybe they were not Vikings.

"What'll we do with her?" one of the men asked.

"I think we better take her to the castle, Louis."

"My Renee could use another hand. I could take her home with me."

"No, Phillippe. 'Tis not explainable to Lord Henry's men. Another hand in your hut? You could be hanged. What is found is Lord Henry's."

"But," Louis said, still holding Marie's shoulders, "if we take her to the castle she will tell them about the deer."

"Aha! Then I know what we must do. Give her and the deer to Lord Henry. We must say we shot it for him."

"Phillippe, you are as dumb as this child here. You know the penalty for shooting Lord Henry's deer."

Marie tried to squirm away, but Louis tightened his grip.

"But if we bring him a girl . . ." Phillippe leaned over to face Marie. "Your father? Where is your father, girl?"

"Dead," Marie whispered, looking only at the grass around her bare feet.

"And your mother?"

"They took her." She began to cry.

"Ah, see, Louis . . . she has no one to claim her. And we cannot claim her. We must do it this way. Maybe we can come back for the deer with one of Lord Henry's horses."

"I don't know," Louis said, releasing his hold on Marie's shoulders and grabbing her arm when she tried to run from him. They began to walk, Louis pulling Marie with him.

"Trust me, Louis. It will be good. We will tell Lord Henry we thought the deer was a bear attacking this girl. Only, what will we do if the child tells what happened?"

"We will cut her throat," Louis promised, jerking Marie's arm.

For a long time before they reached the castle, Marie saw it on the hill. People in her village had talked about the big castle but she never knew anyone who had seen it. It covered the whole mountain top.

Louis pulled her along through the trees. Again and again she tried to pull her arm free of his grip, but it was no use. She began to see small huts in clusters among the trees. The closer they came to the edge of the trees the more huts there were.

Small children played in the mud in their doorways. Women came out of their huts to stare at the two men and the girl passing. In a clearing Marie saw people chopping down tall grass. Some were putting grass across poles like hanging clothes out to dry. Marie had never seen so many people before. The Norsemen wouldn't dare attack here, she thought. There would be too many people.

Two men on horses wearing red and gold clothes stopped them at the bridge.

"We bring a gift to Lord Henry," Louis told them, thrusting Marie in front of himself. "And we seek an audience with Lord Henry."

"For what purpose?" one asked.

"We would tell him of a deer, where it lies. . . ."

"You can tell me," the other said. "I will tell

248

my Lord where it lies. I will get it for him. But how long has it been dead? We do not want sick meat."

"Lord Henry knows of us. We talked together one day in the woods. It would please him. We think if you would announce us we could talk." The two horsemen spoke together in low tones and then one said, gruffly, "Follow us." Marie walked in front of Louis and Phillippe. They entered the castle courtyard where they were ordered to wait. A young man dressed in a long, white tunic, came out from an archway. He looked at the three in front of him and frowned.

"My Lord does not see peasants. These guards say you have been spoken to by Lord Henry. Why do you lie?"

It was Phillippe who ventured. "Please, Squire, we did talk with Lord Henry in the wintertime past, when he was hunting and one of his horses became lame. We came upon him and he was uneasy because he said it was his favorite horse—one he had had since he was knighted."

Not being silenced by the squire Phillippe dared to continue. "His men were going to shoot an arrow into his horse when Louis here offered that he might be able to fix the horse's leg. He put a piece of tree limb to it and tied it with his belt and it limped off, but it seemed to be all right. Lord Henry was most grateful to Louis and wanted to know his name and said he would help him sometime if he needed it."

"And you think I will believe all this and that you can come here now and collect something?" The squire sneered. "There is something you want?"

"Oh, no, Squire," Phillippe said quickly. "We would only tell him about a deer . . ."

"You are dirty as my Lord's pigs. And this child, why is she here? Does she come to beg from Lord Henry also?" Marie trembled. The sound of his voice reminded her of the Norsemen.

This time Louis tried. "Respectfully, Squire, if you would only tell our Lord that we are here to make him an offer and please let him know that we are the ones who helped him with his horse last winter?"

The Squire looked again at the three standing before him, weighing his choices.

"Wait here," he ordered and then he left.

The three, alone in the large, stone courtyard looked up at the high enclosed building, at the many archways opening to inner areas, at the multi-colored banners hanging from the walls above them and at the corridors leading in all directions. They looked down at the shiny cobblestones, polished by all who had walked over them in the hundreds of years the castle had stood.

Marie heard a woman singing as she looked up to a room above them. The voice reminded her of her mother and she felt sad. Louis saw a woman, her hair piled up into the shape of a cone, looking down at them from one of the upper archways. She glanced at him, then turned and disappeared. He became fearful. Yet he must stay to explain the deer. If he did not, harm would come to him and his family.

The Squire returned and his voice had a different sound. "Lord Henry will see you. He will meet you in the slaughter room. He is watching cook butcher an elk."

The floor was slippery with blood in the slaughter room. Phillippe grabbed Marie's arm when she started to fall. She tried to release her hand from his, but once again she was caught. She saw the cook splattered with blood, his hands covered with it, and the table dripped blood to the floor. A large hulk of an animal lay on the table where the cook was slicing meat from its bones.

A man standing across the table was dressed in clothes so shiny Marie wanted to smooth her hands over it. Someone must have spent their whole life embroidering the gown-like covering he wore over his blouse. She looked at his hair. It had ringlets and it too was shiny. She thought of her father and his dirty, torn tunic, his snarled hair and she longed for him. She stifled a cry. The cook glanced at Marie.

"What is this child doing here?" the cook demanded.

"Marcel," Lord Henry asked the squire, "are these the peasants? You said nothing about a child."

"It is with my pardon, my Lord, but these are the men who would speak to you. And they said they have a gift. I think maybe it is the child."

"Speak then," Lord Henry said, directing his

attention to Phillippe and Louis, yet looking back and forth to the animal on the table as the cook carved on it.

"My Lord," Phillippe began, "we come with the gift of this child to you. She looks in good health and we think she will be a good worker for you. We found her in the woods. We believe she escaped the raid on Navron. We make you a gift of her."

Lord Henry only glanced at Marie. He turned to his squire, "Marcel, take this dirty child away. Blanche will do with her. Now, you," he said, pointing to both Phillippe and Louis as Marcel led Marie out of the room, "you may go."

"My Lord," Louis started, "do you remember one day last winter when your horse was injured and your men were going to kill him. Do you remember that I put a splint on his leg and. . . ."

"Yes," Lord Henry said slowly, scrutinizing Louis and Phillippe. "Yes, I remember something like that. You're the man, are you? And what do you want?"

"Pardon, my Lord, but you did say you might help us if we needed it sometime."

"Yes," he agreed, "Yes, I do remember. That horse. He is yet my best horse. Yes, I am . . ." Marie thought he was going to smile. "What is it you want?"

As they all watched the cook carve the elk into small hunks, Louis explained.

"We have a deer in the woods we would like to give you because. . . . we know it is your deer, as all deer in the woods belong to you. We would like to use one of your horses to bring the deer in, to give it to you."

"And that, you say, is a favor from *me* to *you?*"

"Yes, pardon, my Lord, it would be a favor if you would allow us to bring you the deer."

"You are clever men," Lord Henry said, looking away from the bloodied table and at the two men. "All three of us know the favor is that you will be dungeoned for killing one of my deer. You are clever."

"Pardon, my Lord," Phillippe said, "it was the child. When we first saw the child in the woods something was about to attack her. We did not take the time to learn what it was. We thought it was a bear. There have been sightings of bears in the woods, my Lord. We ask your understanding that we did not knowingly kill our Lord's deer. But having killed it we would like to bring it to you."

Lord Henry laughed. "You must be the smartest peasants on my lands. You have talked yourself our of punishment, maybe even death. Do not talk about bringing me the deer. Tell Marcel where it is and he will have my men get it."

"Thank you, my Lord," both men said. Dismissed, they backed out of the room.

Marie walked hurriedly alongside Marcel through the windy corridors. He pulled on her short arms making her go faster than she wanted to. She glanced at the passageways and the large rooms covered with cloth on the floors. Marie, who had often swept the dirt floor of her cottage in Navron, wondered why anyone would put cloth on the floor. Marcel led her down winding stone steps to a room where many women sat peeling potatoes and carrots and stirring large pots on a great stove. They stopped to see what Marcel had brought them. One of the younger women, wiping her hands on her apron, went up to Marcel. Not looking at Marie, she asked, "And what do we have here, Squire? You have brought us some more help?" "I am looking for Blanche. Where is Blanche?"

"Blanche, is it?" the young woman asked. "And why is it you want Blanche when I can help you?" A large-breasted woman who had been stirring one of the pots on the stove walked over to the younger lady, taking her by the hand and leading her back to the table. She then turned to Marcel. "Blanche is out in the vegetable garden, Squire. I will get her for you."

"No. I will find her." He grabbed Marie's arm again and walked her out of the kitchen. Marie would have liked to stay. Her stomach was hurting. She had not eaten since she pulled the roots from the ground. The kitchen smelled good to her. She wanted to ask Marcel if she could eat something, but she couldn't seem to talk. And his grip on her arm hurt.

Marcel found Blanche directing a man who was gathering vegetables. "Do something with this girl," Marcel ordered Blanche. "Lord Henry gives you charge. She was found in the woods." He dropped Marie's arm and left.

Marie felt Blanche looking at her, looking at her hair, her torn dress, her bare feet. Marie saw that Blanche had shoes and she remembered the women in the kitchen. They had shoes too. Blanche took one of Marie's hands and held it in her own, looking at the palm. Blanche's hand felt warm and gentle. "I see you haven't done much work," Blanche said. "What do they call you?"

"Marie."

"Where do you come from?"

"Navron."

"Ah . . . the raid. Is anybody left?"

Marie started to cry. Blanche pulled her next to her large body. Marie covered her face in Blanche's apron and cried.

"There . . . there. . . ," Blanche soothed. "We'll put you in with the Armands. They have many little ones. You'll soon be all right. Come with me," she said, and once again Marie was being led, but this time by a soft, warm hand.

The Armand's hut was far away from the castle. There were many huts around in the same place in the woods, near the clearing where the people had been reaping the hay when she had walked with Louis and Phillippe.

Mama Armand scowled when she saw Blanche bringing Marie to their hut. "It's another mouth to feed."

"She'll work for you," Blanche reassured Mama Armand. She patted Marie on the head and left her.

255

"Don't just stand there," Mama Armand said, "Get yourself out into the sheep hut. Colette and George are shearing. You help them."

Marie shook her head. "I don't know how. . . ."

"You'll learn. Out that way," she pointed.

"Please ma'am," Marie tried, "I haven't had anything to eat for a long time. Do you have. . . ."

"Nothing. We have nothing. Papa brings our share of the grain tonight."

"I'm hungry," Marie started to cry.

"We're *all* hungry, child. Now get out there. When we sell the wool we can fill our stomachs. Now you be hungry like the rest of us."

In the shed, Colette ran the rusty shears over the sheep's back, tearing, more than cutting the wool, while George held the squirming sheep. Both children looked sideways to see Marie in the shed's opening. They went on with their work.

"I'm here to . . . to help . . ." Marie said.

"Well then, come here. You hold her front parts. She never likes this," George told her.

Marie stepped up to the sheep slowly. "Here, come on," George said. "Grab her by the legs. We'll turn her over. There . . . that's better . . . Who are you?"

"I'm Marie. I'm to live with Mama Armand."

Colette stopped her clipping and glared at Marie. "Are you now? We don't have enough food and now we have *you!*"

Marie and George turned the sheep on its side and waited for Colette to start shearing.

"I am to live with Mama Armand," Marie re-

256

peated. Colette came toward Marie with the shears. George dropped his hold on the sheep and moved himself between the two girls. Marie put her knee on the sheep's stomach and held it down by herself. George and Colette stared at each other.

"I have to stay with Mama Armand." Marie held the squirming sheep. "Blanche brought me. She said I belong to Mama and Papa Armand."

Colette was quiet a moment, then she said, "If Blanche brought you, then you are right, then you have to stay." The three children continued their work, until Papa Armand brought them a sack for the wool.

That night, after Mama had given them each a piece of bread and a cup of barley soup they all slept on the floor in the one-room hut, the three tired sheep shearers, Mama and Papa, and three more of the Armand children, all younger than Marie.

Falling asleep on the straw, Marie snuggled next to Colette and Annette for warmth. She thought of the food her mother would fix for dinner. She imagined herself back in Navron with her own family.

Her mother always said they were very poor, but Marie never remembered having only a piece of bread and a cup of watery soup for dinner. She wished she were sleeping on her own straw pad, the one her father had made for her in the corner. She remembered how the Norsemen had run their swords through her father and then ridden off on her father's horse. She started to cry, silently so no one would know.

She wished Colette's warm body next to her were her mother's. She had never known what it was to be lonesome before. In this crowded hut she felt all alone. She knew she could never again crawl next to her mother where she slept. She could never again get warmth and love from her mother.

"How old are you, girl?" Papa Armand asked her the next morning when the family went out to hoe the weeds away from the potatoes.

"Ten, sir."

"And good manners. That'll help. Ten's getting old," Papa Armand considered. "Colette, here's a year younger. Works the ground real good though."

Marie's hoe, a tree limb with a thin, crooked piece of metal, weighed heavy in her small hands. She struck the ground trying to dislodge the weeds from around the potato plant, but the metal was too light to chop the weeds away. She dropped the hoe and began to pull the weeds with her hands.

"Marie's a comely one," she heard Mama Armand tell Papa.

"Yes. And that's a sure problem. Must get her a husband before Lord Henry finds her one."

Papa Armand told Mama about a boy who had traveled with his father yesterday, when they brought the wool to Toulon.

"He's a good boy. I'll talk to his father. This here Marie will fetch a price. Betrothed maybe a year, then married. This way it keeps her with us, but gets her promised."

Marie, pulling weeds on the opposite side of the row from Mama and Papa Armand, waited to hear what Mama would say, but she said nothing. Why did Papa say they had to find a husband before Lord Henry finds her one?

She remembered when her father had talked about making arrangements for her marriage, but the plans had not been completed. She pulled harder on the stubborn weeds, then accidentally pulled up a potato plant. She held it up in the air, looked at the many, round, new potatoes. She pulled off one small potato, rubbed the dirt on her sleeve, and bit into it, chewing it quickly and swallowing. She pulled off another potato and ate it. She saw the shadow fall across the plant she held and then Papa Armand's big feet in front of her.

He knocked her to the ground, took the potato plant from her hands and replanted it. He grabbed her by the shoulders and shook her so she thought the food in her mouth would fly out.

"I should beat you," he said. "If we eat the potatoes when they are small, we will starve in the winter."

Marie's thoughts flew to the kitchen in the castle where there were pots of different foods steaming on a stove, and food on cutting tables waiting to be washed and cooked.

"I'm hungry," Marie cried, getting up. Papa Armand knocked her to the ground again.

"We are all hungry." He stomped to the opposite side of the row of plants.

"But there is food here," Marie said.

"Marie," Mama said across the row of potatoes, "you must not talk to Papa unless he talks to you. You will be beaten. It is best you learn that now, or when you are married your husband will beat you."

Marie sank to the ground and whimpered. "Come, girl," Papa spoke not unkindly. "Get to work now. See how Colette is tearing away the weeds."

When the potatoes were ready for harvest all the children and Papa and Mama trailed out to the potato field. The whole clearing next to the castle was filled with people bringing in their potatoes. Marie was beginning to feel close to her new brothers and sisters, and as long as she stayed out of Papa's way, she was seldom scolded or hit. The Armands brought in ten sacks of potatoes.

"Three sacks, George," Papa told his son. "Go up to the castle. The gateman will take them. Be sure you give him our name."

"Why," Marie whispered to Colette, "why don't we keep all the sacks? Why is Papa giving our food away?"

"You don't know anything," Colette told Marie. "We all have to give Lord Henry our share. It is our payment to him."

"For what?"

"For letting us stay on his land."

It was the same when the apples were picked. George brought a basket up to the castle. It was the same when the sheep were sheared again, half of the money Papa got for the wool was sent up to Lord Henry. When Papa requested from Lord Henry permission to

260

send his son, George, to school in Toulon, Lord Henry gave his permission. But Papa would have to pay money to Lord Henry because George's services to the Lord's land would be lost if he went to school.

"I cannot pay," Papa told his son, as they all sat in the hut on a winter night. "And as I cannot pay, you cannot go to school. You will be as I am. . . . but I had hoped you could learn to read."

"I want to go Papa," Colette spoke up. "What if I go to school? Maybe Lord Henry will not ask you to pay for not having a girl in the fields."

"Humph. Girls do not go to school."

"But, Papa. . . ."

"Quiet, girl," Mama ordered "Do not speak to your father unless he speaks to you."

Marie would have asked if she could go to school, but she dared not. She looked at George who was twining two pieces of straw, concentrating on a design. She saw that water dropped from his eyes onto the straw.

One day Papa walked across the fields to their hut with another man and a boy. Marie saw that the boy was about as big as George. Papa looked proud. He called everybody together inside the hut and made his announcement.

"This is Petre. He will marry Marie. It is arranged."

Marie looked at Petre who looked at the dirt floor. The other children looked from Petre to Marie.

Mama asked, "When?"

"At the next harvest. We will go through the winter. Marie will be here for the planting and for our harvest. Arnold here has promised a bride price for Marie. He will pay us two milk cows."

"Oh!" Mama smiled. "That is a good price!" "We'll get one cow tomorrow and two more when Petre comes to take Marie away."

A sadness came over Marie. She saw that Mama and Papa were happy and Petre's father was laughing, but she could not feel happy. To think of leaving here made her want to turn her head away from the others' happiness. She looked around the hut, looked longingly at the one table, the cook pot, the water jug, the straw mats. She would miss these things and she would miss Colette, and George, and the three little ones. And Mama was nicer to her lately. She didn't want to go away. She moved next to Mama and put her hand in Mama's hand. Mama squeezed it and Marie wanted to cry, to tell her she wanted to stay, but she knew she couldn't say anything or Papa would hit her.

Petre never looked at her. When they went out of the hut Papa and Arnold talked together with Petre standing aside, and then the two men shook hands. Marie and the others watched from inside. Papa strode off, his arm around Arnold's shoulders. When they were out of sight, Colette came over to Marie and hugged her. Then George and the little ones hugged her too. She felt warm and cold at the same time.

When Marie saw Petre's father, Arnold, leading a cow toward their hut the next day, she thought happily of the milk they would have to drink. That would be good. Then she remembered why he was bringing the cow.

Mama called to the children, "Come here. See what we will have." They all gathered around her.

"Our cow?" one of the little ones asked, "will that be our cow?"

"Hmmmm," Mama Armand murmured. "We will have milk . . ."

"But Marie will have to go away," Colette sulked. "We get a cow but Marie has to go away."

One little girl tugged at Marie's ragged skirt. "Don't go away, Marie. Won't you stay with us?" Marie picked her up in her arms and held her close to her body.

"It's a fine cow I bring for Monsieur Armand," Arnold announced.

Marie, still holding the small girl in her arms, felt herself shoved out in front of Mama Armand. "And a fine wife we have for your Petre," Mama said.

Papa and George appeared from the clearing, their hoes across their shoulders. "Aha," Papa said, striding up to the cow. "You are here. Let me see what you have brought."

He threw down his hoe and ran his hands over the cow's back, down its rump, and then he knelt down and pulled on the cow's teats, squirting the warm milk into his mouth.

"She's a good one." He stood up.

"As good as any of Lord Henry's . . ." Arnold bragged. "And now, we make the arrangements."

"Yes, yes," Papa said quickly.

"This girl," Arnold said, pointing to Marie. "She is ours."

"After the harvest. It was agreed. She stays for the planting and the harvest."

"Hmmmm," Arnold mumbled.

"It was agreed." Marie heard the beginning of anger in Papa's voice.

"Yes," Arnold finally answered.

"She is a good worker, this one," Papa said. He took Marie by the upper arm and held her off by his side, looking at her. "Been here since Epiphany. Never sick."

Arnold nodded but said nothing.

"And she'll live longer than that cow."

"Yes," Arnold said and walked up closer to Papa and Marie. "It is arranged, then. I will come back with my Petre after the harvest."

"And you will bring another cow," Papa reminded him.

"Yes, yes. As we agreed."

The two men shook hands and Arnold walked off. Marie went to Mama. "What is going to happen, Mama?" she asked.

"You will have a husband, child. After next harvest. Did you not listen? It is agreed."

Marie turned to watch Papa leading the cow to a thin tree where he tied her.

"That was your betrothal, girl," Mama explained. "Now you are spoken for."

Colette objected. "Marie is only going to be eleven, Mama."

"That is the good time," Mama told the two girls. "Before any man gets to Marie. If she lets a man spoil her before she is married, we can get nothing for her."

Mama had more to tell the girls. "So you be careful, now," Mama advised Marie. "And you too, Colette. You are getting bigger now. Do not let the boys or any men get to you, or you will be as the dung from that cow."

Papa came back from tying the cow. He had heard his wife's advice. "And not too soon to marry," he told Colette. "You will be next, my little one. It is the best for you."

Colette dared not question him for fear of being hit. But it was as though he read the question in her mind.

"If we do not marry our girls early, Lord Henry will lay claim to you. He will find husbands for you himself, put them on this land and we no longer will have the use of our land."

Days later when Squire Marcel and three of Lord Henry's vassals galloped up to Mama and Papa Armand's hut, they found it empty. All the family were out in the fields. Marcel's men untied the cow, walked it through the woods, out into the clearing and up to Lord Henry's cow shed, where the other cows brought in from the fields were being milked.

In the evening when Mama, Papa and the whole family returned from the fields, George was the first to notice that their cow was missing. He ran around the woods asking the other people about the cow. Had it gotten loose and wandered off?

"Didn't walk away by itself," a neighbor told him. "Squire Marcel come and took it."

"Took it? Why?" Papa asked.

"Don't know," the man answered. "I stayed out of their way. Don't do a man any good to question the Squire. Don't want my head to roll."

"It was our cow," Mama protested. "Give to us for Marie's wedding."

"I'll go up the hill and ask to get it back," Papa said. That worried Mama.

"After supper, Papa, think more on that. If you go up the hill . . . you might never come back."

Papa thought about that and then insisted, "It's my cow."

That's what he said to the vassal standing watch by the cattle shed.

"The cow, the cow Squire Marcel brought you . . . it is a mistake that he, . . . I gave one of my girls to marry for the cow."

"Squire tells it the girl weren't yours to give. Squire tells it the girl was Lord Henry's . . . so the cow is his."

"But . . . she was given to me."

"None of my interest, man. All these cows belong to Lord Henry."

"Then I will see Lord Henry."

The vassal laughed. "Our Lord does not explain to peasants. Best protect your head, good man."

"Then I will see Squire Marcel."

"You are a fool, old man . . . go away now or you will bring me trouble."

"Squire Marcel will . . ."

"Go away." The man yelled and reached for the sword in its sheath.

Papa moved away, looked back at the man, then at the shed. He was going to walk back to the shed, but the man drew his sword and glared at Papa. He remembered Mama's words, "You might never come back."

He walked down the hill, longing for the cow he had had only a few days.

"But what now of Marie?" Mama wanted to know. They sat all huddled together on the floor of the hut, Mama spooning a few mouthfuls of soup into each outstretched cup.

"She goes to Petre," Papa said. "Arnold gave us the cow."

Marie, warmed by the hot soup and the glow from the twig fire, looked at Mama and thought of her mother. She would never see her again and now she did not want to have to leave here and maybe never see Mama Armand and the children again.

But the time came. Papa had asked the priest from Lord Henry's castle if he would come and say the words that would marry Petre and Marie after the harvest. Lord Henry had to give permission for the priest to perform the wedding, but first Papa had to pay Lord Henry two extra sacks of potatoes for the priest.

Papa grumbled to Mama that a man should get richer when he gives a girl child, not poorer. But he would not let his grumbles be heard outside his own hut.

After all of the crops were in from the fields and there was the sting of winter in the air,

Arnold came walking through the clearing up to their hut. Marie shuddered when she saw Petre with a cow, walking behind his father. Papa took a rope and tied the cow to a tree, wondering if Lord Henry would come for this one too.

The children gathered flowers and tucked them in Marie's hair. Mama hugged her and about that time the priest rode up to their hut on a red, velvet-draped black horse. They all encircled him, with Marie and Petre standing in front. Sitting on his horse he blessed them, reminded Marie to be obedient to her husband, and then he rode off.

Mama brought some cups of cider and flour cakes from the hut. They sat on the grass, the smaller children laughing at Marie with the flowers in her hair, Colette holding Marie's hand.

"I didn't like you when you first came here," Colette said, "but now I want to cry because you are going away."

Marie, feeling the warmth of the tears in her eyes, could not say anything. She feared she would let all her tears fall if she tried to talk so she pinched her lips together and smiled.

Papa and Arnold were laughing. George and Petre were tossing sticks in the mud pond, each one trying to knock over the other's stick. When George's stick toppled over, hit by Petre's stick, George bumped Petre. Petre knocked George to the ground and soon they were wrestling and giggling in the mud. Their fathers pulled them apart.

"It's a long walk home, Petre," his father told

him. "And soon it is going to get dark. Take your wife and let's go."

Papa and Arnold shook hands. Mama and the children all gathered around Marie crying. This time Marie didn't try to control her tears. The three trudged out into the clearing. Arnold first, then Petre, then Marie. She turned every few steps and waved at the group standing by the hut.

They had been walking in the dark many hours when the three of them arrived at Arnold's cottage at the far side of Lord Henry's lands. Arnold opened the door to a dark room, dimly lit by a single candle. Marie could see someone lying in the corner.

"This is Martha . . . Petre's mother," Arnold told Marie. "She cannot walk."

"Come here, girl," Marie heard from the corner. "Let me see you. Ah, you are a pretty one. Yes. It will be good to have you here. Petre, get us some berry juice . . . here, help me up, girl. I will sit on the bench." Marie and Petre each put their arms around Martha and dragged her to the bench by the wooden table.

Now that she was getting accustomed to the light, Marie could see the room. Then she saw that there were two rooms. She had never lived in a house with two rooms.

"Does anyone know about Petre's wedding . . . any of our neighbors?" Arnold asked his wife.

"I have not told," Martha replied.

"Good. Then maybe we can get some sleep tonight." He pulled his tunic over his head, dropped it on the floor, and flopped down on the straw where Martha had been.

"Here, girl," Martha offered, "have a cup of berry juice. That is a long walk you had."

They drank in silence. Martha stared at Marie, Petre, his head bowed, looked at his mug, and Marie looked at the room, at the wooden floor, at the row of dishes on a shelf, and at the door opening to another room.

Martha saw Marie looking at the doorway. "That is Petre's room. And now it is for both of you. I am happy you are here. You will help Arnold and Petre in the fields and you will help me."

After Marie and Petre dragged Martha back to her bed, Petre took the candle and walked into the other room. Marie followed him and slowly sat down on the straw mat. Petre sat next to her, folding his hands around his knees. They watched the candle until it burned down to darkness. Though Marie couldn't see him she felt Petre facing her.

She heard him say, "My name is Petre."

"Yes." she said. "I know."

6

Victorian England*

Through the years Marie worked in the fields
with her husband and with her father-in-law.
In the evening she cooked their meals and
helped her invalid mother-in-law, and then she
fell into a deep sleep on the straw in the room
she shared with Petre. After Petre's father and
mother died, he inherited his father's section
of land, on the condition that he give one tenth
of what he raised to Lord Henry.

Marie gave birth to a child every year for
fourteen years and six of them lived to marry
and have their own children. One daughter
married a neighbor's son who took his family
across the channel to what is now England,

*The life of Helen in this chapter is based on the life of
Caroline Norton, England, 1808–1877.

where they settled in a town later to be called London.

They had many children who also had many children and about half survived, which was better than most in those days. Generations later, about 1830, a male descendant, Thomas, set up a textile company in his home, having learned the trade from his father. His wife, Elizabeth, who had learned to weave as a child in her family's home, worked with her husband in every way. When their three boys were young they too, learned to spindle and weave, and they all contributed to the family income.

Elizabeth designed the fabrics and the whole family worked the loom in the center of their large main room. The steady click-clack of weaving was the heartbeat of their home as it was in many country homes in England at that time.

People from nearby villages and even as far away as what is now France, ordered materials from their home-industry. Elizabeth was not only the designer, but she also maintained the records and shared in reinvesting their money in necessary supplies. Periodically she and Thomas traveled to what are now northern England, Scotland, and Ireland to observe the shearing and to bargain with sheep ranchers for their wool. And when cotton was brought from India, they met the ships at the Liverpool wharfs and bid the highest prices for the best grade of cotton.

This was all about one hundred years after

the steam engine was invented, the machinery that eventually shut down the home industries when the large, puffing metal monsters were installed in huge town buildings known as mills. Because mill goods could be produced cheaper than home goods, most people could not afford to buy hand woven textiles. The looms in those home industries slowed down. Eventually, except for family use, home looms became silent relics of a previous way of life.

Country people were forced to try to find work in towns. They crowded into slums, over-supplying the labor market, and working for near starvation wages. All members of a family needed to work in order for the family to survive. Children as young as five years old worked from six in the morning until six at night, six days a week. As they slept most of Sunday, many mill workers never saw the sun.

Elizabeth and Thomas were more fortunate than most people. When their business was prosperous they had been able to secure a substantial loan to build one of the large mills in town. With her boys in school, and good help at home, Elizabeth spent most of her time at the mill ordering equipment, paying bills, hiring women to weave, children to keep the spindles full, and men to supervise.

After the mill had been in full operation about six months, Elizabeth was shocked when her husband, the man by whose side she had worked since she was sixteen, decided to send her home. Elizabeth had arrived for her day's work, had taken off her hat, and was about to sit down at her desk when Thomas announced, " 'Tis not good that you come to work in a factory, Love. 'Tis best now you stay and manage our home."

Certain that Thomas must be joking, Elizabeth answered lightly, "Is that my silly Thomas talking? With our maid and cook at home, what is there need of me there?"

" 'Tis not right, Love, that you come here everyday. People will say you are low-class like these workers here." He looked out over the rows of looms from their upstairs office. Elizabeth stood next to him and watched the women at work, the few men walking the rows.

"Poor souls," she said.

"Not poor now. They have work . . . thanks to us."

"A couple of pence a day. How can they live? We should pay them more."

"Now, Love. you know we can't do that and make a profit."

Thomas laughed, but Elizabeth did not. "Now be a sweetheart and walk on home. Roland will be coming from school. He will take on your job."

"Roland!" Elizabeth stood up and walked over to her husband who had been sitting at the desk opposite hers. "Roland knows nothing about what I do here. He can't order wool or . . . or pay the bills of lading. What is all this you're saying? I should go home . . . Roland come to work in my place? Roland is the slowest of our boys."

"Well, 'tis time he found himself. He's not

going to go on in school."

"Thomas," Elizabeth questioned, "you're not really thinking of replacing me with Roland?"

His silence was her answer. She finally absorbed the seriousness of her husband's request. She backed away from him. "This is our mill. I am a partner. . . ."

"Well, Love, yes . . . and no."

"What do you mean?"

"Yes . . . you did help . . . I mean, we did start this ourselves, but . . . the law. . . ."

"The law?"

He spoke quickly as though to get it over with. "The law does not recognize a wife as a partner."

"Thomas," she sat down at her desk. "What do I care about the law? We are partners. We have always been partners."

He was silent once more.

"Thomas," she asked, "who have you been talking to? This does not sound like my Thomas. It's those men . . . those, . . . that new merchants' club?"

"They did speak about their wives. It seems," he paused, "I'm the only one whose wife works."

"Thomas, you know I like to. . . ."

He slapped his desk with his open palm. "You can't do this anymore." Then he hesitated. "Oh, it's not . . ." He went to her and put his hands on her shoulders. "It's not I don't want you here. I think about being here with-

275

out you and," he walked away and looked out over the working women again, "it will just be work. Together you and I," he turned to her, "we were building. . . ."

"Well, then, why. . . .?"

" 'Tis the way things go now, Love. If our business is to . . . you know, we have that big loan to pay. I need to get along with the brokers, the bankers. This mill has to . . . I have to do business with them and the other merchants. We must socialize with them, Love. 'Tis best you are not a worker here when we gather with the other businessmen and their wives."

Now it was Elizabeth's turn to be silent.

" 'Tis for our family, Love." Once again he went to her and put his hands on her shoulders. "It would not be good for our family if the mill does not go well. I must not be looked down on."

"How could you be?"

"They say only low-class men permit their wives to work."

Slowly Elizabeth rose from her chair, arranged her hat on her head, looked around the room, walked over to look at the workers, then she walked out of their office and shut the door. The next day their seventeen-year-old son, Roland, took his mother's desk next to his father's.

Roland showed little interest in paying bills or keeping records of employees and their production. "I'd rather supervise the weavers, Father," he announced. "These bills of lading confuse me."

"You must learn to do this work, Son. Someday when I'm gone ... you will be the manager."

But Roland was impatient and not good with numbers. Thomas saw that it took many more hours to get the office work done than when Elizabeth worked by his side, but he could not ask her back. The Merchants Association had elected Thomas into full membership and he would not jeopardize his standing.

Roland often left his desk to stroll behind the rows of women working at the looms. Now and then he stopped to cuff the ears of a small child asleep on a pile of cotton. "Get to work or you'll not get your soup at the lunch bell." The child would scurry to fill the spindles, too tired to cry.

When Roland passed behind the working women they seemed to hunch their shoulders as though pulling into themselves away from him. He ignored the older women, but the younger ones were as magnets. He could work just so long at his desk and then he needed to "walk the rows," as he called it.

His father, aware of Roland's attraction for his workers, attempted to get him to change his ways.

"You're the owner's son, Roland. You should have higher aims than a mill worker."

"It's nothing serious father. I'm not looking to marry one."

"Well, son, now that you speak of it, 'tis time to think of it. You're eighteen now. You have a yearly income."

"And you think I want to marry one of them?" He waved his arm in the direction of the looms without looking toward the women.

"I don't know what you're thinking. I'm saying we should start. . . ."

"We?"

"Yes. Your mother and I have been talking about . . ."

"Mother!"

"Yes. 'Tis as it should be. There is a young lady . . . a daughter. . . ."

"Oh . . . and you have chosen for me?"

"We would choose only well for you, son. Hear what I have to say."

Roland put both hands in his pants pockets and leaned against the wall of the office. "Well," he said, "go on."

"Your mother has met the wives and daughters of the Merchants' Association. You know, they take tea together at times."

Roland was quiet.

"There is a certain young lady your mother has spoken of. Her mother and father are disposed to her marrying well. Her name is Helen, I believe. She is an only child. . . ."

"And will inherit their mill?"

"No, son. She does not come from a mill family. Her father is a . . . something in the English parliament."

"Ah . . ha. She could get me an appointment. I could get away from this place and all. . . ," he pointed out at the work room, "all its smells."

It was settled easily. Helen's parents invited Roland and his parents to their home for a dinner. A week later Roland took Helen and a chaperone for a ride in his father's open carriage. He spoke of the boredom at the mill and she spoke of poetry.

"You read poetry?" Roland asked.

"Yes. And I write it."

Except for that, Roland could find nothing much to dislike. She was not pretty, but neither was she ugly. Her family was obviously upper-class and had been for many generations, though he calculated they probably had more prestige than money.

"I would like to move into some government position, and get out of the mill," Roland announced. "It smells of sheep dip."

Helen sympathized. "I have heard the mills are terrible places."

"Yes." The horses trotted through the green-hedged countryside as Roland spilled out his dreams of living the genteel life, away from clanging looms, and sniveling children. "I'm going to have a fine home, a position where I wear gentlemen's clothes, and a wife who knows how to entertain the important people."

"My, you do know what you want," Helen told him.

It was only a week after that ride in the country that he asked her to marry him. "If your parents give their consent."

It was arranged. In exchange for marrying her, Roland asked that Helen's father get him an appointment as an attorney's assistant, a position which would grow in prestige as the attorney's clientele increased. It would also give Roland an opportunity to become an attorney, or solicitor as they were called.

Elizabeth and Thomas were pleased with their son's marriage. Elizabeth, never having had a daughter, was especially drawn to Helen.

"You see what it means, Love, when my wife doesn't work," Thomas reminded his wife at the wedding. "Look at all these people here. We are in the company of Magistrates and Peers. And you, Love, you made this possible."

Helen and Roland moved into a flat furnished by Helen's parents. There were only three rooms but there was a small alcove off the hall where Helen set her poetry books and her writing materials. They hired a woman named Mary to keep the place tidy and to wash their linens.

Roland never again went to the mill. After taking a long time to dress each morning, he left their house about ten o'clock and rode a waiting carriage into town. His absence gave Helen the long, sustained periods by herself in her quiet house for her writing. After many months she had enough confidence in her poetry to send one to Claredge House Press.

When the acceptance and a check arrived in an afternoon mail she held back her excitement until Roland returned that evening. She greeted him in their small entrance hall, extending the check to him, and smiling with the pride of having succeeded at something she had not previously thought possible.

"What's this?" he asked, fingering the check. "Real money?"

"Of course it's real. It's from my writing." She backed away, squared her shoulders, and announced with a wide smile, "I sold a poem. My first published poem."

"Ah . . ha." Roland again examined the check. "Very good my dear wife," he nodded, then folded and put the check into his vest pocket. He saw that she was expecting more from him. He kissed her on her cheek, took the evening newspaper from the hall table and went into their sitting room.

"Congratulations, my dear," he said as he sat down to read the paper. "Keep it up. God knows, we can use the money."

And that was true. Roland's appointment had offered him escape from the mill and it had offered prestige, but very little money. He frequently asked Helen if she would talk to her father again about a different appointment.

"He can use his influence," Roland urged her. "We need more money. Even your father knows that."

"Father says this is a learning position for you. You can become a solicitor yourself if. . . ."

"Well surely, my dear, he can find me a solicitor who can pay more. One who has better clients. Now that we have a child on the way . . . a grandchild coming, your father will want to do better by us."

Even as Helen gave her parents the news about her child, and even as they were congratulating her, she asked if her father could find Roland a better job.

He sighed and shook his head. "He's only been with this position a short time."

"I know, but, father. . . ."

He could not refuse the pleadings of his only child. He found another position for Roland, but told Helen he did not wish to ask his friends for any more favors. Helen relayed this to Roland.

Roland's response was to yell, "You bring no money into this marriage, so the least you can do is get your influential friends to help me."

Helen did not tell him she was through asking her family's friends for favors. Instead she told him, "As you are in a sour mood, though I have just brought you news of a new position, I am going into my study to work. I have an essay to send to my publisher by next week." She left their sitting room.

In her alcove she took out papers and began to read where she had left off writing. Not long after that the curtain separating her alcove from the hall was pulled aside. Roland stood in front of her.

"You do not walk out of the room when I am talking to you."

"I have to finish this. . . ."

"Your ways are too good for me. You and your high-class family. Your high-handed ways. Your writing . . ." He grabbed Helen's papers and tore them in two and then in two again, dropping the pieces to the floor.

Helen looked at her writing scattered around the alcove. "Do you realize you have destroyed the words that feed us?" she asked quietly.

Roland then grabbed her by her hair and pulled her to him until they were face to face. He hit her cheek with his fist, shoved her back in the chair, and left. She heard their outside door slam and then she began to cry. She found her cloak, and though it was dark, she ran the long distance to her parents' home.

Their maid answered the door and pulled her into the foyer when she saw Helen's bruised face. Her mother, alarmed by the commotion, came running down the stairs. Helen told her what had happened.

"Father . . ." Helen said, crying, "I want to ask him what I should do."

Her mother held her close in her arms. She, too, was crying. "Your father is very ill, my dear. After you left today . . . I was going to send for you."

"What is it?" Helen's trouble no longer seemed important.

"I don't know." Her mother wiped her tears from eyes that immediately filled again. "The doctor thinks it is his heart."

Helen tried talking to her father as he lay in his bed, barely breathing, but he didn't seem to hear her, and he never opened his eyes. Helen was glad he couldn't see her swollen face. Why should he worry about her in his last hours?

She stayed with her mother through the funeral days. Together they cried at the edge of the grave, holding close to each other.

Roland tried several times to see Helen at her mother's house, but she refused to see him.

"He's not a gentleman, Mother. I shall never go back." But his letter, delivered by a special messenger softened her heart.

"My dearest," it read, "I have been a bad person to you. You are a delicate flower and I have hurt you. How could I do so terrible a thing? I beg you to forgive me. My life is empty without you. Please return to your loving husband in forgiveness and I will promise never to strike you again. Yours in love and kindness forever, Rollie."

"It is for my child, Mother, I must return. My child will need a father. It would be selfish of me to deny that."

"Helen, dear," her mother asked, "can you trust him to do what he says? That was a dangerous thing he did to you. He might have killed you."

"But he didn't. I will return and we will start over."

When she returned home Roland was more amiable than Helen ever remembered him. He even complimented her on her essay, published during her stay at her parents' home.

"You are quite successful, my dear wife," he told her at their dinner table. "Proceeds from your copyright should supplement our income quite amply."

Things went well for a long time, until one

night when Helen was seated in their living room reading a book after having nursed and settled their newborn son. She heard Roland come into the room and demand that she get up.

"That's my chair," he announced.

"Is it indeed? It has never been anybody's chair before. And there are other chairs in this room." She resumed her reading. He tore the book out of her hands and made as if to strike her, but she ducked and ran to their bedroom, shutting and locking the door. He banged on the door and demanded that she open it.

"More of your high-handed manners," he shouted, "locking yourself out of my bedroom. Who do you think you are, the Aristocracy? Just because I came from a mill family does not mean you shall treat me as an inferior!"

"Please go away. I need to rest and you're disturbing the baby."

Behind the door Helen clutched the bedstead and watched the signs of awakening on her baby's face.

"Let me in my lady, or I shall break this door down."

Mary, their household help, alarmed by the noise, came in from the kitchen.

"Roland," Helen implored from behind the locked door, "please leave me some time to rest."

He threw his weight against the door and it cracked and then splintered.

"Mercy me!" Mary exclaimed.

"Out of my way," Roland told Mary. He pushed her aside and knocked the door to the floor. Helen stood facing him, her hands behind her back. "And now," he started to swing at Helen, but Mary grabbed his arm. Once more he flung Mary aside and then hit Helen on her cheek. Helen put her shawl to her face and ran out into the hall. He followed her and knocked her against the wall before she made her escape out the front door. Roland started to follow her and then stopped.

"Mary," he ordered, "take care of that noisy baby." He went into the living room and sat squarely in the chair where Helen had been sitting. He lit his pipe and then picked up a pamphlet to read. When Mary passed through the living room into the kitchen, carrying the baby, Roland, not looking up from his reading ordered, "Mary, get a carpenter to fix the bedroom door."

Once again Helen ran to her parents' home. An older male cousin who was visiting her mother opened the door and hurried her inside. After hearing Helen's story, they both begged her to leave Roland once and for all.

"What is he doing to you?" her mother asked. "Here you are again, arriving in the night beat up and hysterical. You shall leave him . . . get a divorce."

"Don't be hasty, Aunt," her cousin advised. "It would be best to keep this out of the courts. A woman has little chance. . . ."

"Then what can she do?"

"She can leave. Take the child and leave, but make no ruckus about it."

Helen agreed to think about it. And in the days that followed she found it was near impossible to think of anything else. Though she missed her baby, she knew Mary would take care of him. She was not afraid that Roland would harm him. It was on Helen he laid his anger.

In a few days a letter came from Roland, again by special messenger. He begged her forgiveness, wrote of what a beast he had been, said he missed her greatly and if she would deign to live with him again he would be the exemplar of a gentleman.

Though she was not entirely persuaded of his good intentions, she told her mother and her cousin that she would return. When they both protested, she explained, "I am carrying another child."

As before, their home was without anger for a short time. But soon Roland reverted to frequent outbursts over petty annoyances, mostly about money, and about his slow advancement in the legal profession. He always made it clear that, because Helen had brought no dowry into the marriage, she was obliged to arrange promotions for him through her father's friends. Though it was embarrassing for Helen to call on the Magistrate to persuade Roland's employer to advance Roland, it was the easiest way to keep peace in their home.

Whatever time Helen had away from caring

for her baby, supervising Mary, or being with Roland, she spent on her writing. Her publishers were eager for whatever she would send, because their readers were waiting for her work. Roland seldom if ever read her essays or poems, but he always cashed the checks that came to her. When the checks were slow to arrive he would write her publishers letters over Helen's objections, and demand early remittance.

Weeks after Helen's mother had died suddenly, Helen made plans to visit her cousin's family, a half day's carriage ride away. Roland went along with the idea until they were ready to leave. Then as the carriage arrived, he told her they weren't going, that it was too far to travel. In the meantime, Veronica Simmons, one of Roland's clients who was attracted to him, had unexpectedly come for a day's visit and was playing with the new baby.

The carriage waited outside, Helen's cousin waited far away, Roland insisted they all stay home. Helen insisted they all go, except of course for Veronica. Mary stood by listening to the loud argument. In the end Helen said, "Very well then, as Mary is here to take care of the boys, and as I cannot let my cousin wait unknowingly for us, I will go by myself."

At her cousin's she was miserable. She stayed the night as had been arranged, but left the next morning and returned to her home, dismissing the carriage after the driver put her luggage on the steps. She turned the key in the lock but the door would not open beyond a few inches. It was held fast by the night chain. Mary came to the door and spoke through the opening.

"Master's gone, Ma'am. Took the babies."

"Took the babies? Gone where? Let me in, Mary!"

"Can't Ma'am. Master gave me orders. Said he'd put me in prison if I let you in." Mary looked down at the floor. "Said I'd be giving away his property if you came and . . ."

"Came and what, Mary?"

"Came and got your things."

"Mary . . . this is nonsense. Where did he go? You take the chain off right now."

"Went with that Simmons woman." Mary made no move to remove the chain.

"Mary!"

In tears Mary cried, "Can't Ma'am. The Mister said the house and everything in it was his and if I let you in I'd be breaking the law. I can't Ma'am."

"I'll see that you do. I'll be back here with the police." Helen ran down the steps and then ran more than walked to the constable's office.

"Can't do anything about it Ma'am," she was told. "Man's house is his house. That's the law. I gotta go by the law, Ma'am."

"It's my house too. My money bought it. My writing."

"Sorry Ma'am. Do you have someone you can go to . . . a relative?" Mary thought of her mother and wanted to cry. She must not let go now. There was too much to do. She would go to a friend's. She would go to the daughter of her father's friend, the Magistrate. It was an embarrassment, but she had no choice.

The next day she met with the Magistrate in his office. He told her she had no case against her husband.

"Sad as it is, Helen, that is the law."

"Then I'll get a divorce." When he didn't respond she asked him, "That is possible, isn't it?"

"It is unlikely."

"Unlikely!"

"Helen, sit down. You are too excited. This will wash out. Roland will come back and he'll ask you back. Isn't that the way it went before . . . each time?"

"Yes. But this time I won't go back. I will get my babies . . . and a divorce." She walked back and forth in the small office.

"Helen that is not likely. No point in deluding yourself."

"But why is it not likely? My husband has beat me, he has stolen my children, my money, everything. . . ."

"A divorce, Helen, is an Act of Parliament.

Only three petitions from women have ever been granted. Petitions from women are not even considered."

"But my case is extreme. I was hit . . . and hit again."

The Magistrate looked at her kindly. "Helen, that is no case. You went back to him each time. You forgave him. That means you have no case against him."

Helen sat down in one of the large leather chairs.

"Stay at my daughters until you can settle somewhere else."

"Not being disrespectful of your opinions, Sir, I'd like to talk to another jurist, or solicitor."

"Of course. That is wise for you. Do not take only my opinion. Circumstances vary. Maybe you have a better case than others." He helped her from the chair, held both her hands in his and walked her to the door.

"My heart hurts to see you so badly treated," he told her, patting her hands before she left.

At Helen's appointed time to meet with the

new solicitor, he asked her, "It's a divorce you are seeking?"

"Yes, I. . . ."

"You don't know that can't be done?"

"What can't be done?"

"A petition. A woman can't petition for a divorce."

"I understand a few have been granted."

"So few as to make them non-existent."

"But my case, my husband . . ."

"Yes. I know. It's probably your husband beats you, won't let you see your children, or won't let you have your personal belongings."

"How do you know?"

"They're all the same."

"What about adultery?"

"That's to be expected."

"To be expected!"

"A man's. Not a woman's."

Helen felt her breath quicken. "Tell me sir. What is the difference between a husband's adultery and a wife's?"

"Very simple, Ma'am. If a man commits adultery it is no crime against his wife, but if a woman commits adultery, she may produce an heir to her husband's fortune, and he not know it is not his."

"But when a husband," Helen said, "commits adultery, what of the heirs he is producing for his friends to raise as if they were their own? What of the bastards he is fostering on poor women to raise by themselves in poverty, what of. . . ."

"Madam, please be more discreet. If you are

292

an adulteress, of course you have no place in my office."

"Sir," she said, rising, "I am not the adulterer in my family. It is my husband . . . my husband whom English law protects at every turn." She walked out of his office, past the stares of the secretary and other clients waiting on long, wooden benches.

After days of despair and loneliness she made another attempt to see her children at her home. This time, to her surprise, Roland met her at the door instead of Mary and he even invited her inside. Her children ran to her and nuzzled themselves in her arms. Tears ran down her cheeks. She wiped them on little Henry's hair. "My dears . . . my dears. . . . Mummie has missed you so."

"Mummie, please come home," little William begged. "Then Veronica can go home."

"Veronica?" Helen looked at Roland. "Veronica? She is here? Living here?"

"Yes. She's taking care of the boys."

Helen stood up, holding her baby, Henry, in her arms. "I've come for my boys and my clothes, and my writing."

"Yes. Yes." Roland was agreeable. "You shall have the boys . . . in good time. I have an agreement here, my solicitor drew up this contract." he held up a piece of paper.

"A contract?" Helen asked. William was clinging to her skirt as Henry wiggled in her arms.

"Yes, I have it right here." He held out a paper. "You agree to turn over one half of your mother's inheritance and the boys are yours."

"You would have me buy my own children?"

"Now don't put it that way," he smiled. "If we were together I'd be spending half of your inheritance now, wouldn't I?"

"You are vile!" She held her baby next to her, then released one hand and put it on little William's shoulder. She looked at the father of these children and said, "But, of course, you know I'll do it."

"The contract then . . . we'll sign it." Roland pulled a chair up to a table. He signed two papers and extended the pen to Helen. "I agree to give you the children, you agree to give me one half of your inheritance." He handed her the two papers. She signed them both. He took one and handed the other to her.

"Good!" Roland said and smiled. "You deposit the money in this account," he handed her a slip of paper, "and when the money is there I will send the boys to you."

As soon as the bank opened the next morning, Helen deposited the large sum of money and went home to wait. She did not expect the children to be sent that day, but when they did not arrive the next day or the day after she went to her old home and rang the bell. Mary answered the ring.

"All gone, Ma'am. Went to Scotland with Mrs. Simmons."

"Gone? The babies? But that can't be!"

"Gone, Ma'am. They're all gone. Seems Mrs. Simmons has a place in Scotland."

"But the contract?"

"The what, Ma'am?"

"Never mind, Mary." She retraced her steps back to her own small apartment and then on to her solicitor's.

"But I have a contract!" she shouted at him. She put the paper on his desk. He didn't look at it.

"Madam. You have no contract. A married woman can make no contract."

"But my husband, he is a solicitor, and his solicitor drew up this contract . . ."

"Madam, just because one is a solicitor does not make him honest. If your husband asked you to sign this. . . ."

She completed the sentence for him. "He knew it was worthless."

Her solicitor nodded. She spoke quietly. "He knew . . . he knew . . . he tricked me . . . and he used his own children. . . ."

"It appears so."

"I'll bring him to court. I'll expose him. Surely I'll get my children then."

"Madam. There is no way. The children are his."

"I can sue him. I may not have a contract, but. . . ."

"I will not take your case to court, nor will anyone else. You cannot sue your husband Ma'am. The law recognizes a husband and wife as one, and that one is the husband."

"And I cannot petition for a divorce. This English law is a monster, protecting husbands who steal children, steal their wife's inheritance, their clothes, and even their means of an income. I hear from my publisher now that my husband is demanding the money from

295

my copyrights and they are sending the money to him, because, they say, my earnings are his. No wonder he will not give me a divorce. I live like a pauper while he spends my money."

"Madam. . . ."

"I know . . . there is nothing I can do . . . legally. But I will . . . I will do . . . something."

From what was left of her mother's inheritance Helen rented a small apartment with a gas jet cooking stove, and a bathroom down the hall. Here she resumed her writing in bitterness and sorrow. She ached to see her babies and wrote occasional notes to Roland in Scotland, hoping to gain his friendship. If she were ever to see her sons again it could only be by his good will. She knew he didn't have much good will toward her. She asked for him to at least return the beginning of a novel she had been writing, as Claredge Press was anxious to see it.

"They may give me an advance of money on it," she wrote. "As you know I am living on very little money and need all I can get."

When he was in London, Roland found the writing she spoke of, took it to Claredge's and obtained the advance of thirty pounds. He brought her the writing but kept the money. Six months later when the novel was completed and the first copies were sold, Claredge's sent her an accounting, but no money. They had been instructed by Roland's solicitor to send all royalties to her husband. She was further advised that henceforth all money from all of her copyrights would be sent to him as his wife's earnings were legally his.

Helen wrote Roland and asked him for the money anyway, and she also asked to see the children. "William must be talking now and no doubt Henry is walking and getting into everything. I would so love to see them." But she was denied.

She decided that maybe she could appeal to Roland through his mother, Elizabeth. Surely she would know what a mother's sorrow could be.

Elizabeth received her warmly in her large home. "You look tired," Elizabeth said. "Here let us take tea in the sitting room. This living room is too large to be cozy." She gave instructions to her maid and then settled herself and her massive skirts into a needlepoint chair which Helen had admired.

"Thank you, Helen. I did this needlepoint myself. It's what I love to do. But tell me about yourself."

"You know my circumstance," Helen said.

Elizabeth's mood became somber. "Yes. I know. And I've seen your little ones at times. Roland has brought them here to stay when he is in London."

"Are they . . . what do they look like? Does William have any new teeth? Oh, I have tried to keep the pictures of them in my mind, but, it is so difficult." Without wanting to she began to cry.

Elizabeth went to the couch where Helen sat and put her arm around her. Helen wept on Elizabeth's shoulder as she had wept alone in her bed at night.

"There . . . there," Elizabeth patted Helen's shoulders.

"Do you think you could persuade Roland to let me see my sons?"

Elizabeth continued patting. "I have tried. I have tried many times. It is not right to keep a mother from her children, nor children from their mother. But Roland, I am sorry to say, is stubborn. The more I speak for you, the more he stiffens against you."

"He is even taking my money . . . the money I have earned from my writing."

"I know. I talked to my husband about that.

It is not right. Thomas asked his solicitor, all he told Thomas was that what a woman earns belongs to her husband."

Elizabeth continued. "Thomas told me of the women at the mill, and their children. They work almost all their waking hours and can keep none of their money for themselves. They must give it to their husbands. It is the law, they say."

"It may be the law, but it is not justice. We are not living in primitive times. This is eighteen-fifty. The laws . . . they are wrong . . . we must do what we can to change the laws."

"We? What can we do?" Elizabeth asked.

"I don't know . . . but I know I have to do something. I can write about this injustice. I have a large audience now. Many people read what I write. It is the only thing left for me." She wiped her eyes on a handkerchief from her small purse.

"I wish I could help you," Elizabeth offered. "Sometimes I see those women coming from the mill and I feel ashamed that I am part of their poverty. I think Thomas feels the same way."

"You can help me," Helen said.

"How?"

"Someday when you have my babies here in this lovely home, would you send for me so I could see them?"

"Yes . . . Oh, yes. But Roland, if he, if the boys tell him they saw their mother. . . ."

"I know. If he found out he would not have them brought here again. I will, the baby, Henry will not know me," Helen said with sorrow, "and William . . . well, I will disguise my-self. Leave that to me. I will not risk not seeing them again. Oh it will give me such courage."

"Yes. I know it will," Elizabeth smiled warmly. Yet Helen sensed Elizabeth's hesitation.

"You will be working against your own son," Helen said.

"I'm thinking about that. But, I think I must. I must help you. It's not right what is happening to you."

"Oh, Mother," Helen embraced Elizabeth. "Seeing my children will give me courage. Thank you." She took Elizabeth's hands and held them in her own. "This will give me the strength I need."

7

U.S.A. 20th Century

In her essays Helen hid behind herself, writing as if what happened to her had actually happened to someone else. And of course it had. She was only one of thousands of women whose children and earnings had been taken from them by their husbands.

Her essays brought money to her publishers and to Roland, but not to her. Yet Helen told herself her efforts would be worthwhile if her writing could change things. At first it was only women who bought her essays. Then, as wives discussed what she wrote with their husbands, some men began to wonder about the law and they became part of her growing audience.

Discussions moved from the dining room tables of upper and middle class homes to the various merchants' associations, and to men's clubs. Eventually the question of a woman's right to petition parliament for a divorce was brought to the floor of the House of Commons. There were the usual comments, "It won't be long before they'll expect to vote," and, "Next thing you know they'll want to run for election." There was also the usual hilarity. But not all men laughed.

Elizabeth and Thomas had many conversations about Helen's essays, and especially about a woman's right to petition for a divorce. Thomas, who was ashamed of Roland's treatment of Helen, sided with his wife in these conversations.

"A man has no right to take as his own, what a woman earns," Thomas told her. "You know I've always felt that way, Love."

Elizabeth would agree. "We have only to look at what our own son has done to Helen. It is nothing less than cruelty, and the law permits it."

Thomas' friends in the Merchants' Association, grown in wealth and influence, could affect parliament, and they did. Throughout the country there was a gradual movement to change the divorce laws and women's property laws. And because Helen was the leader of this movement, she was also the target for those who did not want change. Wherever she went men and women singled her out and harassed her. They called her un-Christian, telling her that God meant for man to be the head of woman.

"It's for our own good," one woman yelled at her. "Our men should take hold of our wages." She walked up to Helen on the street. "You will rob us of our only protection," the woman said, holding a squirming child in her arms. "Then what will become of my baby?"

"My dear," Helen paused and smoothed the child's tangled hair, "it is the babies I am writing about. Don't you see, whatever helps mothers, helps children." She patted the child and started to walk away.

The woman shouted after her, "You're from Satan. My husband says you're hurting us women." Helen had heard that before.

"My husband says you'll have it so's all women will have to go to work 'cause men won't take care of us if they don't have the say so. Why should they?"

Helen was tempted to turn back, but she didn't. She was tempted to try to talk to this woman, tormented because her essays had been deliberately misconstrued by the woman's husband. He had something to lose, Helen knew. If his wife could keep her own wages, she could support herself. Then she could either stay with him, or leave him if she wanted to. If she left, he would lose her as his servant.

In spite of the bitter opposition, the idea that women could petition for divorce and own their own wages took hold. In 1870, Helen's mother-in-law, Elizabeth, elderly but still high-spirited, openly invited Helen to her home to celebrate recent parliamentary legislation. Helen's sons, who were now grown men, joined their mother at Elizabeth's house. After Roland died there was no longer a need to keep the secret about the mysterious woman who visited their grandparents.

Elizabeth and Helen embraced at the front door and immediately spoke of their joy.

"It's because of you, dear," Elizabeth told Helen, walking with her arm around her shoulder into the sitting room, "women will be forever indebted to you for your courage and . . . skill. You had the skill to write about . . ."

"Thank you mother, . . . but never forget, you helped. You stood by me. You . . . you gave me heart . . . helped me to see my children."

"Compared to you . . . I did nothing," Elizabeth said. She shook her head and sat down next to Helen on the overstuffed sofa.

Helen contradicted her. "You did everything." She took her mother-in-law's hand in her own. "You did the most important thing." She paused. "When I was at my lowest ebb," Helen said, "you . . . and you alone kept me from despair."

Later at the dinner table, William raised his glass of wine, "Here's to our courageous mother for her Wage Law."

"And for her Divorce Bill," Elizabeth said. "Though I hope you boys won't come up against it."

"It would be difficult for either one of us to get divorced, grandmother," Henry laughed, "since neither of us is married yet."

Yet Henry, who was then managing his grandparents' textile mill, was the first to marry. Settling into a flat in the suburbs of

304

London, he soon became the father of two girls, who were their grandmother's joy in her last years.

William joined the wave of Europeans who immigrated to America at the end of the century. He remained in New York only a few weeks, then boarded a train for San Francisco where he found a job. Several years later he bought himself a home in the fog free part of the town, south of Market Street, married, fathered a son, and wrote to his brother Henry in England to come to California, though Henry never did. Henry was committed to carrying on with his grandparents' textile mill, which he supervised with benevolence.

Years later, in 1906, William and his wife were killed in the San Francisco Fire and Earthquake, but his son survived. A married man with one daughter, he lived in the small San Francisco peninsula town of San Mateo. This was William's granddaughter whose name was Sheila.

She did the usual things girls did growing up in the 1960's, and 70's. A quiet girl, she took piano lessons and practiced each day. She joined the Girl Scouts, and one day to her surprise she was chosen to be a patrol leader.

After she graduated from San Mateo High School, Sheila went to San Mateo Junior College for two years and then commuted to San Francisco State University every day where she earned a Bachelor of Science in business administration, with special awards for her skills in statistics. Another year at Healds' Business College qualified her for interviews for junior management positions with businesses in San Francisco. The federal government with affirmative action legislation had just started to encourage companies to hire minorities and women. Sheila was one of the first women hired by General Container Corporation as a junior manager. Her position as assistant to the Division Chairman paid Sheila a good entrance salary with promise of regular advancement.

She had lived in San Francisco during her year at Heald's and had visited her parents in San Mateo often. But when she started her new job she found she was always short on time. Most of her week-ends were spent either resting from her previous week, or getting her clothes ready for the next week, or getting a hair cut, or buying new shoes, or something she needed for her apartment.

While she liked her job she didn't like the feeling of aloneness in the big, glass-enclosed skyscraper on Montgomery Street. It was difficult to make friends with the other employees. Most of the women were older and all were earning much less. They spoke to her as though she were more important than they were, and she sensed they were resentful. Months after she was hired one of the women told her about three of the division secretaries who had applied for the job Sheila had. At times she felt like an intruder.

The junior managers, all men, treated her casually. Some ignored her. When she gave an opinion at the management meetings, where she was the only woman sitting around the large polished table, the men listened and then went on with what they were deciding. At times she felt invisible.

Her immediate superior, the production manager, met with her every day, passing on the tasks that formerly were his responsibility as he prepared for his advancement. He gave her schedules and reports from their factory and from their suppliers, and he outlined how he wanted the computerized tables to be laid out, and he answered her questions courteously, but Sheila noticed that he seldom looked at her. When he went home, Sheila wondered, did he smile at his wife or just go through the routine of dinner, newspaper, T.V., the same way that he did his work at the office?

The district manager was more friendly. He smiled when he saw her in the elevator and when he popped in and out of management meetings he had compliments and greetings for everyone. Sometimes he stopped by Sheila's office, letting her know that he appreciated how the production schedules were always on time now that she was on the job and he told her he based most of his sales predictions on the accuracy of her reports.

With the long hours of her job she didn't have much of a social life, though sometimes she met with her high school or college girl friends for dinner or a movie. Bonnie, one of her friends from San Mateo High School, was easy to meet for lunch. She worked around the corner in another skyscraper and was always ready to meet Sheila at Dominic's. But Sheila didn't phone her often because all Bonnie talked about these days was the women's movement.

"Of course I'm interested," Sheila answered Bonnie's charge that she wasn't concerned enough about working women. "But" Sheila would continue as she usually did, "I'm doing very well. You could too, Bonnie, if you'd apply for promotions. I don't understand why you don't."

"They are token jobs. Yours is too. Why don't men promote women automatically like they do men. Anytime a woman in our company gets promoted, the bosses walk around like they should be anointed. That's why I don't apply. I'll be a secretary. I'm freer this way . . . not like you."

Sheila paused with her napkin midway to her face. "Oh, I'm sorry, Shea," Bonnie said, calling her by her high school nickname. "I don't mean to get personal."

"That's okay." Sheila thought a moment. She seemed about to say something, and then didn't.

Bonnie looked at her watch, excused herself. "Have to run. The women are having an ad hoc meeting in the lunch room. I'm supposed to report on the Los Angeles convention. It was great! I'll tell you about it later, Shea. Bye."

Besides seeing Bonnie now and then, Sheila was still friendly with Mark, a college classmate she had dated for more than a year. When she was a senior and he had his first job, they had talked about getting married. Then for reasons Sheila couldn't explain she postponed the wedding and later abandoned the idea because Mark was more like a brother to her than a lover. That's the way she felt about him, but not the way he felt about her. When they made love he was passionate and out of control, but she didn't feel part of it.

When she decided not to marry Mark, she knew it would not be fair to continue to see him, even though they had good times together playing tennis and going to the movies. Mark phoned her from month to month and seemed pleased to know she was not involved with anyone else. And she liked his phone calls because they let her know someone cared for her.

She began to wonder how long it would be before there was another man in her life again. It was as if she were in a holding pattern, disappointed that the men where she worked were either married or involved with someone else. There were a couple of unattached single men, but their attitude toward her was distant. One junior manager was outright hostile. He referred to her as, "Stocky, as in taking care of the warehouse stock," joking to his friends in the hallway. As if she didn't know he was referring to her heaviness.

Sheila thought about that remark during the next few days. At first she was hurt and angry, but when she looked at herself in her full length mirror she saw that she was too much overweight. She decided to do something about her figure. She joined a health and swim club across town and set a schedule for herself to work-out on Thursday nights. On her first night, Fritz, the manager, showed her the exercise room, let her see that his eyes lingered on her new blue leotards, and told her to let him know if she needed help with the equipment. Though Sheila had never been athletic she began to look forward to Thursday evenings. She used the pulleys to strain her muscles, and she swam back and forth in the heated pool, taking the week's tension out of her body. Sometimes Fritz came and talked to her at the pool or in the equipment room. It was nice to relax and be friendly with someone.

She found she was smiling more at the women she supervised at work, and she began to disregard the men who ignored her. One whole management meeting passed by without anyone notifying her of the time or place. Her secretary had heard of the meeting from one of the other secretaries.

"Well, we sure know who's important around here." Sheila smiled at her secretary. Several weeks ago she would have had difficulty hiding her hurt feelings. "When the district manager doesn't see my name on the list of people at that meeting, he'll want to know why I wasn't there." Sheila told her secretary. "Would you get a copy of the announcement of that meeting? It will say who it was sent to. My name not on the list . . . well . . . that should tell the story."

Her secretary returned Sheila's smile. "A good idea."

On one of her Thursday health club nights, as Sheila was leaving to go home, she was not completely surprised when she saw Fritz loitering around the dressing room.

"Coffee?" he asked, nodding her head at the cafe across the street.

Briefly Sheila thought she ought to take the next bus back to her apartment to give herself time to press her clothes for tomorrow. She buckled her coat to meet the San Francisco fog waiting outside.

"I think I better get home," she said.

"Ten minutes?" Fritz said quickly, looking at her.

He walked her across the busy street, his arm around her shoulder, steering her around the oncoming cars. When he curled her coat collar up around her ears, she felt taken care of.

For several Thursday nights after that they had coffee in the same cafe. And then one Sunday Fritz drove her in his five year old Toyota to Sausalito where they walked the shop-lined streets hand-in-hand. They ate lunch at a sidewalk restaurant and later bought chocolate-dipped ice cream cones, laughing as they sat on the rocks where the water from the bay washed over the toes of their shoes. In the evening Fritz drove back across the Golden Gate Bridge, through the thick grey fog, with Sheila's head on his shoulder. She was relaxed and warm and happy.

Fritz kissed her when he left her at her apartment. "I'll see you Thursday," he said.

The next day when Sheila went into the District Manager's office for the routine monthly report, he greeted her in his usual cordial manner and then stopped to look at her as though for the first time.

"An attractive dress," he said, hesitantly. Awkwardly he offered, "Would you like a cup of coffee?" He held up his cup. "I'm having a cup."

Sheila wondered if not accepting his offer would offend him. "Yes," she said. "That would be very nice."

He rang for his secretary who soon brought the hot cup of coffee.

"Mr. Waterman," Sheila began, "these charts are . . ."

"David," he interrupted. "Please call me David. You've worked here now . . . is it six months already? You're part of our management team. First names are in order . . . Sheila."

"Thank you, . . . David," she said self-consciously.

Several days later he called her into his office again to discuss an employee she had recommended to the personnel department for a raise. They discussed the pros and cons of the promotion, and David accepted Sheila's recommendation.

"You're a good judge of character, Sheila," he said as they both rose from their chairs.

"Thank you."

"I'm wondering," he said, shuffling papers on his desk, not looking at her, "if you would have dinner with me some night?"

Sheila had been closing her briefcase. She stopped. She couldn't think of anything to say.

She remembered a young man who had been pointed out to her as David Waterman's son. She would never go out with a married man. She clasped and unclasped her briefcase.

"I'm sorry," David Waterman said. "Maybe you have a . . . a boy friend? I didn't mean to upset you. It's just that since my wife died I've . . . well, it would be nice to have dinner with a . . . an intelligent woman again. I didn't mean to upset you," he repeated.

"Oh," she said, "I was surprised. I mean . . ." Now she didn't know what to do. If she refused, would it offend him?

"That would be nice . . . to have dinner with you, but . . ."

"Good," he said. "What night would be good for you? "Or," he noticed her hesitation again. "Suppose I just set the date. Is that all right? What about this Saturday night? Is that too soon? But," he paused, "I hope I'm not . . . you're sure there's not a young man? . . . I don't mean to. . . ."

"No," Sheila answered. She thought about Fritz and Sausalito and his goodnight kiss. "No, there's no one . . . definite. Thank you, Mr. Waterman. Saturday would be fine."

"Call me 'David.' Would seven o'clock be all right?"

She clasped her briefcase firmly and walked toward the door. "Yes . . ." she smiled, "that would be fine." She turned back to the table where they had been working, found a piece of paper and wrote her address on it. He picked it up, returned her smile, put the paper in his wallet and walked with her to his office door.

313

Saturday night dinner at Vanessi's lasted until after ten o'clock. Then they rode through Golden Gate Park in David's Mercedes. They talked of production problems and the future of the corporation. He drove her home around eleven o'clock and walked with her to her apartment door.

"You've made this a pleasant evening, Sheila. Thank you for having dinner with me." On Monday when David met with the managers he smiled at her slightly and then looked away. She didn't see him all that week. She began to wonder if maybe she had done something he didn't like. But after Thursday she didn't have room for David in her thoughts because Fritz dominated her time. After coffee on Thursday night Fritz had insisted on driving her home.

"I'll close up early," he told her. "Wait for me in the lobby at the club."

"Fritz, I can be home by the time you close the club."

"Honey, I don't want you to ride that bus tonight. Can't you see, I want to be with you."

She invited him in to her apartment and when he kissed her she felt it all through her body. When they made love she whispered that she didn't know it could be so wonderful.

They woke up curled together, responding to each other, ignoring the alarm clock that rang on and on.

Showers and breakfast were quick. "I've got to get to work," Sheila told him. "Lock the door when you leave."

The next night Fritz phoned her and stayed at her apartment all night. When they went to a movie on Saturday Sheila could sense that he was planning to stay the night again. She told him she thought it was better if he didn't.

"Don't you like it?" Fritz asked.

"Yes," she said, a little embarrassed at his bluntness. "It's that . . . it's all happening so fast, and . . . well . . . we don't really know each other."

"What's to know? I'm Fritz. Really I'm Fernando Vuelo. But I like 'Fritz' better. And you're Sheila Watson."

"Wellington."

"So okay, Sheila Wellington. You're twenty-four years old? Am I right? Okay. You work in one of those boxes downtown, push a pencil for some guy, make enough to pay for your apartment and a few fancy clothes. Come home every night and eat dinner by yourself. On Thursday you come alive with me. Am I right? Okay. And I'm Fritz, twenty-eight, I drive a 1981 Toyota, make four hundred a week and I send a hundred home to my mom in Texas. Now why don't we pick up a pizza, go back to your place and watch T.V.?"

"Do you," Sheila asked slowly, cautiously, "go home with other women from your club?"

"Oh . . ." he said, "so that's what's bugging you. Okay, it's this way. Me and my girl friend just broke it off. Fact is, she kicked me out. I been living at her apartment for . . . maybe a half a year now. Doing great! Came home one night after work—not too long ago—the lock on the door's been changed. I can't get in. All my stuff is in cardboard boxes in front of the door. I ask the manager, did she leave? No, he says, just didn't want me no more. So, I moved back in my room over the club." He leaned toward Sheila. "Honey, I'm clean." He laughed. "Now how about that pizza?"

She let him stay with her Saturday night, but Sunday she woke up worried about herself. What would her life be like if she went on this way with Fritz? Would she end up kicking him out of her apartment like that other girl?

"I don't want to hurt your feelings, Fritz," she told him the next morning over their toast and jam. "But I would like to be by myself today to clean this apartment and . . . you know . . . get ready . . . go to the laundromat."

"I can help you. Hey. Let me run the vacuum. . . ."

"Fritz, that's nice of you, but . . . I need to, well, wash my hair and. . . ."

"I won't get in your way. Want some of this blackberry jam?"

"No. I mean, yes I'll have some jam, but, no, I like to do my own cleaning. . . ."

"Oh . . . okay. I'll come back tonight."

"Fritz, I . . . let's skip tonight. I need. . . ."

"I'm too much for you?" he laughed.

"No. That's not it. There really are things I need to do."

"Okay, honey. I'll see you tomorrow night."

She telephoned him at the health club and said she was sorry but she couldn't see him that next night either, though she wanted to. But something about him was disturbing her.

When she thought about his making love to her she let her body give in to all the sensations that overtook her, as though he were there in the office with her. She was forcing herself to concentrate on her work and had not heard David Waterman walk into her carpeted office. "Your secretary was away from her desk, so I came in unannounced," he said. He held a file folder in his hand. She stood up, half smiled, and reached for the folder. He reached for her hand. "How have you been Sheila? I've been out of town." He dropped her hand, walked over to the window and looked out toward the rows of skyscrapers facing him. "When I was gone," he talked quickly, almost as if he had rehearsed what he was saying. "I kept thinking about you. Things I like. Your movements. How you stop and think before you say anything. Sheila, I know I shouldn't ask you to go out with me again." He turned toward her and answered her questioning look. "Because . . . you're . . . very young. I keep telling myself, you're only a few years older than my son, Bob."

Sheila was uncomfortable for him. She wanted to say something that would help him, but she didn't know what it could be. She thought of Fritz for an instant, but he didn't seem to have any place here now.

David walked back to her desk where Sheila stood looking down at her hands. "It's a dilemma for me, Sheila. I've known men my age with young girl friends, and I never approved.

And now, here I am."

Sheila still couldn't say anything. Girl friend?

"Maybe," he said, "I should just follow my impulse. That's hard for me . . . Can't seem to throw caution to the wind. I mean, I shouldn't even be here this long when it has nothing to do with business." He walked back to the window again and stood for a moment. "How about you, Sheila? Would you care to keep company with this old man?" That helped her to shift her body and to laugh a little.

"You're not an old man, Mr. . . . David, You're not old."

"I'm forty-four," he declared. "You're twenty-four. And then there's something else."

He looked at her and then back to the window.

"The company," he said. "It's one of those unwritten policies . . . management not dating secretaries. Of course you're not a secretary." Sheila felt strangely disoriented and uncomfortable again. "Nothing ever said about dating managers or department heads," he smiled. "Never had women in those positions before." He looked around the room.

"Sheila," he asked, "would you talk to me about this over dinner tonight?"

She didn't answer.

"At seven. I could pick you up at seven?"

After a long pause, she nodded. "Yes," she said. "I'll be ready."

They met many times after that. They went to musicals in Oakland, walked through Muir

318

Woods in Marin County, drove to San Mateo to visit Sheila's parents, but seldom went any place in San Francisco.

"It's best," David explained one evening when they were sitting at a restaurant in Jack London Square in Oakland, "It's best that the people at the office don't know we're seeing each other outside of business hours."

Sheila guessed he was right.

"Especially," he said, "since your promotion is coming up." Sheila was surprised. He told her the production managers' advancement had been approved and that Sheila was one of three candidates for the position.

"But, do I have a chance?" It seemed unlikely.

"It's more than a chance. You're the one who's been doing the actual work—and doing a good job too."

"Who are the other two?"

"One from our Southeastern Division who wants to come out to the west coast. A man about my age. I know him. The other is a young man in the sales department. He's been wanting to get into production so he can learn more about the whole company. But I don't know. He doesn't get along with people very well."

"I'm the only woman," Sheila said.

"Yes. And that's in your favor. The home office wants more women in top administration. There's only one now and thirty-two men. That's not a good ratio for our affirmative action reports."

"How old is that second man, the one who's

now in sales?"

"He's . . . a family man. Has two teenagers. In his late thirties."

"I'm only twenty-five."

"There you go again. Your age is to your advantage too. Get young administrators and the company can train them the way they want."

Yet Sheila was totally surprised when the promotion was given to her.

"Because she's a woman." She overheard the men talking in the meeting room when they hadn't realized she was about to enter. "A white man doesn't have a chance these days." She stopped, out of their sight.

"A kid. She's nothing more than a kid."

"Sleeping with the boss. That's what I hear. They been sneaking out of town. My brother-in-law saw them at Walnut Creek together."

Sheila slipped back away from the door and returned to her office. She slumped down in her leather chair and wanted to cry. She looked at the flowers on her desk sent to congratulate her. Even her mother had sent a potted African Violet.

The roses from David had been signed simply, "From one who is proud of you." Now they didn't look as beautiful as they had when they arrived. She thought of Fritz. She had been postponing seeing him, missing Thursday nights at the health club because she didn't know what she was doing with him. And now she wondered why she had been slipping out of town with David.

She put her head down on her desk. It seemed she was just letting things happen to her, Fritz on Thursdays and David on Saturdays, and now those awful things they said. Terrible things! She didn't know why she thought of Mark then, except that life had never been complicated with Mark.

Fritz was waiting for her at her door when she went home. Her heart jumped when she saw him and without thinking she walked right into his open arms. They fell into bed and as quickly made love, and then made love again.

"I missed you, Babe. You been avoiding me, but you must'a had your reasons. Give her space, I told myself. When she sees me she'll know she wants me." He laughed, and Sheila smiled, but she knew he was right.

"So what's it gonn'a be, Babe?" he asked. "I move in here so we can live happily ever after?" He got out of bed and pulled on his trousers. Sheila wondered why he never wore undershorts. Mark always wore undershorts, she reflected. And David? Sex hadn't occurred to him, she guessed.

She realized she had not said a word since she saw him at her door. There she was again, letting things happen to her.

"Fritz," she said, mustering determination. "Something happened today at work and . . . I need to . . . Well, would you mind . . ." She stood up and kissed him. He pulled her to him and began to run his hands over her buttocks and thighs. She pulled away.

"Fritz, I don't want to offend you, but would you mind. I'd like to be by myself tonight."

He looked puzzled, but only for a moment.

321

"Oh, sure. Take me in small doses until we get used to each other again. Hey," he asked unexpectedly, "there's no other guy is there? I mean, I can bow out."

"No," she answered. "there's no other guy." She reached for her clothes.

She sat in the dark for a long time after he left thinking about him, about David, and about her promotion and what they had said about it. Now the promotion was hollow. What they said made her not want it. Funny, she mused, wouldn't David be surprised if he knew what people were saying. Sleeping with the boss!

She looked in her address book and dialed Mark's phone number, something she had never done before. She was happy and relieved to hear his voice.

A few weeks later Sheila phoned her mother and father and told them she was going to marry Mark.

"Oh, honey," her mother said. "Nothing could make me happier. You know how we always liked Mark. Never knew why you didn't marry him years ago. And, the man you work with, what's his name? David? Honey, he's too old for you. Dad and I were worried about him. Wait 'til Dad hears about this. You know he couldn't stand that Fritz fellow. Oh, my! When will it be, honey?"

"Soon, Mom. We'll find a date. No big wedding. Maybe go to Reno or Tahoe."

"Oh, honey. Don't do that. I'll get the church here."

But they went to Reno.

Fritz accepted the news almost casually. "You could'a told a guy," he teased. "Don't know why women are so hell-bent on getting married. Well, good luck, Babe. I'm at the club if you ever need me."

It was difficult telling David. She had gone into his office, file folder in hand to camouflage her real reason for seeing him. Thoughts passed through her mind as she walked over to him. She wouldn't ever again have the feeling that she was being hidden as she did when she went out with him. It would be a relief to be out in the open, to go where she and Mark wanted to go, not to search out places where they hoped they wouldn't be seen. And Mark was good to be with, tall, and he wore stylish suits and jackets—always looked good. She didn't think Fritz even had a suit.

"You're getting married?" David asked. "But what about . . . Sheila . . . I thought, but who?"

She explained about Mark. He leaned back in his swivel chair. Let out a sigh.

"You're sure? Have I done something wrong?"

"Goodness, no! Mark's an old friend. I mean . . . we almost got married before."

"I didn't know that. You never said."

"Well, I guess we never talked much about me."

"Sheila," he said, rising from his chair, composing himself, "Sheila." He extended his hand. "I wish you every happiness."

And Mark and Sheila were happy. After the wedding they moved into a large apartment and a year later when their daughter was born, they moved into a flat.

Sheila went back to work when Marcie was three months old. That was the extent of the maternity leave her company would permit.

"We can't hold your position open any longer," the personnel director told her. "It's company policy."

Fortunately a new business called "Nanny Service," had started in San Francisco shortly before Marcie was born so Sheila could go to work knowing that her baby was well cared for.

Though she returned home tired in the evening, Sheila found new energy when she held her baby.

Often Mark would cook their dinner, giving Sheila more time with Marcie. Or, when the weather was nice, they'd put Marcie in a stroller and the three of them would go for a walk in the neighborhood.

When the nanny called at six o'clock one morning to tell Sheila she was sick and couldn't take care of Marcie, Sheila decided there was only one thing she could do. She phoned her office to say she was sick and wouldn't be in. Then she looked forward to a full day of being with Marcie, though she wondered at times about her office. It reminded her of the one day in high school when she had cut her classes. All day long she felt guilty, and wondered what was going on in school.

That evening the nanny phoned again to say she was still not well. Sheila took another day off while the Nanny Service searched their files for a substitute. Mark offered if there were no sitter the third day, he would postpone his out-of-town trip to Portland, though it would mean he might lose out on an important business meeting. But on the third day their nanny returned.

Things went smoothly at home and at work. David was a little distant, but then she was, too. Anyway, no one could even whisper that her second promotion was based on anything except her work. There was even some talk the company might fly her periodically to meet with her counterparts in their midwestern and southeastern divisions. David told her they had never flown any women executives before.

"If that happens," Mark said, "we'll have to coordinate our flying time."

"I know I'd hate to leave the baby. Don't want both of us to be gone at the same time."

"Well," Mark said, reflecting, "that promotion puts you ahead of me. About five thousand a year more. Right?"

"What difference does that make?" Sheila asked. "It all goes in one pot."

"No difference, honey." He hugged her. "Congratulations!"

Yet Sheila wished Mark had been the one promoted. That would have called for a celebration.

When the nanny they had grown to depend on told them she was leaving San Francisco to go back to her home in Missouri, both Mark and Sheila were frustrated.

"We get so our life depends on one person and when she leaves, we're helpless," Sheila said.

"Have you thought, honey, you might quit work for awhile?" Mark asked.

"Sure. I've thought about it. I feel sad sometimes when I leave Marcie in the morning. But I like my job, and I make good money."

"But if it . . ."

"Would be better for Marcie?"

"Yes, I guess that's what I was going to say."

"Mark, do you want me to quit work?"

"Only if you want to. I have to admit, sometimes I fantasize about one of those homes . . .

typical suburban home . . . you at home with the kids."

"You do want me to quit!"

"No! I mean it when I say, only if you want to. I make enough money."

"Mark, it isn't just the money I work for. I like what I do. It makes me feel good. You could have your dream, and I'll still work. We could buy one of those houses . . . maybe in Marin, or over in Concord . . . get a babysitter in the neighborhood. We could commute. Lots of people do it."

They settled in Corte Madera, out of the San Francisco fog in Marin County, a short commute to their jobs. Theirs was a Tudor style home with bedrooms on the second floor, Marcie's next to theirs.

Sheila dropped Marcie off at the babysitter three blocks away at seven fifteen each morning and picked her up again at six o'clock at night. There were three other infants who arrived at the babysitter swaddled in blankets. When one of the mothers brought her baby with a running nose and a low fever, the baby-sitter told the mother she couldn't take care of her baby that day.

"Well, what will I do?" the mother asked. "I have to get to work. There's a sale at the store today. I've got to be there."

"I'm sorry," the babysitter said. "I'd take care of Jackie, but the state law says I can't take care of a sick child as long as I have other children here. I'd lose my license."

Sheila walked past the distraught mother, thankful Marcie was well.

"Maybe you should have a back-up," Mark advised Sheila, that night. "Our baby's going to get sick too."

"Yes, I'm sure you're right." Now and then Sheila thought about finding someone as a stand-by for Marcie, but she didn't do anything about it. "It probably wouldn't work," she said to herself. "By the time I'd need that person, she'd be doing something else." Anyway, as long as Marcie was well, things were fine.

Both Mark and Sheila learned that they were good managers. He paid the bills, she hired the housekeeper. They both cooked and they both shopped, and they took Marcie with them everywhere they could. When Marcie woke up one morning with a fever and was spitting up her formula, Sheila asked Mark if he could stay home and take her to the doctor.

"Today? Not today! I've got a meeting with Henderson today. Dick's picking me up in two minutes. Call your secretary and tell her you're sick."

"I can't do that today. David's arranged with

Josh Benson to go over our records. I have to be there."

"Call David and tell him to rearrange the schedule. I have to run, honey. See you tonight."

"Mark," she implored, holding Marcie in her arms as Mark ran down the steps to the waiting car.

"Honey I told you you should have gotten a back-up."

She called out to him, "I should have gotten a back-up! What about you? Marcie's your baby too."

"Honey," he said, running back up the stairs. He put his arm around her. "Honey," he repeated patiently, "you're the mother." He kissed her and ran back down the stairs.

"Call a neighbor," he said. "Do something. Quit your job. I've got to go." He waved as he got in the passenger side and the car disappeared around the corner. Sheila stood at the top of the steps, holding her crying baby and wanting to cry herself.

After she phoned her secretary to ask David to rearrange her meeting, David phoned her back, and sympathized with her about Marcie. But she thought his tone of voice was critical when he asked, "What do other mothers do?"

"We lie," Debbie, one of the women in the word-processing unit women told her when Sheila asked that same question the next day. "I know I shouldn't tell you, but it's all we can do," Debbie, explained. "If you tell the boss you're staying home to take care of your kid, they act like you ought to look for another job.

So we say we're sick."

"But the company gives us all sick leave," Sheila said.

"Five days a year. That's good, but I've got three kids in elementary school. Five days don't go very far."

"Does your husband help . . . I mean does he stay home when your children are sick?" Sheila thought of Mark. She was still hurt about the way he had left yesterday.

"Sure. Sometimes. But it costs him a day's pay. He doesn't have anything like sick leave."

"So . . ." Sheila started.

"So I lie. We all do." She indicated the room full of women sitting at their computers.

After awhile Sheila asked, "Do you have to work, Debbie?"

Debbie ran her fingers lightly over the computer keyboard. "Are you asking, could we live on my husband's salary? Yes. We'd cut down a lot. But if I gave up my job and my husband supported me, well, I'd kind of feel like he owned me. Not that he would feel that way. It's just how I would feel. I don't want to have any feeling like that."

"I never thought of it that way before," Sheila said. "I think I know what you mean."

"Sure, my husband could give me money. He's generous with me and the kids. But the money I earn . . . it's different. Even though we spend it together, somehow my money means more than money."

"Yes," Sheila nodded. "Of course it does."

"But those other women," Debbie leaned her

head in the direction of the women working at their computers, "most of them have to work. Tammy over there is raising two kids by herself. Lottie isn't married. Sandy's husband doesn't make enough to support himself. They're all . . . like that." She looked at Sheila. "So you see why we need to keep our jobs, even if we have to lie now and then?"

"Yes. I see, Debbie. Thank you."

At the next manager's meeting Sheila brought up the problem of absenteeism. Now that she had several years seniority, the men were more apt to listen to her, especially as absenteeism was a problem in every department.

"I'm glad you brought that up, Sheila," Dan said. Since he'd been appointed to his new job as expediter in the supply department he occasionally sat in on these management meetings. "I've been thinking about recommending we hire an alcohol rehabilitation counselor. The men in the factory are hitting an all-time high in absenteeism, especially on Mondays."

"I think this first discussion," Sheila said carefully "should be limited to just one aspect of absenteeism." This was the first time she had ventured to introduce a management discussion-topic. She knew she needed to proceed cautiously.

"That's a good idea," David said. "Let's not wander all over the company. Work on one problem at a time. I'll call Steve in personnel, see which department is giving us the most trouble."

"That won't tell the whole story." She immediately realized she sounded like she was contradicting David, or might seem to think she knew more than he did. She tried to correct that. "That's the best place to start . . . with personnel. But could we look further than what the figures say?"

"See how much is related to alcoholism?" David asked. "We probably know that."

"Well, no, it's more than that. If you don't mind," Sheila said, "I'd like us to look at how many of the women are taking sick leave and then statistically correlate those figures with the women who have children."

"That would be interesting," Dan said. "It may show us it's more expensive to hire women with children than . . ."

"Oh, no," Sheila interrupted, "That's not what I meant." Worried that she might be hurting the very women she had meant to help, she thought quickly. "How many women employees have children . . . either really young, or in school?"

"Are you saying," David asked, "there's a company problem here?"

"I was wondering if there is more of an absentee problem with women with children, and if there is, if we could help them, maybe change the policy . . . expand the sick leave, or. . . ."

"Help them!" Dan said. "God knows we already help them enough. We give them good pay, sick leave, vacation time. Frankly I think our policies encourage women to work—to leave their kids. Personally I think they ought to stay home and take care of their kids . . .

Oh, I'm sorry, Sheila," he said earnestly, "I forgot about your little girl. Still, that's the way I feel."

"Aren't we talking about something that concerns the union?" the sales manager asked.

"No, the union only covers factory workers," Dan said. Almost under his breath he added, "Thank God!" The other men smiled and nodded.

Sheila tried one more time. "I just think that because this corporation is known for its good personnel policies we could . . . well, it seems to me that our women employees with children have more difficulty than our men employees with children."

"Men employees with children," Dan grinned, "I never think of men in that way."

David brought the discussion to an end. "I'll talk with Steve in personnel, bring some figures to next week's meeting. Hank, you have something you wanted to bring up about our overseas market?"

Sheila drew her shoulders inward, waited through the rest of the meeting, and left the large room when the men did. Back at her office she phoned Bonnie to join her for lunch. "Meet you at Dominic's. I'll be a little late. Hold a table for us, Okay?"

Bonnie greeted Sheila with her wide smile, calling to her over the noise of the small, upstairs restaurant.

"Sheila, it's been so long. The baby must be keeping you busy. How is she?"

"Marcie's fine." Sheila sat down, smiled at

Bonnie and picked up a menu.

Bonnie tilted her head. "But Shea's not fine, right?"

Sheila looked up over her menu. "I'm okay, Bonnie. How are you? Sorry I haven't called."

"Mark? Things not right with. . . ."

"We're fine."

"Then it's the job. You're down about something."

Sheila paused and then nodded in agreement.

Bonnie squinted her eyes. "The same old thing? They don't listen?"

"Oh they listen," Sheila said. She watched the people filling up the restaurant. "They listen," she repeated, solemnly.

"Yes. I know what you mean. Let's order," Bonnie suggested. "The waiter's getting antsy."

When the waiter walked away with their orders, Bonnie continued. "The men listen but they don't hear. With me it doesn't much matter. There are advantages to being just a secretary."

Sheila was quiet, still thinking of the meeting. She turned her fork over and over.

"The trouble with you, Shea, is you think the women's movement is going to keep on going without your help."

Surprised, Sheila didn't know what to say. Finally she told Bonnie, "I'm no . . . activist, but, well, aren't women doing okay? I've got a good job, and other women. . . ."

"Other women, except for a few like you, are

334

right where they were ten years ago."

"I don't feel up to talking about the women's movement, Bonnie. You know I've never been much into it."

"You're into it. As a matter of fact," she said, "you are the women's movement, and . . . just like it . . . you're stuck."

Sheila studied Bonnie's face. "I'm not working in the women's movement."

"You said they don't listen to you," Bonnie said, annoying Sheila by jumping around in the conversation.

"They listen."

"If they do," Bonnie paused, "then that's almost worse, because they don't do anything. What I have seen in my company . . . the women who have been promoted, they have ideas but they're always on the outside. They're being fooled."

The waiter placed a shrimp Louis in front of Sheila and another in front of Bonnie who continued to talk and eat. Sheila picked at her shrimp listlessly.

"Women are not taken seriously," Bonnie announced.

Sheila considered that. She looked at Bonnie for awhile and then told her, "I think you go to too many women's meetings." She put down her fork.

"It's up to us, Shea," Bonnie said firmly.
Sheila frowned.
"It's up to women."
"What is?"
"The world, Shea. The men are destroying

it. Nothing we do is stopping them. Our leaders have gone crazy. They're going to blow us all up."

"Bonnie, you get too involved."

"Too involved?" Bonnie held her fork midair. "You can't get too involved. It's our life. Your life. Your baby's life."

They stopped talking. Sheila put her napkin beside her plate and looked at the remains of her food. She was barely aware of the noise of the restaurant. Blow up the world, Bonnie had said. Anytime she thought of the bomb she found it was too frightening and she turned off her thoughts. Now Bonnie was forcing her to think of it again.

What happened in world affairs didn't interest Sheila very much. She never felt she could do anything about things anyway. But if her baby were to be in the path of the bomb?

"What can I do, Bonnie? March in those parades like you do? What good is that?"

"It shows Washington that lots of us don't like what's happening. We have to let them know."

"Yes . . . I can see that." She looked at her plate full of food. "Bonnie," Sheila said, putting her hand on Bonnie's hand, "I've got to get back to work." She stood up and draped her purse over her shoulder. "Call me, will you?"

Sheila went home that night thinking about the conversation with Bonnie, about the bomb, about Marcie, and wondering about that meeting. Was there something she could have done to make the men at the meeting more interested in what she wanted to say? If she'd been more aggressive? No, they probably would have braced themselves against her then.

When she and Mark were eating dinner, and Marcie was asleep in her room upstairs, she told him about the meeting and about her frustration.

"All I wanted was to give women a few more days leave and not call it 'sick leave'. Not make them have to lie about it. Call it something like emergency child care leave."

"Give women extra leave and not men? I don't think so, honey. That would be discrimination."

"Why? Women stay home when their kids are sick . . . mostly women."

"Sometimes I do," Mark said.

"Not like you used to."

Mark gritted his teeth. "My job's more important now than it was when Marcie was born. They've got me coming and going. You know the tension I'm under."

"Me too, Mark."

"Damn it, Sheila," Mark yelled. he slammed his fork on the table. "Will you quit nagging me."

Sheila stared at him. Noisily he pushed his chair back from the table, threw his napkin into his plate, and walked out the door. He stood on the front porch, shuffling his feet. After a moment Sheila rose and went out to him.

"I'm sorry, Mark. Please come back in. I know your job has you under pressure. I'm sorry. I didn't mean to upset you."

Mark muttered something she couldn't hear.

"Darling," Sheila said, "you do a lot more with Marcie than most fathers do with their children. Those men at work," she smiled and put her hand on his arm, "I'll bet they hardly know they have kids."

Mark didn't say anything. He just looked across the street.

"I apologize, Mark. I didn't mean to nag." He turned and they went back into the house.

"Dessert?" she asked, as she brought two dishes of ice cream into the dining room.

"Sure," he said, and reached for the dish she offered.

She didn't talk about working women with children to anyone, either at home or at work, until about two months later when her secretary told her of two women being laid off because they had been sick too often.

"They're out more than they're in," the personnel director told her when she went to his department and asked about the lay offs.

"Do they have children?" Sheila asked.

"I don't know."

"Are they out more than the men in the factory—I hear there is a lot of absenteeism in the factory, especially on Mondays."

"What are you talking about? Sheila, these women are not in your department. Being the only lady exec doesn't mean all the women are your domain." He forced a smile, but it was not returned.

Sheila decided she had better retreat. An hour later David told his secretary to phone Sheila's secretary to ask Sheila to come to his office.

"You're overstepping your department responsibilities, Sheila. I have to advise you to stay out of personnel problems unless they're in your department."

"Yes, I'm sorry. It's just that I was concerned."

"I know that, Sheila. You have a soft heart for the women who work here, especially the mothers, being one yourself. But the other department managers are getting irritated. Those women are their employees, Sheila."

"Yes. I know."

"I have to tell you Sheila, again, don't overstep your bounds. When you do . . . the men come grumbling to me."

"I'm sorry."

"How are things going?" he asked, a tone of relief in his voice. "Baby okay?"

"She's getting pretty big. Be walking soon." She smiled and talked of Marcie but she wasn't thinking of Marcie. Those women who were being laid off, what now for them? David was walking her toward the door. She turned and looked directly at him.

"I can't help those women?"

"No, you can't," he said kindly. "I'm sorry," he added, opening the door for her.

With the next round of union recruitment, Sheila was hoping the office staff would vote to join the union so they could negotiate for emergency child care leave.

"I don't know much about unions" she said to the labor organizer in the company lunch room, "but wouldn't it be possible to include extra days for women, or for men too, for emergency child care?"

"Sure. But we have to get those women in the union first."

She talked about that with Mark.

"Don't get involved, honey. It's not your business. You're on the other side of the fence."

Mark was right. And considering what David had said about staying away from personnel problems, she had better drop the whole thing.

She stayed away from the women in the lunch room because she could feel they were seeing her as someone who could help them. She would take care of her own problems and the women in the stenographic pool and the computer room would have to do the same. After all, they had a union they could join. There was no union for department heads. She was surprised when she returned to her office after lunch one day to see the union organizer waiting by her door.

"What do you think the chances are," he asked her, "of getting a contract for your white collar workers that would include child care? It's the trend in business. I think we could get your women to join the union with the prospect of a contract like that. Just trying to test the waters here before we dive in."

"I honestly don't know," Sheila said. "I have nothing to say about personnel matters."

"You're in top management. Management negotiates. Lots of companies have child care right in their buildings. Cuts down on absenteeism. Some even have kid's sick rooms. The company gets a good deal—and so do the women."

"What about the men?" Sheila wondered out loud. "Can the men bring their children to these company child care centers? Suppose a woman works someplace else, where there is no child care facility, can the men bring. . . ."

"That's never come up. It's usually for the women. I don't think the men would want to do that . . . still . . ."

"I have a small child myself and I know how hectic it can be at times to find someone to take care of her. So I sympathize with our women here, but I'm not in personnel."

"You can influence negotiations."

She shook her head, "I don't think so."

Once again David told his secretary to phone Sheila's secretary to ask Sheila to come to his office. And once again she was advised to stay out of personnel problems.

"I'm trying to. That organizer came to my office. He wanted. . . ."

"Sheila, I must tell you, for your own good, stay out of this. You're skating on thin ice as it is."

She looked at him directly. "I don't understand. What . . . is something wrong . . . my work?"

"No, it has nothing to do with your work. Dan and the other department heads . . . they say, you're stirring up their women. Sheila . . . be careful. I keep defending you. I don't want to have to . . . Well, you know how it is, how you got your position because of a quota."

"What?" She felt the blood drain from her head, thought she might fall. She leaned against a chair.

"Please don't get anywhere near those personnel problems, Sheila." He looked at her compassionately. "You're the last person in the world I'd want to fire."

She slid down into the chair, forcing herself to look at him. When she could, she smiled. She left the room when he indicated the conversation was over.

"I told you so," Mark said when he came home and found her crying, her head on the kitchen table, Marcie sitting next to her in her high chair. Mark pulled Sheila to her feet and held her as Sheila cried, smoothing her hair.

"You're going to be all right, honey," he said. "They're not going to fire you." She wiped her nose and eyes, kissed him on the cheek and sat down again. "There," he said. "And now a smile." She almost smiled. "They can't fire their only woman department head."

"It's so unfair," she said, wiping her eyes again. "That they'd fire me, for . . . Still, I guess you're right. Fire the only woman? Wouldn't look good on their affirmative action report," she laughed humorlessly.

Mark became more serious. "Don't count on that, honey," he said, mixing himself a bourbon and water. "Don't count on affirmative action. It's pure discrimination."

Marcie banged her spoon on the tray of her high chair, confusing Sheila with the noise. When she watched Mark gulp his drink, something told her she should not question him tonight about what he had just said.

She lifted Marcie out of her high chair, felt her diapers, and took her upstairs to change. When she came down to the kitchen again, Mark was mixing himself another drink. She almost said something about the drinks, but kept herself from it.

The fragrance from the pork chop casserole indicated that dinner was almost cooked. She put Marcie in her roll-about and watched her laugh as she maneuvered around the large kitchen. When Marcie passed Mark's chair, he leaned over and kissed her. Marcie giggled. Sheila split the baked potatoes and filled them with butter and sour cream. She put the salad and the casserole on the table. Mark leaned back in his chair.

"Maybe this is the time, Honey, to beat them to it," he said.

"What do you mean?" Sheila placed their knives and forks on each side of their plates.

"Quit your job." His eyes followed Marcie fondly around the room. "It's time Marcie has a mother, and," he added, "it's time she had a brother. You know how I feel about that."

Sheila knew how he felt about having another child. She wanted one too, but everything would be twice as difficult with two babies.

"Quit your job, honey," Mark said again.

She sat down and spooned the food from the casserole on to their plates. "Mark," she began slowly, "I've told you before, I like my job. Even after today, I don't want to quit. After awhile, when Marcie's a little older, I'd like to have another baby."

"After awhile! That's what you always say. Damn it, Sheila, I make enough money now for both of us. Not as much as you," he added sarcastically.

Sheila held back her words.

"But enough money for us," Mark continued.

They'd been over this conversation before and Sheila remembered, it always ended with anger.

"Why do you hang around on that job anyway?" he demanded. "David always threatening you. And now his boys pressuring him to fire you. I'd get the hell out. Why do you take it? It's an insult to me."

"To you?"

"My wife taking shit off those men."

"Mark! Please!"

"What the hell," he said. he pushed his full plate away and swirled the ice cubes in his glass. Marcie moved her roll-around all over the kitchen floor, babbling.

Sheila looked down at her plate, then got up and took Marcie out of her chair, walked upstairs and went into Marcie's bedroom. She put flannel pajamas on her baby, and rocked her gently in the rocking chair.

She heard Mark downstairs, putting the dishes on the tile counter. She wondered vaguely what he was doing with the uneaten food. Later she heard the motor of the dishwasher and after that the T.V. from the living room.

When Marcie fell asleep, Sheila tucked her in her crib and went into the master bedroom. She undressed, selected clothes for the next day, cold-creamed her face, brushed her teeth and went to bed. She didn't sleep.

Hours later, Mark came upstairs, undressed and got into bed, positioning himself away from her.

"Mark," she said softly, as soon as he had pulled the covers up over his shoulders, "I'm sorry if I make you unhappy." He moved his body slightly. She felt tears rolling down her

345

cheeks. She didn't want him to know she was crying. He would think she was doing it for sympathy.

She lay on her back, unmoving, waiting for him to turn around. He didn't move. Toward morning she fell asleep.